CRUISING GUIDE

to

San Diego Bay

by

Edward and Claudia Bowler

The text of this book is composed in Giovanni Book font.

ISBN 0939837552

Cover design by Rob Johnson

Cover photo courtesy of San Diego Convention and Visitor's Bureau

Charts by Allan Cartography

Editing, indexing, and book design by Linda Scantlebury
linda.scantlebury@stanfordalumni.org

Title page: *Star of India*, courtesy of San Diego Maritime Museum

Back cover: Authors' photo by Hanlan Bowler

Disclaimer:

Cruising Guide to San Diego Bay relies on NOAA charts, Coast Pilots, Light Lists, Nautical Almanacs, other government publications, and personal experience. Charts in this guide contain nautical information reproduced from the National Oceanic and Atmospheric Administration (NOAA) charts; however, these are not intended for use in navigation. Vessels should always be equipped with up-to-date charts of their intended route. Mariners should also keep abreast of chart changes as posted in the Notices to Mariners.

Every effort has been made to ensure each entry is complete and accurate; however, conditions may have changed since the book was published.

The authors and publisher assume no responsibility and disclaim any liability for any injury or damage resulting from the use or effect of any product or information specified in this publication.

Published by Paradise Cay Publications, Inc.
P. O. Box 29
Arcata, CA 95518-0029
website: www.paracay.com   e-mail: info@paracay.com
(800) 736-4509   (707) 822-9063   (707) 822-9163 fax

CRUISING GUIDE

to

San Diego Bay

by

Edward and Claudia Bowler

PREFACE

Cruising Guide to San Diego Bay contains an abundance of information gathered from many sources to make cruising San Diego Bay interesting, safe, easy, and fun. Edward and Claudia Bowler have been cruising San Diego Bay and its environs for twenty-six years. They have spent this past year cruising the west coast of the United States. Their first-hand experience and knowledge contribute to this comprehensive volume to facilitate your travel in this exciting region.

Forty-two detailed sections begin with a brief summary of the desirable characteristics of the harbor area. Each part includes a short history of the area and instructions for land and sea approach, including details of facilities available to boaters in San Diego Bay, Mission Bay, Oceanside, Ensenada, Coronado Islands, and San Clemente Island.

This all-inclusive guide provides charts and pictures of each possible site at which boaters may consider staying in San Diego Bay and adjacent harbors. Charts are simplified, labeled, and easy to read, giving locations of marinas, mooring areas, anchorages, and yacht clubs with all important landmarks and navigational aids necessary for safe arrival. Pictures are clear and accurate, giving boaters a view of local destinations so marinas can be easily recognized upon arrival. Information is provided on size and facilities available at each marina, mooring, and anchorage in the area, along with the local phone numbers of each complex.

Written directions accompany charts to guide you, whether arriving by sea, in your boat, or by land. Latitude and longitude are provided, to set your global positioning system (GPS) for accurate and precise arrival. Information for visiting friends and family regarding nearby hotels, restaurants, and shops is included to make their stay easier and more convenient.

A concise history of the development of each local area provides interesting insight for greater appreciation of San Diego Bay. Local tourist information is provided for all the popular sites along the water and throughout the county. Recommendations are found throughout the volume regarding the best places to eat and explore. Local telephone numbers are supplied for your convenience, as well as up-to-date information on local services within walking distance from your berth. Important boating businesses such as boating supply stores, boatyards, launch ramps, laundry, banks, post offices, etc., are included.

Rules and regulations in the harbor are pointed out to assist in making contact with public officials smooth and uneventful. Names, phone numbers, and addresses are given to facilitate making all arrangements before your arrival, including helpful hints on obtaining visas and licenses from Mexico before setting off into foreign waters. Information is furnished regarding emergency situations, as well as local phone numbers to call for the latest weather information and forecast.

All major attractions in the area are listed, along with local phone numbers for quick, easy reference. Important private and public transportation information, including bus numbers, routes, and information telephone numbers, facilitates your travel anywhere in the county.

Cruising Guide to San Diego Bay provides a wealth of information. History and boating information—including charts, pictures, and details about marinas and anchorages—will make your stay in San Diego, the birthplace of California, a pleasant and memorable experience.

CONTENTS

Preface   6

Introduction: Sailing San Diego Bay   11

ABOUT THE BAY AND BOATING

1.   History of the Bay   13
2.   Geography and Geology   25
3.   Wind, Weather, and Season   29
4.   Tides and Currents   34
5.   Safety and Comfort   38
6.   Navigation and Seamanship   43
7.   Trailer Boating   47
8.   Procuring a Berth   51

ANCHORAGES AND MARINAS

9.   **North Bay**
    Shelter Island Yacht Basin   59
    La Playa Cove Anchorage (Anchorage–A1)   67
    Shelter Island Roadstead (Mooring–A1a, A1b, A1c)   74
    America's Cup Harbor (Mooring–A2)   80
    Naval Sailing Center, Point Loma/Marine   88
       Corps. Recruit Depot Boathouse
    Harbor Island   95
    Cruising Anchorage (Anchorage–A9)   103
    Embarcadero   109
    Laurel Street Roadstead (Mooring–A3)   116
    G Street Mole   122
    Marriott Marina   128

10. **Central Bay**
    Coronado Ferry Landing   136
    Bay Bridge Roadstead (Mooring–A4)   141
    Glorietta Bay Anchorage (Anchorage–A5)   146
    Coronado   152
    Fiddler's Cove   158
    Silver Strand State Beach   164
    Sweetwater/South Bay Anchorage (Anchorage–A8)   169
    National City   174

11. **South Bay**

      Coronado Cays   183

      Chula Vista   189

12. **Mission Bay**

      Mission Bay   199

      Outside Ventura Bridge

      Quivera Basin   205

      Mariner's Basin   210

      Inside Ventura Bridge

      Dana Cove and West Mission Bay   216

      Perez Cove   221

      Campland Marina   225

13. **Outside the Bay**

      Coronado Islands   232

      San Clemente Island   237

      Oceanside   242

      El Coral, B.C., Mexico   250

      Ensenada, B.C., Mexico   255

LAUNCH RAMPS

14. **San Diego Bay Launch Ramps**

      Shelter Island   264

      Glorietta Bay   266

      National City   268

      Chula Vista   270

15. **Mission Bay Launch Ramps**

      De Anza Cove   274

      South Shore   276

      Dana Cove   278

      Ski Beach   280

      Santa Clara Point   282

      Campland on the Bay   284

INTRODUCTION

For centuries San Diego Bay has been an alluring harbor to explorers, military men, fishermen, speculators, city builders, and especially boaters. Her quiet, calm waters, sheltered by the hills of Point Loma, attract all mariners. Protected by a broad headland from the mild northwest wind and swell, San Diego Bay truly is an inviting, beckoning harbor. Today, sailors find an easy reach into the thirteen-mile-long bay from the gentle Pacific swell.

Little rain, wind, or fog affect the fair, year-around weather that attracts visitors from all over the world. Temperatures remain mild year around, since San Diego is actually an irrigated desert with little seasonal change. This neat, clean, organized harbor is uncluttered with heavy commercial shipping, seeing only moderate military presence.

We are not the first to cherish the wonderful attributes of the bay. Other people have noted them, as well:

"We were always glad to see San Diego."

Juan Rodriguez Cabrillo in 1542 reported in his log, "[This is] a sheltered port and a very good one to which they gave the name San Miguel." Cabrillo stayed here only a few days before he moved north to discover more lands for Spain.

Sebastian Vizcaino in 1602, after staying ten days, reported in his log, "Port must be best to be found in all of the South Seas, protected on all sides and having good anchorage."

Father Junípero Serra in 1769 reported in his account, "The missions in the regions which we have seen will all thrive very well because there is good land and sufficient water."

Author and sailor Richard Henry Dana, Jr. in 1835 reported in his book, *Two Years Before the Mast*, "We were always glad to see San Diego; it being the depot, and a snug little place, and seeming quite like home, especially to me . . . "

Alonzo Horton, Father of San Diego, remarked in 1867, "I thought San Diego must be a Heaven on earth . . . I have been nearly all over the United States and that is the prettiest place for a city I ever saw."

Come and find out what navigators, explorers, conquerors, and developers have discovered through the years. Come and explore San Diego Bay.

" . . . best to be found in all the South Seas."

" . . . San Diego is decidedly the best place in California."

Richard Henry Dana, Jr.

Two Years Before the Mast (1834)

About the Bay and Boating

"Man cannot discover new oceans unless he has the courage to lose sight of the shore."

--Anonymous

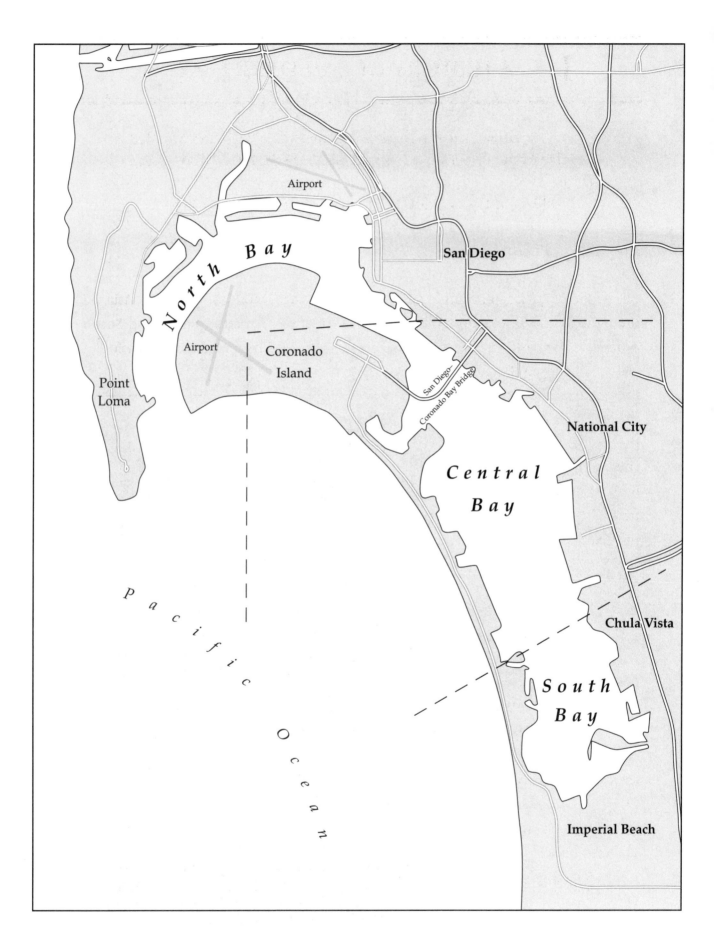

North Bay

Airport

San Diego

Point
Loma

Airport

Coronado
Island

San Diego–
Coronado Bay Bridge

National City

Central
Bay

Chula Vista

South
Bay

Pacific Ocean

Imperial Beach

12

1   A HISTORY OF SAN DIEGO BAY

"At sunset on the second day we had a large and wooded headland directly before us, behind which lay the little harbor of San Diego."

Richard Henry Dana, Jr., *Two Years Before the Mast* (1835)

Prewritten Record

Archeologists report that thousands of years ago, prehistoric man left Asia via the Bering Land Bridge, moving into North America, Central America, and South America. The earliest artifacts found in the San Diego area are from the La Jollan Indians, believed to have been present around 4,000 B.C. Not much is known about these people other than that they were shell gatherers. No one knows why they disappeared, but theories suggest they either moved into more southerly regions or were destroyed by invading tribes.

Later artifacts from 1,000 B.C. tell of the Kumeyaay Indians. They spoke Hokam, a language similar to dialects spoken by Yuma and Mojave Indians of the Colorado River area; therefore, they are believed to have been from that area. Migrating with the seasons, they were hunters and gatherers. They did not plant, nor did they have permanent settlements with substantial structures. They were unable to communicate

San Diego Historical Society

Local Kumeyaay Indians are related to Yuma Indians

with adjacent tribes, as there were many different dialects. They killed and raided neighboring villages using bows, arrows, and war clubs. Daily life was marked by numerous rituals and ceremonies. They had no written language, and were just called by the name of the area in which they resided—Diegueños (San Diego) or Luiseños (San Luis Rey).

These were the tribes present when the Europeans arrived in 1542. Today, about 7,500 native Indians live throughout San Diego County, with 2,500 living on seventeen reservations scattered throughout rural San Diego County.

European Exploration

The Golden Age of Discovery began in 1492, when Columbus discovered the New World. Fifty years went by before Juan Rodriguez Cabrillo, a Portuguese explorer sailing for Spain, arrived with his two ships, *San Salvador* and *Victoria*, in San Diego Bay on September 28, 1542. He named the harbor San Miguel, in honor of St. Michael, the archangel. Cabrillo stayed in the harbor six days, then continued north to explore the coast.

Juan Cabrillo arrived in 1542

Sixty years passed before the next Europeans would frequent these shores. On November 10, 1602, Spanish explorer Sebastian Vizcaino entered the bay with his four ships: *San Diego*, *San Thomas*, *Tres Reys*, and one other. Vizcaino gave the harbor its present name, San Diego. After a short ten days, he left. No written records mention San Diego for another 167 years. Possibly it was the opposing northwest wind and current hindering easy exploration. Rumors of Russian and English interests in the New World prompted Spain to expand its presence along the Pacific coast to establish a military foothold and build missions, leaving missionaries to proselytize and develop the area. To this end, an expedition was formed with Gaspar Portolá leading a land party and Captain Vila, of the Spanish vessel *San Carlos*, leading the sea expedition. They planned to meet in San Diego Bay.

Spanish Influence

Officials gathered in Mexico City in 1769 to plan the expedition to New Spain, beginning their fifty-two-year development of outposts along the Pacific coast. One expedition traveling by sea and the other by land, both left in April, 1769. The sea party arrived first, with the *San Antonio* making port after fifty-seven days; the land party followed, with Father Junípero Serra founding the first California mission on July 16, 1769. A few years later, in 1774, church officials moved the mission from the Presidio to a spot four miles up the San Diego River, to be free of the influence of soldiers in the fort. Here, over the years, they built the first of twenty-two missions, a day's walk from each other. San Diego's Mission de Alcalá would be known as "The Mother of Missions." In 1775, the Indians burned down the mission, killing Father Jayme and thus creating the first martyr in California.

In 1793, British explorer George Vancouver visited the harbor in the ship *Discovery*. With orders to survey the west coast, he visited ports and determined military strength of the fortifications. He reported the bay was not well defended and prompted the Spanish to build a defense on Ballast Point, called Fort Guijarros, in 1803.

Mexican Period

Dead Man's Point, where early explorers who lost their lives are commemorated

Mexican Independence from Spain, in 1821, began the twenty-five-year Mexican period during which the mission system dissolved. The Secularization Act of 1833 turned the church lands into private rancheros. The missions fell into disrepair and in 1846 were abandoned, with some used as barracks. Between the years 1800 and 1831, thirty-one merchant ships visited San

Diego, sixteen of them from the United States. In 1835, one of the most famous visitors, Richard Henry Dana, Jr., arrived in San Diego Bay on the ship *Pilgrim*. Dana wrote much about life along the early Pacific coast in his book *Two Years Before the*

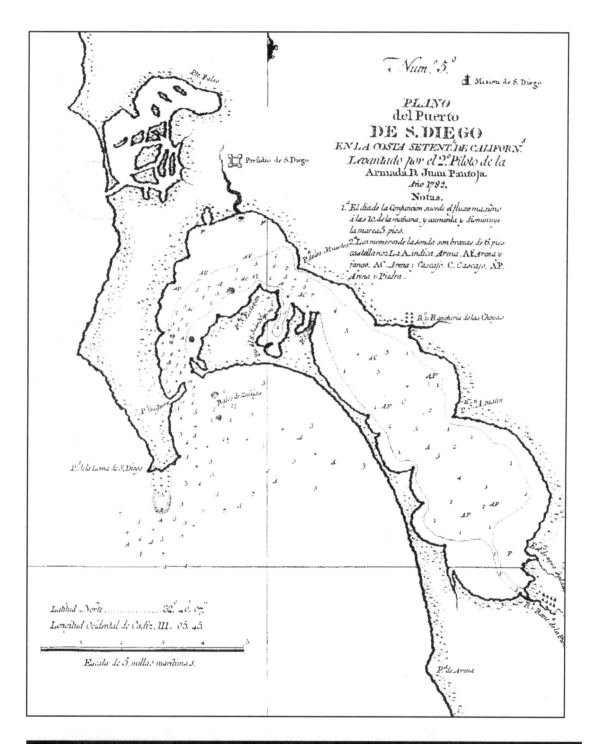

San Diego Maritime Museum

Juan Pantoja map of San Diego Bay, 1782

Old Town San Diego grew during the Mexican period

Mast. In 1845, the last governor of Mexico, Pio Pico, gave lands away before the Mexican War. The USS *Cyane* sailed from Monterey to San Diego Bay in 1846, declaring the town independent of Mexico and making way for California to become the thirty-first state in the United States a few years later.

California Period

In 1850, the first permanent wharf was built at the foot of Market Street, with barracks built at the foot of the wharf a year later. In 1853, "Derby Dyke" was completed to divert the flow of the San Diego River so it emptied not into San Diego Bay, but rather into False Bay, or Mission Bay, in the north. The first lighthouse was built in 1855 on Ballast Point, serving the increasing number of ships coming into the bay. With the discovery of whales in San Diego Bay, in 1859 a small whaling business began, but by 1871 the fishermen needed to go further offshore to find their catch, and the whaling business ceased. By 1860, "Old Town" had grown to a population of approximately 600 people.

San Diego Historical Society

Chinese junks fill the bay in 1887

The Chinese, who first came to the United States in great numbers to work in the gold fields, in 1850 were driven from the fields by the Foreign Miner's Tax; many then found work in fishing, agriculture, and railroads. They came to San Diego, with their junks filling the harbor from 1860 to 1900. They were the first people to start the fishing industry.

San Diego became a developer and speculator's paradise as men saw great promise for the city. Alonzo Horton, later known as the father of San Diego, arrived from San Francisco to make his dream become a reality. Frank Kimball, the father of National City, arrived from San Francisco the following year to ultimately develop railroads in southern San Diego. Surprisingly, gold was not only discovered in central California, but in 1870 in Julian, in east San Diego County, as well, bringing prospectors and more growth to the area. San Diego, the southernmost city of California, became connected to the rest of the state with the Southern Pacific Railroad track. It was completed from San Diego to Los Angeles in 1876, developing excellent trade between the two areas.

Railroad connects Los Angeles to San Diego in 1876

**Hotel del Coronado built by
Babcock and Story in 1889**

Victorian Period

The Victorian period was a time of building and expansion for the city of San Diego, with many great old buildings being constructed. In 1883, John Montgomery flew a glider 600 feet from a hill near the Mexican border; this was twenty years before the Wright brothers and Kitty Hawk. In 1888, Babcock and Story began development of the historic Hotel del Coronado on empty sand dunes across the bay from San Diego, with the dream that rich and famous people would come to this beachside paradise. John D. Spreckles, son of the Hawaiian "Sugar King," bought interest in Coronado Beach Company and Hotel del Coronado in 1889. Spreckles would later become one of the major developers of San Diego and Coronado. In 1908, the "The Great White Fleet," a friendship flotilla of United States Navy ships, visited San Diego on its round-the-world tour, anchoring off Coronado in the San Diego roadstead. The year 1911 marked the beginning of the San Diego tuna fishing industry that would thrive and help build San Diego's economy over the next forty years. The U.S. Navy, in 1912, began the first naval flight training school across the bay at the North Island Naval Air Station. Each of these developments brought more people to San Diego. The oldest functional pier, Broadway Pier, was completed in 1913. It was located at the end of Broadway Street, near the center of town, where it remains today, being used as a scenic park and pier.

The U.S. Navy interest expanded during the wars

World War I Period

This period saw more change and expansion in San Diego. The California/Panama Exposition was held in 1915, celebrating the opening of the Panama Canal. The development of Balboa Park by George Marston began with this event. Dr. Harry Wegeforth, attending the exposition, decided this was an ideal place for a zoo. He began collecting animals in 1916, for what was the beginning of the San Diego Zoo. He gave 100 acres of the park to develop the zoo.

In 1922, the U.S. Naval Training Center began taking its first recruits, marking the beginning of a growing size in the military population. The great *Star of India* came to San Diego in 1927, when it was donated to a group of San Diego historians. In 1928, a new airport was developed at Lindbergh Field on reclaimed tidelands called "Dutch Flats." By 1938, San Diego had become the biggest U.S. naval installation in the country.

San Diego Maritime Museum

Star of India comes to San Diego in 1927

World War II Period

The beginning of World War II initiated a period of growth for the city, increasing its importance as a military town. All military sites in the area grew as the National City tidelands were sold to the U.S. Navy, in 1938, for expansion of the U.S. Naval Station. Hundreds of new military families descended upon the San Diego area. When the Japanese bombed Pearl Harbor, Hawaii on December 7, 1941, destroying or sinking a great number of the country's battleships, six aircraft carriers were all safely docked along the wharfs in San Diego Bay, ready to go into battle. After the bombing of Pearl Harbor, the entrance to San Diego Bay was netted and remained netted until the end of the war.

1938 San Diego becomes the largest naval installation in the country

Suburban Growth Period

After World War II, servicemen returned to San Diego in record numbers. Housing development boomed as people moved to the suburbs, where housing was less expensive. The development of Mission Bay, in 1945, created a premier water park that developed into the world's finest aquatic

Mission Bay Park completed in 1945 as "World's Finest Aquatic Playground"

playground. The success of Mission Bay Park spurred the city of San Diego to further bay development. In 1952, construction began on Shelter Island, designed to be the premier yacht harbor on San Diego Bay. In 1960, University of California at San Diego was added to the California University system with their prime La Jolla location. Sea World opened in 1964 as a welcome addition to Mission Bay Park. The success of the Shelter Island development prompted creation of Harbor Island, with the airport expansion of Lindbergh Field in 1964.

After years of debate and quarreling, the San Diego-Coronado Bay Bridge was opened in 1969, and the Coronado ferry took its last trip across the bay. San Diego's beautiful harbor continued to be a major tourist attraction with the 1980 development of fourteen-acre Seaport Village along the downtown waterfront. In 1987, a smaller version of the Coronado Ferry, carrying only passengers, was brought back to ply the waters of the bay between Broadway Pier and the Coronado Ferry Landing.

Today, men and women continue to dream what San Diego can become, as they are drawn to this beautiful, temperate bay city. Expansion and development proceed with the Convention Center, the new ocean-front ball park, and the Golden Triangle, as San Diego remains "America's Finest City."

San Diego continues to be "America's Finest City"

2 GEOGRAPHY AND GEOLOGY

"Everyone was desirous to get a view of the new place. A chain of hills, beginning at the point (which was on our larboard hand coming in), protected the harbor on the north and west, and ran off into the interior, as far as the eye could reach. On the other sides the land was low and green, but without trees."

Richard Henry Dana, Jr., *Two Years Before the Mast* (1835)

Rocks and land masses tell a story, much like the pages of a book. The earth has a radius of 2,200 miles, with the outside covering, or crust, where all the visible change takes place, about forty miles thick. Within the crust are the earth's plates, shifting, pushing, rising, and sinking. The two plates most familiar to Americans are the Pacific plate, extending under most of the Pacific Ocean, and the North American

San Diego is built on an ancient sea floor

plate, extending from the middle Atlantic Ocean to the west coast of North America. These two plates meet at the San Andreas Fault, passing through all of southern California, and shifting at a rate of approximately two inches per year. This fault begins above San Francisco, running inland, paralleling the coast to Los Angeles, to terminate near the Salton Sea. It is one of the most rapidly deforming areas in North America. Rose Canyon Fault is a major fracture line close to San Diego. Beginning in the ocean off Del Mar, running south between Miramar and Mount Soledad, it ends in San Diego Bay and is a major concern to San Diegans. Scientists determined Mt. Soledad and Point Loma to be slowly rising, while Mission Bay and San Diego Bay are slowly sinking, due to plate pressure. Change occurs gradually at a rate of five to eight inches per one thousand years—nothing we have to worry about.

While plate shifting causes lifting and sinking of land masses, independent rising and falling of world seas occur with different climates, as the polar ice expands and contracts over thousands of years. Variations in sea level have been great; in earlier times the great seas have extended to the Mojave Desert and the Grand Canyon. Present day San Diego is built on top of an ancient sea floor.

North San Diego coast has sea cliffs and terraces

San Diego County coast has sea cliffs and terraces in the north, while the south contains coastal plains and mouths of major river valleys, with estuaries, deltas, and barrier islands. Embayed coasts are common on the east coast, Gulf Coast, and northwestern United States, but few exist in southern California. Generally, the

South San Diego contains river valleys and estuaries

coast is straight, with uniform cliffs made of uniform material. Mission Bay, Mission Beach, and Pacific Beach are lowlands on a former delta formed by the San Diego River, while San Diego is on lowlands on a former delta formed by the San Diego River, Sweetwater River, Otay River, and Tijuana River.

When European explorers first arrived, San Diego River flowed primarily into San Diego Bay. Mission Bay was earlier called "False Bay," where deep-draft vessels could enter until 1810. A large flood in 1821 changed the course of the river, causing it to enter both bays. After a few more floods, the flow into San Diego Bay was reduced to a small stream. Silt was carried downriver, forming barriers across openings to the sea called bars. Because San Diego was the primary harbor, a dyke, "Derby's Dyke," was constructed in 1853, to completely stem the river flow into San Diego

Bay. More flooding in 1855 destroyed the dyke, opening the small stream into San Diego; however, the primary flow continued into Mission Bay. In 1949, a controlling flood channel was finally created to tame and control the San Diego River at its outlet.

Because of this wonderful geology, where shifting continental plates cause rising and falling land masses, with independent rising and falling of the world's oceans, we have the geography of gentle sloping river valleys ending on beach barriers, creating the beautiful, protected, calm, and sedate San Diego Bay.

3 WIND, WEATHER, AND SEASON

"This wind [the southeaster] is the bane of the coast of California. Between the months of November and April (including a part of each), which is the rainy season in this latitude, you are never safe from it: and accordingly, in the ports which are open to it, vessels are obliged, during these months, to lie at anchor at a distance of three miles from the shore, with slip ropes on their cables, ready to go to sea at a moment's warning. The only ports which are safe from this wind are San Francisco and Monterey in the north and San Diego in the south."

Richard Henry Dana, Jr., *Two Years Before the Mast* (1835)

The weather map provides a framework for forecasting the weather. Surface charts are plotted as information is received from stations every six hours. The lines on the chart, called isobars, reflect equal barometric pressure. These lines form around two types of centers: low pressure centers, called "lows"; and high pressure centers, called "highs." Movement of these centers creates weather patterns. Heavy lines on the weather map show fronts, or boundaries between weather systems. Fronts can be warm, cold, or stationary. Wind generally blows nearly parallel with isobars; the more closely packed the isobars, the greater the wind force. A changing barometer indicates changing weather, with a rapidly falling barometer meaning an increase in wind, while a rising barometer indicates a decrease in wind. Over this low-altitude weather system is the tubular, horizontal, high velocity stream of air called the jet stream. It helps control the direction and path of passing fronts and pressure systems.

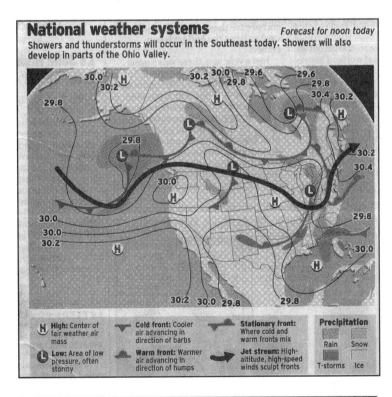

National weather systems Forecast for noon today
Showers and thunderstorms will occur in the Southeast today. Showers will also develop in parts of the Ohio Valley.

H High: Center of fair weather air mass

L Low: Area of low pressure, often stormy

Cold front: Cooler air advancing in direction of barbs

Warm front: Warmer air advancing in direction of humps

Stationary front: Where cold and warm fronts mix

Jet stream: High-altitude, high-speed winds sculpt fronts

Precipitation: Rain, Snow, T-storms, Ice

The weather map is very important in predicting weather

Two types of wind are measured: true wind, when wind velocity is measured with the object standing still; and apparent wind, when velocity is measured with the object moving. Wind velocity is measured with an anemometer in units of nautical miles per hour. An easy way to refer to wind velocity is the Beaufort Scale, which relates wind velocity to sea surface conditions:

Beaufort Scale of Wind Force and Its Probable Wave Height

Beaufort number	Description term		Wind speeds		Wave height (m)	
	Wind	Wave	knots	m/s	probable	maximum
0	Calm	-	< 1	0 - 0.2	-	-
1	Light air	Ripples	1 - 3	0.3 - 1.5	0.1	0.1
2	Light breeze	Small wavelets	4 - 6	1.6 - 3.3	0.2	0.3
3	Gentle breeze	Large wavelets	7 - 10	3.4 - 5.4	0.6	1.0
4	Moderate breeze	Small waves	11 - 16	5.5 - 7.9	1.0	1.5
5	Fresh breeze	Moderate waves	17 - 21	8.0 - 10.7	2.0	2.5
6	Strong breeze	Large waves	22 - 27	10.8 - 13.8	3.0	4.0
7	Near gale	Large waves	28 - 33	13.9 - 17.1	4.0	5.5
8	Gale	Moderately high waves	34 - 40	17.2 - 20.7	6.0	7.5
9	Strong gale	High waves	41 - 47	20.8 - 24.4	7.0	10.0
10	Storm	Very high waves	48 - 55	24.5 - 28.4	9.0	12.5
11	Violent storm	Exceptionally high waves	56 - 63	28.5 - 32.6	11.5	16.0
12	Hurricane	Exceptionally high waves	64 - 71	32.7 - 36.9	14.0	> 16

Local winds, as sea breezes, occur because the land heats up faster than the sea, causing an onshore wind that typically starts in the late morning and continues into the late afternoon. Land breezes occur because of reverse conditions—the land cools more rapidly, while the sea stays at a constant temperature, with the flow of air from the land to the sea beginning about midnight.

West Coast weather is influenced not only by weather patterns, but also by topography and the Pacific high. Coastal mountains generally act as a barrier to storms, minimizing their effects. The Pacific high in the north Pacific increases in the summer months and weakens in the wintertime, pushing storm tracks above southern California. The coast between Point Conception and the Mexican border generally runs west to east and is therefore protected from storms coming from the northwest. All these factors contribute to the generally mild weather in southern California.

San Diego generally has fair weather in contrast to other coastal areas of California, Oregon, and Washington. Weather generally comes from the northwest during the majority of the year; however, during the summer it can occasionally come from the southwest. When a cold front comes from the northwest, the wind changes and comes from the south just before the front arrives.

Average temperatures in the area are 55° F in the winter and 75° F in the summer, with afternoon sea breezes from the west and northwest at ten to fifteen knots. Occasionally in the autumn, dry, hot winds ("Santa Ana" winds) blow off the land. Periodically, strong winter storms from the northern Pacific approach the area in the mid fall to late spring. Winter is the rainy season, with January being the wettest month. January through March is the wettest period of the year.

San Diego generally has fair weather

Fog is prevalent in the fall and winter, with the foggiest month being in December. The fog commonly comes in late at night and stays until the early morning, dissipating during the day. The fog is most common at Point Loma; it thins out further inland from the point.

Wind is strongest in the summer months of March through September, with winds of seventeen knots or greater, two percent of the time. The wind commonly blows from 10 A.M. to 4 P.M., being greatest in the south San Diego Bay area. Off Shelter Island and Harbor Island the wind is more moderate, being in the lee of Point

You won't see this in San Diego

Loma. Winds are generally from the west and northwest; however, in the spring the direction can be from the southwest. Sea breeze and land breezes are present year around, keeping temperatures mild throughout the year.

Mariners should be aware of two special conditions in southern California: "Santa Ana" wind, which is an offshore wind from the desert, most commonly occurring in late autumn or winter. Although fairly infrequent, it can be violent with winds of greater than fifty miles per hour. Also, tropical

Winds are usually strongest in the summer

cyclones originating off Mexico can be a concern in the summer and autumn months. Fifteen cyclones are usually found each season off the Mexican coast, and often the tail end can be felt as far away as San Diego.

An excellent source to determine weather is the National Weather Service.

National Weather Service
1144 W. Bernardo Ct. #230
San Diego, CA 92127
(858) 675-8700
www.wrh.noaa.gov/sandiego

Weather is broadcast on weather channels on the VHF radio. There is a telephone recorded message at 1-858-289-1212, and weather warning flags fly at the west end of Shelter Island above the Harbor Police station.

4   TIDES AND CURRENTS

"The *California* had got under way at the same moment and we sailed down the narrow bay abreast, and were just off the mouth and gradually drawing ahead of her, were on the point of giving her three parting cheers, when suddenly we found ourselves stopped short and the *California* ranging fast ahead of us. A bar stretches across the mouth of the harbor, with water enough to float common vessels, but, being low in the water, and having kept well to the leeward as we were bound to the southward, we had struck fast, while the *California*, being light, had floated over."

Richard Henry Dana, Jr., *Two Years Before the Mast* (1835)

Tides are the rise and fall of water levels around the earth. They originate in open ocean, but are most notable and significant close to shore. Tides occur primarily because of two forces: gravitational and centrifugal. Gravitational force is the inward force of the earth and the outward pull of the heavenly bodies, especially the sun and the moon. Centrifugal force is the outward force caused by the earth's rotation. Forces are generally in balance—however, not exactly in balance at various locations on the earth—therefore, tides result. The moon, being closer to the Earth, exerts twice the force of the sun; consequently, tides usually follow the phases of the moon. Generally, two high tides and two low tides occur during the day, with maximum and minimum recordings

Low tide can put you aground

occurring about one hour later each day. The west coast of the United States is noted for the large inequity between the two high tides and low tides. The average differences between the highs can be one to two feet, while the differences between the lows can be two to three feet. The ebb tide is generally stronger and lasts longer than the flood tide.

Current in the bay can be up to five knots

Understanding tides is essential for safe navigation, especially for deep-draft vessels. Knowing the time for high and low tides and being aware of shallow water is important to prevent grounding. Tidal information also allows us to calculate whether we can safely pass under fixed structures, such as bridges and power cables. Tide forecasts for numerous harbors on the Pacific coast are published in newspapers and tide books for San Diego Bay. Tide table booklets are usually found around harbor businesses or can be purchased at the local boating store.

The mean tidal range in San Diego Bay is 4.0 feet, while the diurnal range is 5.7 feet. The maximum tide in the bay is 8 feet.

Current is the horizontal movement of water. Currents in the bay are caused primarily by the tide. Other minor currents are ocean, river, and wind currents, but these have minimal effects on San Diego Bay. Slack water is a point when no discernible flow of water occurs, usually at the turning of the tide. The California current is the primary ocean current affecting the Pacific coast. This south-flowing current extends 300 miles off shore, flowing at a rate of 0.2 knots. During the months of July through February a countercurrent, the Davidson Current, flows in a northerly direction close to shore. Wind-driven currents will be created by a steady wind lasting twelve hours or more. Their velocity will generally be two percent of the wind velocity. Understanding current is important because it will affect the course and speed of your boat.

Current in San Diego Bay is generally set in the direction of the channel and ranges from a velocity of 0.5 knots to a maximum of 5 knots. Near the south end of Zuñiga Jetty there is a slight set toward Zuñiga Shoal on the ebb tide. Vessels should be careful passing Ballast Point because there is sheer, caused by the crosscurrent deflection from Ballast Point. Near the ends of piers, strong eddies with irregular velocities and direction make docking difficult.

Strong eddies can occur around piers and docks

Shoal areas in San Diego area are marked on the charts; however, mariners should be especially aware of common obstructions in San Diego Bay:

- A submerged jetty across the main channel from Ballast Point is where many boaters go aground.
- Shoal water exists at the east and west end of Shelter Island where vessels trying to cut the corner into Shelter Island Yacht Basin and America's Cup Harbor find themselves aground on the muddy bottom.
- Caution should be taken north of the Coronado Ferry Landing, as water becomes very shallow near the shore.
- Shallow water exists between piers "8" and "15" under the Coronado Bay Bridge.
- Shoal water exists between the northeast end of the Naval Amphibious Base and buoy "1" at the entrance to Glorietta Bay.
- Numerous shoals exist in South San Diego Bay south of the Sweetwater Channel; therefore, always stay within the main channels.

The above areas are common locations where boaters have trouble; consequently, special attention should always be given to these areas when navigating San Diego Bay.

5   SAFETY AND COMFORT

"This was our last port. Here we were to discharge everything from the ship; clean her out, smoke her, take in our hides wood and water and set sail for Boston."

Richard Henry Dana, Jr., *Two Years Before the Mast* (1835)

Operating your boat in a safe condition requires attention to a myriad of items. Good skippers understand their duties and obligations, knowing they are responsible for passenger safety from the time they leave the dock until they return. Lists help us remember all we need to do before we go boating. To improve your safety and comfort when operating a boat, consider the following three areas: boat equipment, leaving the dock, and fueling.

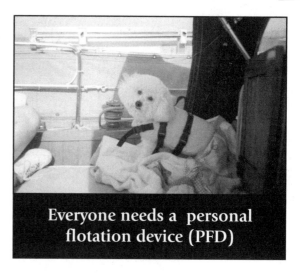

Everyone needs a personal flotation device (PFD)

Minimally, contemplate having the following aboard your boat:

- ❑ Operator's license (if required)
- ❑ Ship's papers (registration or documentation)
- ❑ Life preservers for each person
- ❑ Throwable floatation aid
- ❑ Fire extinguishers
- ❑ Visual distress signals
- ❑ Horn and/or bell
- ❑ Anchor and anchor line
- ❑ Compass
- ❑ Charts and navigation books
- ❑ Boat hook
- ❑ Paddles or oars
- ❑ Toolkit and spare parts
- ❑ Dock lines
- ❑ Flashlight and spare batteries

Life preservers are of vital importance. In the past, they have been large, bulky, and uncomfortable to wear. Today, with improved technology, one can wear small inflatable bands, like suspenders.

Be prepared for all eventualities; don't wait for emergencies to happen. Planning and checking can relieve stress and anxiety, as well as prevent embarrassment.

New, comfortable PFD are available

Before leaving the dock, make sure:

- ❑   Bilge is free of fumes and water
- ❑   Fuel supply is at a proper level
- ❑   Fuel system is free of leaks
- ❑   Engine oil and transmission fluid are checked
- ❑   Battery is charged and electrolyte levels checked
- ❑   Gauges and indicator lights are working
- ❑   Engine cooling system is full
- ❑   Electronic gear is functional
- ❑   Drive belts are operational
- ❑   Navigation lights are operational
- ❑   Steering and shift mechanism are operational

Many boating accidents occur while fueling. Gasoline fumes are heavier than air and form an explosive combination. Careful attention to proper fueling practices will greatly reduce the risk of calamity. Consider the following checklist:

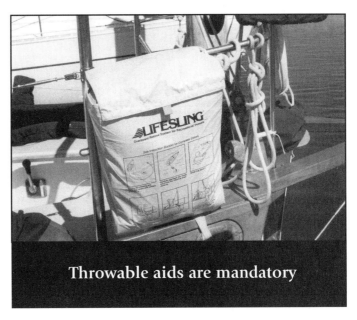

Throwable aids are mandatory

- ❑ Fuel in daylight
- ❑ Put out all flames
- ❑ Prohibit smoking
- ❑ Shut off engine and all electrical equipment
- ❑ Close all portholes, doors, and hatches
- ❑ Have all passengers step off boat
- ❑ Keep pump nozzle in constant contact with filler pipe
- ❑ Fill tanks only ninety-five percent full to allow for expansion
- ❑ Wipe up any spillage
- ❑ Open all closed compartments
- ❑ Turn on bilge blower
- ❑ Check for fuel leaks
- ❑ Sniff bilge for vapors

Careful attention while fueling

In addition to the required equipment, please consider the following equipment for safety and comfort:

- ❑ Spare anchor and rode
- ❑ Bilge pump (automatic and manual)
- ❑ First Aid kit
- ❑ VHF Radio
- ❑ Binoculars
- ❑ Clothing, extra
- ❑ Spotlight
- ❑ Spare tiller
- ❑ Swim ladder
- ❑ Fenders
- ❑ GPS

Cruising for twenty-one months, traveling 4,500 miles and visiting ninety-seven ports and anchorages, we discovered five items that make life aboard more enjoyable:

Weather protectors protect you from the sun

1. **Proper Clothing**: Layer clothing so as temperatures rise or fall, items can be added or removed as the situation requires. Wearing waterproof clothing on the outside is important, because saltwater-drenched clothing never dries. The wind decreases temperature, making it feel cooler out on the water; make sure a warm jacket is always nearby. When guests are visiting, suggest they limit items to a medium-sized duffel bag, since space is usually limited on boats.

2. **Weather Protectors**: Dodgers provide great protection from wind, rain, and ocean spray. We also added a sun/rain awning, for further protection from the elements. Don't forget sunscreen and a hat to protect your skin from the destructive rays of the sun. Keeping hydrated with fluids throughout the day is essential.

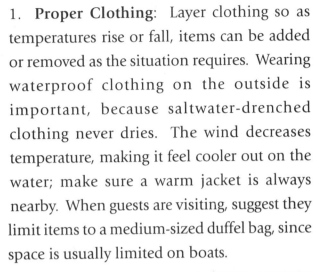
Weather protectors add comfort

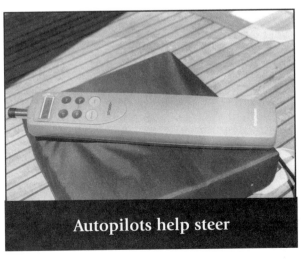
Autopilots help steer

3. **Autopilot**: Traveling long, unobstructed distances for hours is tedious; however, once we added the autopilot, we were free to do other things while the miles passed by.

4. **Heaters**: Traveling north, with summer turning to fall, the temperature started dropping. This was a chilly reality for southern California boaters, and our need for heaters grew, going from no heaters to four heaters in our twenty-eight foot boat.

5. **Plastic Bags**: Moisture on boats seeps into every cupboard and corner, especially paper products and clothing. Heaters and dehumidifiers are essential, while using zip-lock plastic bags to store items helps preserve freshness.

Plastic bags keep moisture out

Finally, consider joining one of the excellent towing services in the area. A minimal fee provides members with unlimited free towing, fuel delivery, parts delivery, jump starts, and ungrounding. Emergency services are provided twenty-four hours a day, rain or shine, 365 days a year. Joining one of these companies even provides for a much-needed boating lobbyist in Washington, D.C.

Sea Tow (888) 473-2869

Tow Boat U.S. (800) 493-7869

Vessel Assist (800) 399-1921

Towing services help in emergencies

6 NAVIGATION AND SEAMANSHIP

"As we drew down near, carried rapidly along by the current, we over hauled our chain and clewed up the topsails. 'Let go the anchor!' said the captain; but either there was not chain enough forward of the windlass, or the anchor went down foul, or we had too much headway on, for it did not bring us up. 'Pay out chain!' shouted the captain; and we gave it to her; but it would not do. Before the other could be let go we drifted down broadside on, and went smash into the *Lagoda*."

Richard Henry Dana, Jr., *Two Years Before the Mast* (1836)

Navigation

Navigation is the science of directing movement of a boat from one place to another in a safe and efficient manner, with the use of charts. Charts, being road maps of the sea, are vital for safe boating because they show exactly where to go and not go.

Charts are vital for safe boating

In the United States, nautical charts are published by the National Ocean Atmospheric Administration (NOAA) of the Department of Commerce. Nautical chart #1 is a booklet explaining all the nautical terms and symbols. Four colors are used to describe the Earth's surface: white for deep water, blue for shallow water, green for tidal areas, and gold for dry land. Careful examination of the chart shows the boater depths, depth contours, height of objects, nature of bottom, hazards, dredged channels, prominent landmarks, and vertical clearances.

Charts divide the Earth into a grid system of latitude and longitude. Latitudes are parallel lines running east and west, measuring distance north and south of the equator. Longitudes are meridian lines running north and south, measuring distance east and west of Greenwich, England. Using this grid system of latitude and longitude, any position on the Earth can be found accurately.

The U.S. Coast Pilot, also published by the National Oceanic and Atmospheric Administration (NOAA), is a set of books describing channels, anchorages, tidal and current information, and navigational hazards. The local Coast Guard district publishes a weekly *Local Notice to Mariners*, reporting changes to charts and Coast Pilots.

The U.S. Aids to Navigation System marks all waters of the United States, including lakes and waterways connecting to the high seas. The system is maintained by the U.S. Coast Guard. Aids to navigation warn of danger, help pilot a boat safely, and aid in finding a position in a body of water. They consist of buoys, anchored floating objects, and beacons that are permanently fixed to the shore. Shapes, colors, lights, and numbers all help the mariner to identify his position. The lateral system using green and red markers, identifies port and starboard sides along a route. Added to these are ranges indicating the centerline of a channel and sound signals, which are all intended to promote safe boating. The *U.S. Coast Guard Light Lists* describe and locate all lights, buoys, and beacons maintained in the United States

Careful piloting prevents grounding

Navigation Rules—traffic rules for boats—are designed to prevent collisions. Inland Rules and International Rules are two sets of rules affecting boaters; however, both are very similar, with the main tenet being to avoid collisions at all cost. Rules explain right-of-way, overtaking traffic, speed, operating with restricted visibility, and navigation lights. The unwritten law of the sea requires a mariner to come to the aid of another mariner in distress. This code also contains a "Good Samaritan" clause to limit liability of those who render assistance.

Seamanship

Seamanship is a broad topic that could include boat construction, design and maintenance, boat handling, lines, knots, splices, and anchoring.

Lines today are all synthetic. Three types of lines are commonly used in boating: nylon, polyester, and polypropylene. Nylon is the most common, as it is low cost and has stretchable qualities. Polyester line is more expensive, with a breaking strength approximately ten percent less than nylon; however, it does not stretch. Polypropylene line is the least expensive of the lines and floats.

Nylon line secures the boat to dock

Three knots commonly used in boating are: 1) the figure eight knot, a stopper knot; 2) the cleat hitch, to tie a boat to a dock cleat; and 3) a bowline, probably the most versatile knot in a sailor's chest because it is easily tied and untied and does not slip. Other common and popular knots, each with its own purpose,

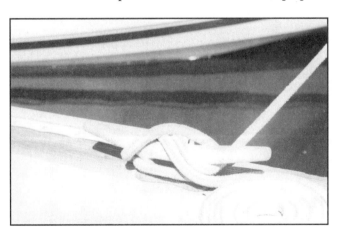

The common cleat hitch is useful

are: square knot, sheet bend, clove hitch, and anchor bend.

Anchoring is an art requiring knowledge and practice to achieve proper results. Three common anchors used are the Danforth, CQR, and the Bruce. The Danforth, with twin sharp flukes, is designed for high penetration in sand and mud. The CQR, shaped like a plough, will not dig as deep, but will penetrate weeds, sand, mud, and rocks. The

Bruce is designed to resist breaking out through 360° change in direction of the pull. Multiple anchors are needed for the varied conditions along the coast. The rode, or anchor line, can be either synthetic line or chain. The preferable synthetic line is nylon because of its great strength and ability to stretch without damage to its fibers. Chain does not have natural stretch, but it is resistant to chafe. Proper technique is important to keep the boat fastened to the bottom. The commonly accepted normal scope of rode is seven to one (7:1).

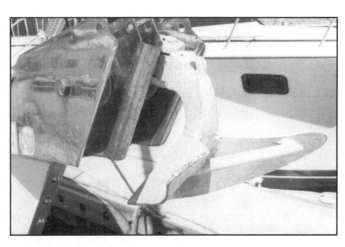

Every anchor has a specific purpose

Further study of these subjects is certainly appropriate. Excellent instruction is provided

U. S. Power Squadron offers excellent courses

by the U.S. Coast Guard Auxiliary and the U.S. Power Squadron, who have organizations all over the country. To find a local squadron near you, contact:

U.S. Coast Guard Auxiliary
9449 Watson Industrial Park
St. Louis, MO 63126
1-877-875-6296
www.CGAux.org

U. S. Power Squadron
P. O. Box 30432
Raleigh, NC 27622
1-888-367-8777
www.USPS.org

7 TRAILER BOATING

"There is nothing, absolutely nothing, half so much worth doing as messing about in boats."
Kenneth Grahame, *The Wind in the Willows* (1908)

Trailerable boats represent ninety percent of recreational boats in the U.S. today. They are easily transported to lakes, rivers, and oceans, while providing savings in slip, storage, and maintenance fees. This allows more people to enjoy the pleasure of boating.

Trailer selection begins with size of boat and distance to travel. Short hauling of small vessels requires lightweight trailers, while large boats that travel at high speeds, for long distances, require heavy-duty trailers. Trailers, like water, should support all areas of the hull. Support from rollers or padded bars should maintain hull shape, with extra bracing at the transom.

90% of recreational boats can be trailered

Trailer tires are subject to greater stress

Trailer tires, usually smaller than automobile tires, turn at a greater rate and produce more stress; therefore, they require greater air pressure. Wheel bearings on a trailer are critical, since wheels turning at high speeds create extreme heat. Bearing protectors keep waterproof grease under pressure to protect bearings. Boats should be attached to trailers with the winches, as well as numerous tiedowns, especially on the transom.

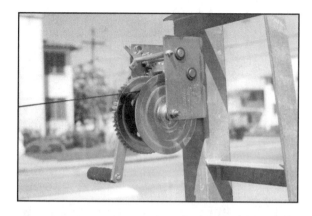

Winches should have an antireverse lever

Use dual safety chains, crossed

To prevent accidents, make sure the winch has an antireverse lever and lock.

The trailer hitch is very important. Hitches come in five gross-weight classes, with universal sizing sequences to prevent them from being overloaded. The hitch should be welded to the frame of the vehicle, while the trailer ball should be secured with a nut and lock washer. The weight of the trailer rig must not exceed the load capacity of the trailer hitch.

Tongue weight should be approximately ten percent of the weight of the rig when the coupler is parallel to the ground. Incorrect tongue weight makes driving hazardous. Too much weight on the hitch makes the vehicle difficult to steer, while too little makes the trailer tend to fishtail.

Dual, crossed safety chains are recommended; their chain-breaking strength should be rated at one and one-half times the maximum gross trailer weight.

Safety is important when pulling a trailer. Careful attention must be paid to such factors as enlarged side mirrors, wheel jacks, spare tires, parking wheel, wheel chocks, and emergency flares. A pretrip checklist is very helpful. Consider the following:

- ❏ emergency equipment: spare trailer tire, trailer jack, proper size lug wrench, wheel chocks, road flares, reflectors, extra bulbs, fuses, etc.
- ❏ additional rear-view mirrors installed
- ❏ equipment inside boat secured
- ❏ coupler seated on ball and locked
- ❏ safety chains fastened correctly
- ❏ electrical harness connected and lights working
- ❏ boat securely attached to trailer
- ❏ tongue jack in full upright position and locked
- ❏ projections over stern marked with red flag or light
- ❏ masts, boat tops, antennas lowered, tied down, or removed
- ❏ correct air pressure in tires
- ❏ lug nuts tight on all wheels

Trailer selection begins with size of boat

Set up your boat as much as possible before entering the launch lanes. Remove tiedowns, disconnect trailer lights, attach lines to the boat, place fenders, insure drain plug is in, and put outboard in up position. Before launching, wait for your wheel bearings to cool down so as not to draw cold water into the bearing. Unless absolutely unavoidable, keep the

Match tow vehicle to boat

trailer hubs out of the water. Tow vehicle tires should be kept out of the water to insure traction. Turn tow vehicle engine off, place vehicle in gear, set parking brake, and place chocks under the wheel once boat is in the water. Launch the boat with bow and stern lines attached, to control the boat. Clear the ramp as soon as possible, driving to a designated parking space. Finish preparing the boat at the dock.

Returning to the dock, let your passengers out first and use the same bow and stern lines to guide the boat to the trailer. Winch the boat onto the trailer. Remove the drain plug, and drive the tow vehicle back to the parking lot where the boat and trailer can be made ready for transport. Remember always to tow your boat with the propeller in an upright position.

Maintain and store your boat and trailer by washing down, inspecting and rotating tires, lubricating wheel bearings regularly, and placing light grease on early corrosion. Reduce tire pressure when the boat trailer is in storage for a long period of time.

San Diego Bay provides excellent opportunities for trailerable boats, with four large modern ramps throughout the bay. Mission Bay also provides fine access for trailerable boats, with six ramps at various locations throughout the park. Come and try them all.

8   PROCURING A BERTH

"We were always glad to see San Diego; it being the depot, and a snug little place, and seeming quite like home, especially to me , . . "
Richard Henry Dana, Jr., *Two Years Before the Mast* (1835)

A common perception among cruisers is that San Diego Harbor is "cruiser unfriendly." This is not entirely true. The San Diego Unified Port District realizes the harbor is a major tourist attraction in San Diego, in addition to being an important revenue source for the enveloping cities. Therefore, it is extremely important to keep the bay and the surrounding harbors spotless. They actively discourage "boat bums" and derelicts from the harbor. The vast majority of boaters do not fall into this category, but are concerned with the environment—clean air, clean water, freedom from pollution, elimination of noise, and retention of unspoiled natural habitat—while at the same time they want to keep waterways open for boating pleasure. The Port District encourages use by concerned, environmentally conscious boaters.

To insure a pleasant and enjoyable stay in San Diego Bay, plan ahead and know your objectives. Decide what you want to do while you are in San Diego. Are you going to haul out, visit the tourist attractions, do maintenance, rest and relax, visit friends, or are you just passing through and stopping for fuel and supplies? Determine how long you want to stay while you are in San Diego. Will you be staying for the weekend, a week, a month, a year, or permanently? Do you need a slip, or can you be happy swinging on a mooring or at an anchorage? Determining these factors will help you decide what preparations to make, guaranteeing an enjoyable stay in San Diego.

If you are planning to stay at a slip, always call ahead to determine space available at the yacht club or marina. If they are extremely crowded or if you have a large boat, you may need to pay to reserve a slip before you arrive. Many times yacht clubs need to check the registry to determine if clubs have reciprocal privileges, also checking the calendar of events to insure space is available at the guest dock.

If you are planning to stay at a mooring, call or write ahead to insure one is available when you arrive. The San Diego Unified Port District controls all moorings.

The San Diego Bay Mooring Office issues a renewable permit, valid for up to one year. Persons interested in mooring their vessel to a port mooring must obtain a mooring permit from the San Diego Port District. Because of the high demand, each mooring area may have a waiting list. To apply, complete an application and submit your current vessel registration or documentation, along with an application fee. Each applicant may submit only one application. To apply in person, make an appointment with the mooring office. To request a mooring application for San Diego Bay, write:

> San Diego Unified Port District Mooring Office
> 2890 Shelter Island Drive
> San Diego, CA 92001

Mooring office is at the west end of Shelter Island

Prior to receiving a mooring permit all applicants must have their vessels inspected by the U.S. Coast Guard Auxiliary. Courtesy Marine Examinations (CMEs) are conducted every Saturday at the Auxiliary Inspection dock between 8 A.M. and 4 P.M. The inspection dock is located along the quay at the north end of the Laurel

Street Roadstead (Mooring–A9). The address is:

Vessel Inspection Dock
2320 N. Harbor Drive
San Diego, CA 92101

This inspection may be conducted no more than six months prior to the date of receiving a mooring permit. Please contact the mooring office with any questions.

If you are planning to stay at an anchorage, less preparation is necessary. Free anchoring permits are controlled by the San Diego Unified Port District Mooring Office and are issued for thirty days at a time. Boats and owners must be from outside San Diego County, as this anchorage is intended for boats transiting the San Diego area. Persons interested in anchoring their vessel must obtain a permit from the San Diego Port District. During popular summer months such as August, September, October, and November, when everyone is traveling south to Mexico, there may be a waiting list; however, the port opens up additional anchorages to accommodate all boats. To apply, complete an application and submit your current vessel registration or documentation. To

Mooring office

apply in person, make an appointment with the mooring office. To request an anchoring application for San Diego Bay, write:

San Diego Unified Port District Mooring Office
2890 Shelter Island Drive
San Diego, CA 92001

Please contact the mooring office with any questions.

San Diego Unified Port District Mooring Office (619) 686-6227
San Diego Harbor Police (619) 223-1133

If you arrive without a plan including prior preparations, you may indeed come to the conclusion that San Diego is an "unfriendly harbor." Plan before you leave, call in advance, write ahead, and you will enjoy all San Diego has to offer.

Anchorages
and
Marinas

"The bay was as deserted and looked as dreary as before and formed no pleasing contrast with the security and snugness of San Diego."

Richard Henry Dana, Jr., *Two Years Before the Mast* (1835)

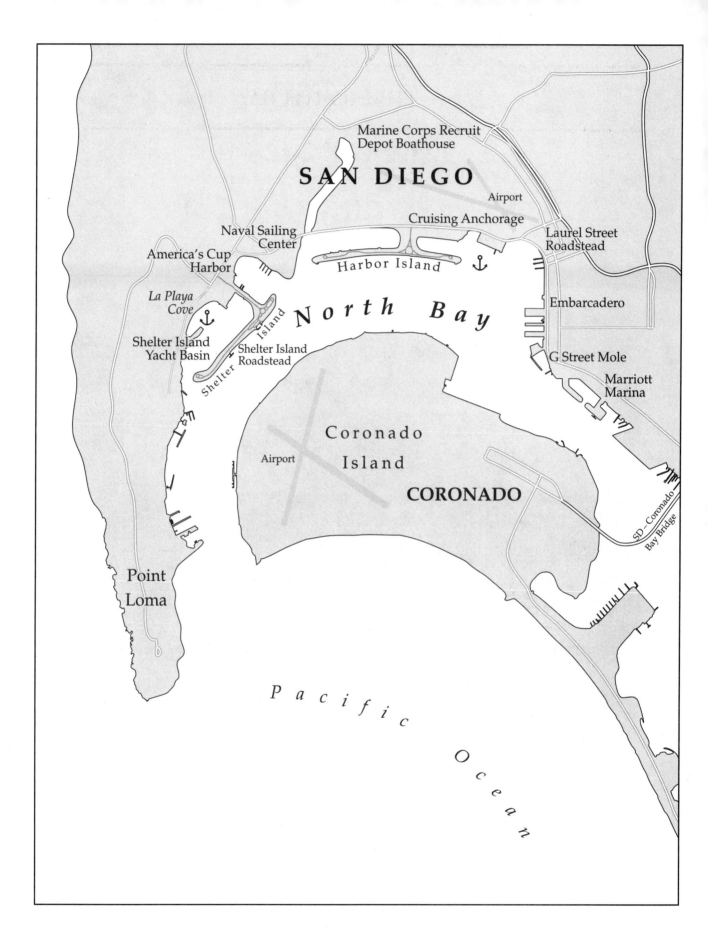

Marine Corps Recruit
Depot Boathouse

SAN DIEGO

Airport

Naval Sailing
Center

Cruising Anchorage

Laurel Street
Roadstead

America's Cup
Harbor

Harbor Island

*La Playa
Cove*

Embarcadero

Shelter Island
Yacht Basin

Island

Shelter Island
Roadstead

Shelter

N o r t h   B a y

G Street Mole

Marriott
Marina

Coronado
Island

Airport

CORONADO

SD – Coronado
Bay Bridge

Point
Loma

P a c i f i c   O c e a n

9   THE NORTH BAY

"The harbor [San Diego] is small and landlocked; there is no surf; the vessels lie within a cable's length of the beach, and the beach itself is smooth, hard sand, without rocks, or stones."
Richard Henry Dana, Jr., *Two Years Before the Mast* (1835)

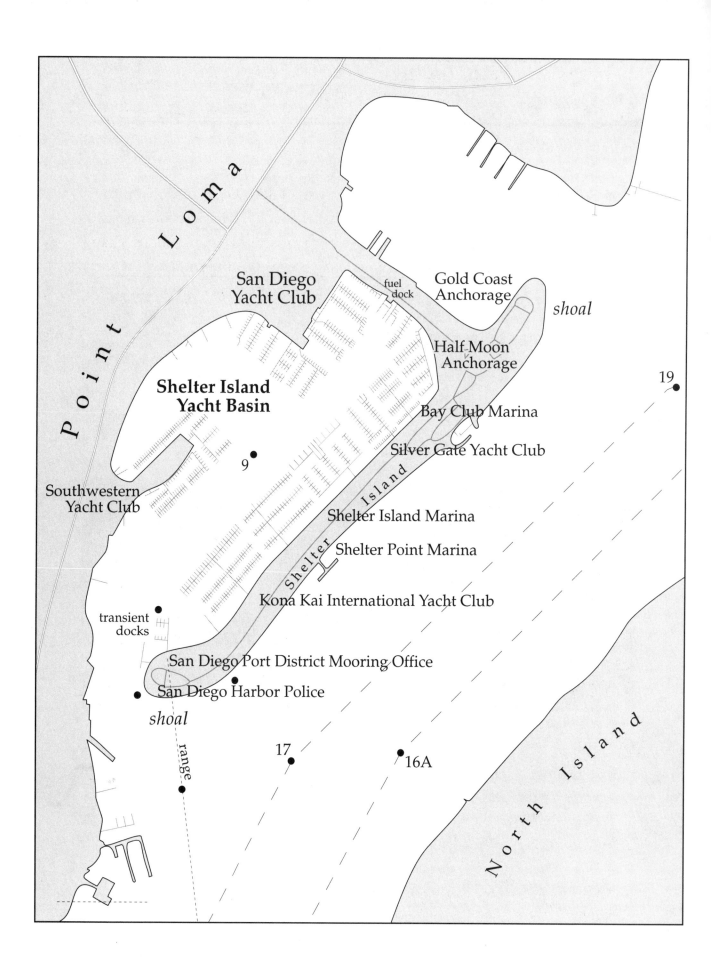

Point Loma

San Diego Yacht Club

fuel dock

Gold Coast Anchorage

shoal

Half Moon Anchorage

Shelter Island Yacht Basin

Bay Club Marina

9

Silver Gate Yacht Club

Southwestern Yacht Club

Shelter Island

Shelter Island Marina

Shelter Point Marina

Kona Kai International Yacht Club

transient docks

San Diego Port District Mooring Office

San Diego Harbor Police

shoal

range

17

16A

19

North Island

Shelter Island Yacht Basin

NOAA Charts #18773, #18765, #18766, #18772

Latitude 32°42.3' N, Longitude 117°14.1' W

(Entrance to Shelter Island Yacht Basin)

Shelter Island is the hub of boating activity in San Diego. The first private docking facility as you enter San Diego Bay, Shelter Island offers all services needed by the boating community—yacht clubs, marinas, boatyards, engine shops, chandleries, hotels, and restaurants—all surrounded by green grass and palm trees. Everything is here to satisfy your boating needs, along with great views of the San Diego skyline.

Entrance to Shelter Island Yacht Basin

The earliest record of the small sandbar off La Playa area in San Diego Bay was on Spanish charts dated 1769. The shoal was always a hazard to navigation. It would appear at low tide; early San Diegans would then row out to the sandy island to fish and picnic. The U.S. Navy and the port district would periodically deposit harbor dredging material here to further expose the hazard.

Plans to develop the shallows off La Playa were proposed as early as the 1930s, but no action was taken. In 1948 John Bates, Director of the San Diego Port District, pushed for development of a two million dollar project to create an "island" peninsula 300 feet wide by 6,000 feet long on the sand bar off La Playa in San Diego Bay.

He went door to door promoting the plan, which became known as "Bates' Folly." Funds were approved and construction began in 1949, with completion in 1952.

Today, Shelter Island is the heart of boating activity in San Diego County. All boating services can be found in the area. Within Shelter Island Basin are Bay Club Marina, Gold Coast Anchorage, Half Moon Anchorage, Kona Kai International Yacht Club, San Diego Harbor Police, San Diego Unified Port District Mooring Office, San Diego Yacht Club, Shelter Island Marina, Shelter Point Marina, Silver Gate Yacht Club, Southwestern Yacht Club, and U.S. Customs. All these facilities are located in and surrounded by beautiful Shelter Island Park, with its green grass, palm trees, concert pavilion, and children's playground. Toward the west end of Shelter Island is the Tuna Fisherman's Monument memorializing the birth of the west coast tuna fishing industry and mariners lost at sea. At the western tip of the island are the Japanese Garden and Friendship Bell, built in 1958, recognizing the eternal friendship between San Diego and her Japanese sister city, Yokohama.

Harbor Police dock and U. S. Customs at west end of Shelter Island

Japanese Garden and Friendship Bell

Land Approach

Two miles north of downtown San Diego, exit Interstate 5 at Rosecrans Street. Drive west on Rosecrans Street past the U.S. Naval Training Center, and turn left on Shelter Island Drive, three miles from the freeway. Proceed on Shelter Island Drive, where you will find all services.

Sea Approach

Approaching San Diego Bay seaward from the north or west, you see only the green headlands of

Point Loma, hiding the city of San Diego behind the hills. All boating traffic must approach the entrance from the south. From this perspective, from a distance of twenty-three miles you see the yellow scar on the south end of Point Loma with the flashing, fifteen-second, white beacon of Point Loma light. San Diego entrance buoy "SD" (latitude 32°37.3' N, longtitude 117°14.8' W) marks the entrance to the bay. Care should be taken to avoid the kelp surrounding the harbor entrance. Staying within the main channel or following the 100-foot-depth-or-greater bottom contour line will help you avoid all attached kelp. Keep an eye out for floating kelp, which can also foul your prop. Upon entering the harbor, in the lee of Point Loma, be careful of the partially-submerged Zuñiga Jetty, extending one mile from North Is-land, on the east side of the channel. Once abreast of buoy "5" follow the Shelter Island range light (353° true) into the bay. Continue to be careful across from Ballast Point, where a submerged jetty grounds many boats. Proceed down the main ship channel. Past Ballast Point and U.S. Naval Submarine Base, at buoy "15" leave the channel and travel northwest to the west end of Shelter Island (latitude 32°42.3' N, longitude 117°14.1' W). Pass between the west end of Shelter Island and Point Loma and enter Shelter Island Yacht Basin.

> Local Weather Service (858) 289-1212
> Sea Tow (888) 473-2869
> Tow Boat U.S. (800) 493-7869
> Vessel Assist (800) 399-1921

Anchorage and Berthing

No anchoring is allowed in Shelter Island Yacht Basin. The nearest short-term anchorage is La Playa Cove, directly northeast of the yacht basin between Southwestern Yacht Club and San Diego Yacht Club. Anchor with a San Diego Mooring Office permit for sev-enty-two hours over a weekend only. The San Diego Harbor Police and the San Diego Moor-ing Office are located on the western tip of Shelter Island. Check with the mooring of-fice for transient slips, anchoring permits, and mooring permits. San Diego is a port of en-try, so clear customs here as you enter back into the United States.

Transient docks adjacent to the Harbor Police docks

Shelter Island Yacht Basin contains numerous private marinas. The first marina on the starboard side is the 523-slip **Shelter Point Hotel and Marina**. Docking facilities are available for boats twenty-four to 180 feet in length, with all conveniences, including hotel club house, health club, spa, picnic area, beach, swimming pool, tennis courts, and restaurants. Within the hotel and marina are the offices of **Kona Kai International Yacht**

Shelter Point Marina

Club, where slip and facilities may be available for transient yachts of yacht club members with reciprocal privileges.

The next marina on the starboard side is the 188-slip **Shelter Island Marina**, with space to accommodate boats from twenty to seventy feet in length. It is associated with the Island Palms Hotel, with all facilities available for slip holders, including telephone, cable TV, shower, laundry, pool, spa, restaurant, lounge, fitness room, and dockside room service.

The adjacent facilities belong to **Silver Gate Yacht Club**, where 170 slips accommodate boats from twenty-four to sixty feet in length. A friendly group of

Silver Gate Yacht Club

people here emphasize racing and cruising, with a restaurant, bar, clubhouse, and dry storage all available. Yacht club members may have reciprocal privileges; a transient slip may be available.

The **Bay Club Marina**, with 180 slips to accommodate boats thirty-two to forty-five feet in length, is the following marina on the starboard side of Shelter Island Yacht Basin. It is associated with the Bay Club Hotel, so slip holders have use of water, electricity, restrooms, showers, phones, restaurant, swimming pool, and health club.

Bay Club Marina

At the east end of the basin is **Half Moon Anchorage**, with 180 slips accommodating boats thirty to fifty feet in length. Humphrey's Half Moon Inn and Suites provides a pool with restaurant facilities, besides such usual amenities as water, electricity, showers, restrooms, and laundry.

Half Moon Anchorage

Gold Coast Anchorage

At the end of the basin is **Gold Coast Anchorage**, a thirty-five-slip marina for boats ranging from forty feet to 120 feet in length. Gold Coast Anchorage has water, electricity, restrooms, showers, and phones.

On the north side of the basin are San Diego Yacht Club and Southwestern Yacht Club.

San Diego Yacht Club, at the northeast corner of the basin, has 565 slips, sharing fame with skipper Dennis Conner, who brought the America's Cup back to the United States from Australia in 1987. (They then led an unsuccessful defense, losing the cup to New Zealand in 1991.)

San Diego Yacht Club

Southwestern Yacht Club

Southwestern Yacht Club, on the northwest side of the basin with over 380 slips, is known as one of the friendliest and most active yacht clubs in San Diego. As a yacht club member with reciprocal privileges, you may find a transient slip for a short period of time at either one of these clubs. Always call ahead to determine slip availability.

Bay Club Marina (619) 222-0314

Gold Coast Anchorage (619) 225-0588

Half Moon Anchorage (619) 224-3401

Kona Kai International Yacht Club (619) 223-3138

San Diego Harbor Police (619) 223-1133

San Diego Unified Port District Mooring Office (619) 686-6227

San Diego Yacht Club (619) 221-8400

Shelter Island Marina at the Island Palms Hotel (619) 223-0301

Shelter Point Hotel and Marina (619) 224-07547

Silver Gate Yacht Club (619) 222-1214

Southwestern Yacht Club (619) 222-0438

U.S. Customs (619) 223-1133

Facilities

Bait and tackle	Shelter Island Bait and Tackle (619) 222-7635
Bank	
Boatyard	Driscoll Boatyard (619) 224-3575
	Kettenburg Marine (619) 221-6930
	Koehler Kraft Yard (619) 222-9051
	Nielsen Beaumont Marine (619) 222-4253
	Shelter Island Boatyard (619) 222-0481
Chandlery	Downwind Marine (619) 224-2733
	San Diego Marine Exchange (619) 223-7159
	West Marine (619) 225-8844
Convenience store	
Exercise room	
Hotel	Bay Club Hotel (619) 224-8888
	Humphrey's Half Moon Bay (619) 224-3411
	Island Palms Hotel (619) 222-0561
	Shelter Point Hotel (619) 221-8000
Ice	
Laundry	
Post office	
Restaurants	Fiddler's Green (619) 222-2216
	Humphrey's Restaurant (619) 224-3411
	Sam Choy's Bali Hai (619) 222-1181
Sail Loft	North Sails (619) 224-7018

Ullman Sails (619) 226-1133

Shops
Swimming
Telephones
Tennis courts

Attractions and Transportation

In the early evening, sailors, racers, and cruisers enjoy spinning yarns around the hundreds of boat models, pictures, and half-hulls at Fiddler's Green Restaurant on Shelter Island. Within walking distance of the marinas, all types of stores offer all marine facilities. Major tourist attractions of San Diego are still quite a distance from the harbor, however; you will need some type of transportation to visit them.

Shelter Island Pierson's fuel dock

Public transportation, bus #28, runs along Rosecrans Street, stopping at a variety of stores along the main thoroughfare and ending up at the Old Town Transfer Station, which offers connections to all parts of San Diego County.

San Diego Water Taxi provides a unique service throughout San Diego Bay. For a nominal fee they will pick you up at your boat or slip and deposit you anywhere on the bay.

Attractions

Balboa Park (619) 239-0512
Belmont Park (619) 491-2988
Cabrillo National Monument (619) 557-5450
Flying Leatherneck Aviation Museum (858) 693-1723
Marine Corps. Recruit Depot Museum (619) 524-6038
Mission Bay Park (619) 221-8900
Mission Basilica San Diego de Alcalá (619) 281-8449

Old Town State Historical Park (619) 220-5422

Presidio Park Historical Site (619) 297-3258

Qualcomm Stadium (619) 641-3100

San Diego Chamber of Commerce (619) 232-0124

San Diego Maritime Museum (619) 234-9153

San Diego Sports Arena (619) 224-4176

San Diego Zoo (619) 234-3153

San Diego Visitors Center (619) 276-8200

Sea World (619) 226-3901

Seaport Village (619) 235-4014

Transportation

Amtrak (800) 872-7245

Becker Auto Rental (619) 298-5990

Enterprise Rent-A-Car (619) 225-0848

San Diego Cab (619) 232-6566

San Diego Metropolitan Transit District (619) 322-3004

San Diego Trolley (619) 231-8549

San Diego Water Taxi (619) 235-8294

California Brown Pelican

La Playa Cove (Anchorage–A1) (see chart on page 71)
NOAA Charts #18773, #18772, #18765
Latitude 32°43.0' N, Longitude 117°14.0' W (Center of La Playa Cove)

La Playa Cove, or "Beach" Cove, is the best anchorage in San Diego Bay. It is calm, quiet, and well protected behind the hills of Point Loma, yet close to stores, shopping, and the excitement of Shelter Island. Swim, fish, walk on the beach, walk to town, or just view the activity in the quiet bay. This anchorage is for seventy-two hours on weekends only; a permit is required. The San Diego Unified Port District Mooring Office, at the west end of Shelter Island, next to the Harbor Police, issues permits for your weekend stay.

La Playa Cove

Richard Henry Dana, Jr., arriving at the cove in 1834, wrote about it in his classic adventure book *Two Years Before the Mast*. As a Harvard student in 1815, he began to lose his eyesight. Leaving school, he signed on the trading brig *Pilgrim*, sailing from Boston around Cape Horn to California, where goods were traded for hides. His writing tells of the early California ports of Monterey, San Pedro, Santa

Barbara, Dana Point, and San Diego. In San Diego he stayed on shore at a house in La Playa where hides were preserved for the trip back to Boston. He gives a vivid account of early life around San Diego Bay:

"We sailed leisurely down the coast before a light, fair wind, keeping the land well aboard, and saw two other missions, looking like blocks of white plaster, shining in the distance. . . . At sunset on the second day we had a large and well-wooded headland directly before us, behind which lay the little harbor of San Diego. We were becalmed off this point all night, but the next morning which was Saturday, the fourteenth of March, having a good breeze, we stood round the point, and hauling our wind, brought the little harbor, which is rather the outlet of a small river, right before us. Everyone was desirous to get a view of the new place. A chain of high hills, beginning at the point, protected the harbor on the north and west, and ran off into the interior as far as the eye could reach. On the other sides the land was low and green, but without trees. The entrance is so narrow as to admit but one vessel at a time, the current swift and the channel runs so near to a low, stony point that the ship's sides appeared almost to touch it. There was no town in sight, but on the smooth sand beach, abreast, and within a cable's length of which three vessels lay moored, were four large houses, built of rough boards, and looking like the great barns in which ice is stored on the borders of the large ponds near Boston, with piles of hides standing round them, and men in red shirts and large straw hats walking in and out of the doors. These were the hide houses."

Dana also writes of the San Diego Mission, whose conception began in 1768 with the Spanish "Sacred Expedition" to settle California. Captain Gaspar de Portolá led the land expedition, with Franciscan priest Father Junípero Serra accompanying the group that set out from Baja California in 1769. A group of three ships under the leadership of Captain Vila left La Paz early in the same

Sailing in La Playa Cove

year to meet the land group in San Diego. After four months at sea, two stricken ships arrived in the bay to await Portolá, while the third never arrived. After a long, difficult journey the Portolá group arrived. Here Father Serra built the mission on top of Presidio Hill, overlooking the bay.

Mission San Diego de Alcalá the first mission in California

In 1773 the mission was moved away from the fort up the San Diego River to its present location. The Mission San Diego de Alcalá prospered slowly, with records in 1800 showing 16,000 Indians baptized. Earthquakes in 1803 and 1812 damaged and destroyed much of the mission. Dana writes of the mission in 1834:

"From the presidio, we rode off in the direction of the mission which we were told was three miles distant. The country was rather sandy, and there was nothing for miles which could be called a tree, but the grass grew green and rank, there were many bushes and thickets, and the soil is said to be good. After a pleasant ride of a couple of miles, we saw the white walls of the mission, and, fording a small stream, we came directly before it. The mission is built of adobe and plastered. There was something decidedly striking in its appearance: a number of irregular buildings, connected with one another, and disposed in the form of a hollow square, with a church at one end, rising above the rest, with a tower containing five belfries, in each of which hung a large bell, and with very large rusty iron crosses at the tops. Just outside of the building, and under the walls stood twenty or thirty small huts, in which a few Indians lived, under the protection and in the service of the mission. Entering a gateway, we drove into the open square, in which the stillness of death reigned. On one side was the church: on another, a range of high buildings with grated windows: a third was a range of smaller buildings, or offices, and the forth seemed to be little more than a high connecting wall. Not a living creature could we see."

One year before Richard Henry Dana Jr. wrote these words, the Mexican Government passed the Secularization Act of 1833 taking all lands away from the church, which caused the missions to fall into disrepair. In 1846 the San Diego Mission closed. Its buildings were used as a barracks until 1862, when President Abraham Lincoln restored the San Diego Mission to the Catholic Church. In 1976 the "Mother of the Missions," the first of twenty-one California missions established a day's walk between sites, was honored by the Pope with the title of Basilica. Today church services are still given throughout the week, with restoration ongoing.

Around the bay much has changed since Dana's time. La Playa is still flat, wide, and sandy, but the hide houses are gone, replaced by multi-million-dollar homes overlooking the bay. The anchorage is filled with yachts that squeeze between Southwestern Yacht Club and San Diego Yacht Club. A short row to shore and a walk down Bessemer Street to Scott Street will place you in the center of the San Diego yachting business district, with sail makers, engine shops, boatyards, rigging shops, and chandleries. This is a convenient location to work on your boat.

Land Approach

Two miles north of downtown San Diego, exit Interstate 5 at Rosecrans Street. Drive west on Rosecrans Street past the U.S. Naval Training Center and Shelter Island Drive, and four miles from the freeway turn south on Bessemer Street. La Playa Cove will be at the end of the street.

Sea Approach

From the ocean, proceed down the main ship channel of San Diego Bay in the lee of Point Loma. Pass Ballast Point and the U.S. Naval Submarine Base, and at buoy "15" leave the channel, traveling northwest to the west end of Shelter Island. Pass between the west end of Shelter Island and Point Loma, entering Shelter Island Yacht Basin. Halfway into the basin between Southwestern Yacht Club and San Diego Yacht Club is the white sandy beach of La Playa Cove (latitude 32°43.0' N, longitude 117°14.0' W) on the north side of the basin.

Local Weather Service (858) 289-1212

Sea Tow (888) 473-2869

Tow Boat U.S. (800) 493-7869

Vessel Assist (800) 399-1921

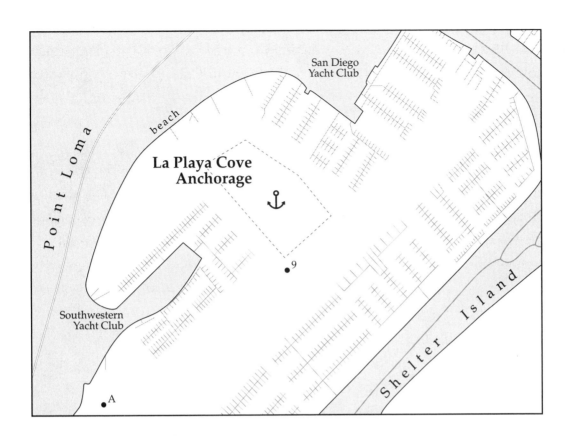

Anchorage and Berthing

La Playa Cove is for weekend anchoring of recreational boats with permits only. No mooring buoys are present. The nearest slips are located on Shelter Island, and the nearest long-term anchorage is found in the Cruising Anchorage (Anchorage–A9) off the east end of Harbor Island. Call or stop by the San Diego Port District Mooring Office to obtain a permit. The cove offers good holding ground to anchor in nine to twelve feet of water in soft sand and mud. Wind is usually light from the northwest, but during winter storms the wind comes in strong gusts over the Point Loma hills. During popular summer months, pick up permits early, as the limited weekend permits go quickly. Relax at anchor in this quiet cove, where you can watch all the bay activity, survey the expensive homes overlooking the bay, swim or row to shore, or walk along the sandy beach to the shops, stores, and restaurants on Shelter Island.

San Diego Harbor Police (619) 223-1133
San Diego Unified Port District Mooring Office (619) 686-6227

Facilities

Bait and tackle	Shelter Island Bait and Tackle (619) 222-7635
Bank	
Boatyard	Driscoll Boat Works (619) 224-3575
	Kettenburg Marine (619) 221-6930
	Koehler Kraft Yard (619) 222-9051
	Nielsen Beaumont Marine (619) 222-4253
	Shelter Island Boatyard (619) 222-0481
Chandlery	Downwind Marine (619) 224-2733
	San Diego Marine Exchange (619) 223-7159
	West Marine (619) 225-8844
Convenience store	
Fuel	Pearson's (619) 222-7084
Hotel	Shelter Point Hotel (619) 221-8000
	Holiday Inn San Diego Bayside (619) 224-3612
	Vagabond Inn Point Loma (619) 224-3371
Ice	
Laundry	
Post office	
Restaurants	Brigantine (619) 224-2871
	Fiddler's Green (619) 222-2216
	Miguel's Cocina (619) 224-2401
Sail loft	North Sails (619) 224-7018
	Ullman Sails (619) 226-1133
Shops	
Swimming	

Attractions and Transportation

All types of stores are within walking distance of the anchorage. Shelter Island is close to all marine facilities. Major tourist attractions of San Diego are still quite a distance from the harbor; you will need some type of transportation to visit them.

You can catch bus #28, which runs along Rosecrans Street, stopping at a variety of stores along the main thoroughfare, or you can take it to the Old Town Transfer

Station to transfer to transportation to all parts of San Diego County.

Attractions

Balboa Park (619) 239-0512
Belmont Park (619) 491-2988
Cabrillo National Monument (619) 557-5450
Flying Leatherneck Aviation Museum (858) 693-1723
Marine Corps. Recruit Depot Museum (619) 524-6038
Mission Bay Park (619) 221-8900
Mission Basilica San Diego de Alcalá (619) 281-8449
Old Town State Historical Park (619) 220-5422
Presidio Park Historical Site (619) 297-3258
Qualcomm Stadium (619) 641-3100
San Diego Chamber of Commerce (619) 232-0124
San Diego Maritime Museum (619) 234-9153
San Diego Sports Arena (619) 224-4176
San Diego Zoo (619) 234-3153
San Diego Visitors Center (619) 276-8200
Sea World (619) 226-3901
Seaport Village (619) 235-4014

Transportation

Amtrak (800) 872-7245
Becker Auto Rental (619) 298-5990
Enterprise Rent-A-Car (619) 225-0848
San Diego Cab (619) 232-6566
San Diego Metropolitan Transit District (619) 322-3004
San Diego Trolley (619) 231-8549
San Diego Water Taxi (619) 235-8294

Shelter Island Roadstead (Moorings–A1a, A1b, A1c) chart p. 76
NOAA Charts #18773, #18765, #18766, #18772
Latitude 32°42.8' N, Longitude 117°13.6' W (Off Shelter Island Roadstead)

Shelter Island Roadstead is a central, turbulent mooring area close to all the boating activities and facilities on Shelter Island. A short row ashore lie a sandy beach with grass and palm trees and the walking paths of Shelter Island Park, which lead to Shelter Island Drive, the major boating center in San Diego. All moorings are controlled by the San Diego Unified Port Mooring Office and require a use permit valid up to one year.

Shelter Island Roadstead

The U.S. Navy built Zuñiga Jetty at the north end of Coronado in 1894 to further protect San Diego Bay, but the narrow, shallow channel between Ballast Point and North Island still limited access to the bay. In 1907, the entrance bar was dredged to twenty-eight feet with the bay's first dredging. However, in 1908 "The Great White Fleet," a group of US Navy ships on a round-the-world cruise, decided not to attempt the harbor, but stayed anchored out in the San Diego Roadstead off the Silver Strand Beach. As bay dredging continued over the years, more areas were opened to a greater number of ships. The most common place for early ships to anchor was south of Ballast Point close to the present location of Shelter Island Roadstead.

Historic Point Loma Light

In 1855, the first lighthouse along the southern California coast was built on the bluff of Point Loma. Sailors soon found the light too high, often obscured by fog, and not visible at great distances. Not until thirty-six years later, in 1891, was the light put at its present location, just above sea level, at the southern tip of Point Loma where it is more easily seen. Falling into disrepair, the original lighthouse was turned over to the U.S. Park Service in 1932 and restored as the Cabrillo National Monument, commemorating the founding of San Diego by Juan Rodriguez Cabrillo on September 28, 1542.

Today, the main ship channel is wide and dredged to forty-two feet. Dredging is now ongoing to increase the depth of the channel to accommodate the huge aircraft carriers of the twenty-first century. Seventy-foot Point Loma Light sends a flashing message twenty-three miles to alert and welcome mariners to a safe harbor.

Shelter Island is accessible with a short row ashore to the white sandy beach. Nearby

Modern day Point Loma Light

grassy lawns and palm trees surround the "island," whose walking paths connect to hotels, restaurants, chandleries, boatyards, engine shops, and sail lofts, which all abound in this exciting boating community.

Land Approach

Two miles north of downtown San Diego, exit Interstate 5 at Rosecrans Street. Drive west on Rosecrans Street past the U.S. Naval Training Center, and turn left on Shelter Island Drive, three miles from the freeway. Proceed on Shelter Island Drive to the Shelter Island Launch Ramp. Park here; the Shelter Island Roadstead is east and west of the launch ramp.

Sea Approach

From the ocean, proceed down the main ship channel of San Diego Bay in the lee of Point Loma. Pass Ballast Point and the U.S. Naval Submarine Base. Between buoys "17" and "19" leave the channel, traveling northeast to the center of Shelter Island and the Shelter Island Roadstead (latitude 32°42.8' N, longitude 117°13.6' W).

Local Weather Service (858) 289-1212
Sea Tow (888) 473-2869
Tow Boat U.S. (800) 493-7869
Vessel Assist (800) 399-1921

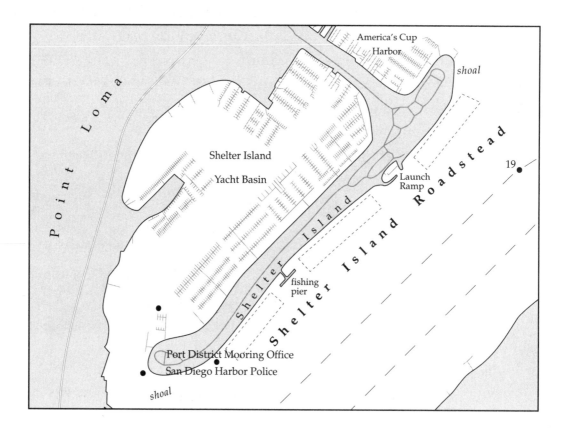

Anchorage and Berthing

No anchoring is allowed in Shelter Island Roadstead. The nearest anchorage is in La Playa Cove in Shelter Island Yacht Basin, or the Cruising Anchorage (Anchorage–A9) off the east end of Harbor Island. No slips are available in this area; the nearest slips are in Shelter Island Yacht Basin or America's Cup Harbor. Shelter Island Roadstead contains forty-four single point mooring buoys intended for boats nineteen to fifty-five feet in length. Mooring is allowed by permit only. Persons interested in mooring their vessel to a port mooring must obtain a mooring permit from the San Diego Port District Mooring Office. Permits are valid for up to one year and can be renewed. Because of high demand, each mooring area may have a waiting list. To apply, complete an application and submit your current vessel registration or documentation along with an application fee. Each applicant may submit only one application. To apply in person, make an appointment with the mooring office, or to request a mooring application for San Diego Bay, write:

> San Diego Unified Port District Mooring Office
> 2890 Shelter Island Drive
> San Diego, CA 92001

Prior to receiving a mooring permit all applicants must have their vessels inspected by the U.S. Coast Guard Auxiliary. Courtesy Marine Examinations (CMEs) are conducted every Saturday at the Auxiliary inspection dock between 8 A.M. and 4 P.M. The inspection dock is located along the quay at the north end of the Laurel Street Roadstead (Mooring–A9). The address is:

> Vessel Inspection Dock
> 2320 N. Harbor Drive
> San Diego, CA 92101

This inspection may be conducted no more than six months prior to the date of receiving a mooring permit. Please contact the mooring office with any questions.

The Roadstead moorage, in the lee of Point Loma, is protected from the northwest winds in the afternoon; however, it is adjacent to the main shipping channel of San Diego Bay, with a great deal of rocking and rolling. Surge is minimal, but heavy boat traffic makes the mooring uncomfortable. The San Diego Mooring Office is located on the west end of Shelter Island.

> San Diego Harbor Police (619) 223-1133
> San Diego Unified Port District Mooring Office (619) 686-6227

Facilities

Bait and tackle	Shelter Island Bait and Tackle (619) 222-7635
Bank	
Boatyard	Driscoll Boat Works (619) 224-3575
	Kettenburg Marine (619) 221-6930
	Koehler Kraft Yard (619) 222-9051
	Nielsen Beaumont Marine (619) 222-4253
	Shelter Island Boatyard (619) 222-0481
Chandlery	Downwind Marine (619) 224-2733
	San Diego Marine Exchange (619) 223-7159
	West Marine (619) 225-8844
Convenience store	
Dinghy dock	
Hotel	Bay Club Hotel (619) 224-8888
	Humphrey's Half Moon Inn (619) 224-3411
	Island Palms Hotel (619) 222-0561
	Shelter Point Hotel (619) 221-8000
Ice	
Laundry	
Park	
Parking	
Post office	
Restaurants	Fiddler's Green (619) 222-2216
	Humphrey's Restaurant (619) 224-3411
	Sam Choy's Bali Hai (619) 222-1181
Sail Loft	North Sails (619) 224-7018
	Ullman Sails (619) 226-1133
Shops	
Swimming	
Telephone	

Attractions and Transportation

All types of stores are within walking distance of the mooring. Shelter Island Roadstead is close to all marine facilities. Major tourist attractions of San Diego are still quite a distance from the bay, needing some type of transportation to visit.

Public transportation, bus #28, runs along Rosecrans Street, stopping at a variety of stores along the main thoroughfare or taking you to the Old Town Transfer Station for transportation to all parts of San Diego County.

Attractions

Balboa Park (619) 239-0512
Belmont Park (619) 491-2988
Cabrillo National Monument (619) 557-5450
Flying Leatherneck Aviation Museum (858) 693-1723
Marine Corps. Recruit Depot Museum (619) 524-6038
Mission Bay Park (619) 221-8900
Mission Basilica San Diego de Alcalá (619) 281-8449
Old Town State Historical Park (619) 220-5422
Presidio Park Historical Site (619) 297-3258
Qualcomm Stadium (619) 641-3100
San Diego Chamber of Commerce (619) 232-0124
San Diego Maritime Museum (619) 234-9153
San Diego Sports Arena (619) 224-4176
San Diego Zoo (619) 234-3153
San Diego Visitors Center (619) 276-8200
Sea World (619) 226-3901
Seaport Village (619) 235-4014

Transportation

Amtrak (800) 872-7245
Becker Auto Rental (619) 298-5990
Enterprise Rent-A-Car (619) 225-0848
San Diego Cab (619) 232-6566
San Diego Metropolitan Transit District (619) 322-3004
San Diego Trolley (619) 231-8549
San Diego Water Taxi (619) 235-8294

America's Cup Harbor (Mooring–A2) (see chart page 82)
NOAA Charts #18773, #18765, #18766, #18772
Latitude 32°43.2' N, Longitude 117°13.0' W
(Entrance to America's Cup Harbor)

America's Cup Harbor is a compact, central mooring area close to all boating activity on Shelter Island. Moorings are controlled by the San Diego Unified Port District Mooring Office. Sheltered from the northwest wind, in the lee of Point Loma, it is only a short row ashore to restaurants, hotels, boatyards, chandleries, and night spots on Shelter Island. Staying here allows unlimited time to do boat maintenance and repair, or to visit all the sights of San Diego.

Bali Hai Restaurant at entrance to America's Cup Harbor

A map of San Diego in 1863 shows La Playa, Roseville, Old Town, Middle Town, New Town, and National City as the major population centers around the bay. The land just north of America's Cup Harbor is considered Roseville.

The Chinese, early residents of this area, began San Diego's famous fishing industry. Junks filled the bay as they fished for barracuda, mullet, sheepshead, and abalone. Fishermen sold much of their catch fresh, and racks lined the shore as abalone was dried for export to China, where it was considered a delicacy. Abalone shells were also shipped to Hungary, where they were used to make buttons.

The 1882 Chinese Exclusion Act, 1888 Scott Act, and 1892 Geary Act had a profound effect on the Chinese residents, forcing them to leave the industry and the area. Other immigrant groups filled the void as the Portuguese and Italians carried on the fishing industry that was becoming part of the U.S. Pacific coast tuna fleet. This big industry began in 1911 and was centered in San Diego. Many years later, in 1950, John Bates spearheaded the development of Shelter Island, naming the east harbor, "Commercial Basin." The commercial fishing fleet randomly anchored in the center of the basin, where it was the hub of fishing activity. With changing laws, the tuna fleet is no longer centered in San Diego.

In 1987, Dennis Conner of the San Diego Yacht Club brought the America's Cup to San Diego, which became the center for the cup defense. During those four years of preparation, "Commercial Basin" became "America's Cup Harbor" as boats prepared for the race. Today, pleasure boats are snuggly moored in the center of the harbor while boating activity surrounds the bay.

Shelter Cove Marina

Land Approach

Two miles north of downtown San Diego, exit Interstate 5 at Rosecrans Street. Drive west on Rosecrans Street past the U.S. Naval Training Center, and turn left on Shelter Island Drive, three miles from the freeway. Proceed on Shelter Island Drive to a parking lot across from San Diego Marine Exchange; stay here while visiting America's Cup Harbor.

Sea Approach

From the ocean, proceed down the main ship channel of San Diego Bay in the lee of Point Loma. Pass Ballast Point, the U.S. Naval Submarine Base, and Shelter Island, and at buoy "19" leave the channel and travel east to buoy "1," the entrance to America's Cup Harbor (latitude 32°43.2' N, longitude 117°13.0' W). Pass outside of buoy "1," as there is shoal water between the east end of Shelter Island and the buoy.

Local Weather Service (858) 289-1212

Sea Tow (888) 473-2869

Tow Boat U.S. (800) 493-7869

Vessel Assist (800) 399-1921

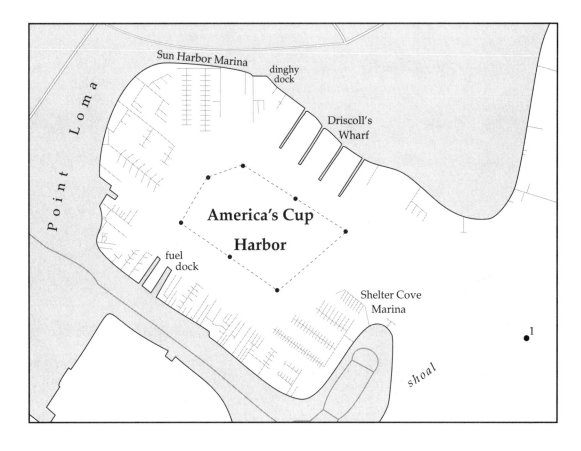

Anchorage and Berthing

No anchoring is allowed in America's Cup Harbor. The nearest anchorage is west in La Playa Cove, on the north side of Shelter Island Yacht Basin. Located here are 180 double-point moorings in the center of the harbor for pleasure boats from nineteen to sixty-five feet in length. All moorings are controlled by the San Diego Unified Port District. A renewable permit is issued by the San Diego Bay Mooring Office, valid for up to one year. Persons interested in mooring their vessel to a port mooring must obtain a mooring permit from the San Diego Port District. Because of the high demand, each mooring area may have a waiting list. To apply, complete an application and submit your current vessel registration or documentation, along with an application fee. Each applicant may submit only one application. To apply in person, make an appointment with the mooring office. To request a mooring application for San Diego Bay, write:

San Diego Unified Port District Mooring Office
2890 Shelter Island Drive
San Diego, CA 92001

Moorings in America's Cup Harbor

Prior to receiving a mooring permit all applicants must have their vessels inspected by the U.S. Coast Guard Auxiliary. Courtesy Marine Examinations (CMEs) are conducted every Saturday at the Auxiliary Inspection dock between 8 A.M. and 4 P.M. The inspection dock is located along the quay at the north end of the Laurel Street Roadstead (Mooring–A9). The address is:

Vessel Inspection Dock
2320 N. Harbor Drive
San Diego, CA 92101

This inspection may be conducted no more than six months prior to the date of receiving a mooring permit. Please contact the mooring office with any questions.

Driscoll's Wharf

Sun Harbor Marina

Slips are also available in America's Cup Harbor at three private marinas. **Shelter Cove Marina** is just west after entering the harbor. It has 161 slips for boats twenty-eight to seventy feet in length. Electricity, water, restrooms, showers, phone, TV, laundry, fitness center, and recreation room make this a convenient place to stay. **Driscoll's Wharf** has 125 slips to accommodate boats from twenty-five to one hundred feet in length. Restrooms, showers, electricity, and water are provided, and they may have space at a guest dock. **Sun Harbor Marina** is located at the northeast corner of the harbor with 120 slips accommodating boats ranging from twenty to fifty feet in length. Restrooms, showers, phones, water, and electricity are available. Always call ahead to determine slip availability.

Driscoll's Wharf (619) 222-4930
San Diego Harbor Police (619) 223-1133
San Diego Unified Port District Mooring Office (619) 686-6227
Shelter Cove Marina (619) 224- 2471
Sun Harbor Marina (619) 222-1167

High Seas fuel dock in America's Cup Harbor

Facilities

Bait and tackle	Shelter Island Bait and Tackle (619) 222-7635
Bank	
Boatyard	Driscoll Boatyard (619) 224-3575
	Kettenburg Marine (619) 221-6930
	Koehler Kraft Yard (619) 222-9051
	Nielsen Beaumont Marine (619) 222-4253
	Shelter Island Boatyard (619) 222-0481
Chandlery	Downwind Marine (619) 224-2733
	San Diego Marine Exchange (619) 223-7159
	West Marine (619) 225-8844
Convenience store	
Dinghy dock	
Exercise room	
Fishing boats	Fisherman's Landing (619) 221-8500
Fuel dock	High Seas Fuel Dock (619) 523-2980
Hotel	Holiday Inn San Diego Bayside (619) 224-3612
	Shelter Point Hotel (619) 221-8000
	Vagabond Inn Point Loma (619) 224-3371

Ice

Laundry

Parking

Post office

Restaurants   Fiddler's Green (619) 222-2216

                             Miguel's Cocina (619) 224-2401

                             Point Loma Seafoods (619) 223-1109

                             Red Sails Inn (619) 223-3030

Restrooms

Sail Loft   North Sails (619) 224-7018

                             Ullman Sails (619) 226-1133

Shops

Showers

Telephone

Attractions and Transportation

All types of stores are within walking distance of America's Cup Harbor, and all marine facilities are available in this compact area. However, it is still a distance to the major tourist sites in San Diego, requiring transportation to visit them.

Public transportation, bus #28, runs along Rosecrans Street, stopping at a variety of stores along the main thoroughfare, or going to the Old Town Transfer Station to connect with transportation to all parts of San Diego County.

Attractions

Balboa Park (619) 239-0512

Belmont Park (619) 491-2988

Cabrillo National Monument (619) 557-5450

Flying Leatherneck Aviation Museum (858) 693-1723

Marine Corps. Recruit Depot Museum (619) 524-6038

Mission Bay Park (619) 221-8900

Mission Basilica San Diego de Alcalá (619) 281-8449

Old Town State Historical Park (619) 220-5422

Presidio Park Historical Site (619) 297-3258

Qualcomm Stadium (619) 641-3100

San Diego Chamber of Commerce (619) 232-0124

San Diego Maritime Museum (619) 234-9153

San Diego Sports Arena (619) 224-4176

San Diego Visitors Center (619) 276-8200

San Diego Zoo (619) 234-3153

Sea World (619) 226-3901

Seaport Village (619) 235-4014

Transportation

Amtrak (800) 872-7245

Becker Auto Rental (619) 298-5990

Enterprise Rent-A-Car (619) 225-0848

San Diego Cab (619) 232-6566

San Diego Metropolitan Transit District (619) 322-3004

San Diego Trolley (619) 231-8549

San Diego Water Taxi (619) 235-8294

Fisherman's Landing

Naval Sailing Center, Point Loma (see chart page 91)
Marine Corps. Recruit Depot Boathouse
NOAA Charts #18773, #18765, #18766, #18772
Latitude 32°43.5' N, Longitude 117°12.9' W (Off Naval Sailing Center dock)

The U.S. Naval Sailing Center on Point Loma and the Marine Corps. Recruit Depot Boathouse are government property whose use is limited to active duty, retired military, and Department of Defense personnel and their families only. These are two of three military marinas in San Diego Bay, the only ones on the mainland side of the bay. In quiet, centralized marinas between Shelter Island and Harbor Island, they are close to tourist sites in downtown San Diego. San Diego Lindbergh Field is within walking distance.

Entrance to the Naval Sailing Center, Point Loma

San Diego's large, natural harbor and strategic location have always interested the military. The Spanish army first established a fort on Presidio Hill in 1769. After visiting English Captain George Vancouver criticized the fort's vulnerability, in 1793 a new fort was built at Ballast Point—Fort Guijarros ("Fort Cobblestones"). It was present from 1797–1835. The U.S. Navy's first official business in the bay was in

1846, when the USS *Cyane* sailed from Monterey to San Diego Bay. Landing on July 29, they pulled down the Mexican flag and claimed San Diego as part of the United States. Since that time the U.S. Navy's presence has increased with each war. Initially the bay was used as a supply depot in 1848. The Marine Corps. Recruit Depot began operations in 1915. Then in 1917, North Island became a naval air station with such other expansions as the Submarine Repair Base (1921), Navy Hospital (1922), Navy destroyer base, San Diego Naval Station, Navy Amphibious Base (1943), Navy Electronics Laboratory (1945), Navy Supply Corps at the Navy Pier, and the Naval Repair Facility.

Naval Sailing Center, Point Loma

The U.S. Marine Corp. is the branch of the armed services especially trained for amphibious assault and operations. It is a separate branch of the armed forces with the Department of the Navy. First established in 1775, the Marine Corps. has been the first to fight in almost every major war of the United States, while making over 300 landings on foreign shores. The 399-acre Marine Corps. Recruit Depot, built on the bay tidelands known as "Dutch Flats," came to San Diego in 1920. It is the oldest Marine Corps. installation on the west coast, training nearly 17,000 recruits annually.

The U. S. Navy has long had a major presence in San Diego

Today, San Diego is headquarters for the Eleventh Naval District that includes Southern California, Arizona, and Nevada. The navy controls twenty miles of San Diego Harbor where San Diego and the U.S. Navy are mutually interdependent. The navy's presence is more alive in San Diego than in any other city in the nation.

Land Approach

Two miles north of downtown San Diego, exit Interstate 5 at Rosecrans Street. Drive west on Rosecrans Street past the U.S. Naval Training Center, and turn left on Nimitz Boulevard, two miles from the freeway. Proceed on Nimitz Boulevard until it terminates at the gate of the Fleet Anti-Submarine Warfare Training Center. The Naval Sailing Center is on the east edge of this facility.

Sea Approach

From the ocean, proceed down the main ship channel of San Diego Bay in the lee of Point Loma. Pass Ballast Point, the U.S. Naval Submarine Base, and Shelter Island, and at buoy "19" leave the channel and travel southeast to the western tip of Harbor Island. The Naval Sailing Center (latitude 32°43.5' N, longitude 117°12.9' W) is directly across from the west tip of Harbor Island. Continue north under the two bridges (minimum vertical clearance nineteen feet) into the Marine Corps. Recruit Depot Estuary; the boathouse and docks will be at the north end of the estuary.

> Local Weather Service (858) 289-1212
> San Diego Harbor Police (619) 223-1133
> Sea Tow (888) 473-2869
> Tow Boat U.S. (800) 493-7869
> Vessel Assist (800) 399-1921

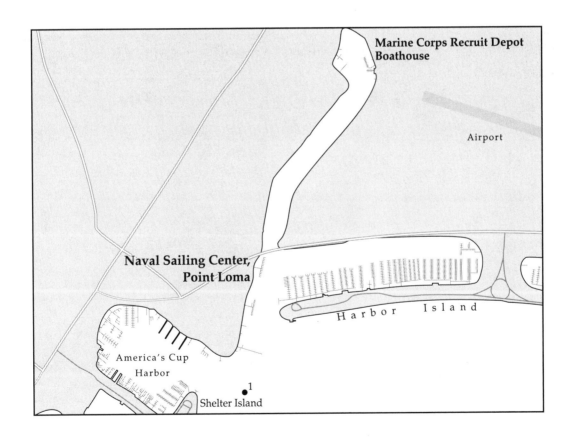

Anchorage and Berthing

No anchoring or mooring is allowed at the U.S. Naval Sailing Center. The nearest anchorage is at the Cruising Anchorage (Anchorage–A9) across from the east end of Harbor Island. The **U.S. Navy Sailing Center**, located in a park-like setting across from the west end of Harbor Island, is near the former San Diego River exit into San Diego Bay. It contains 100 slips for boats ranging from twenty-four to fifty feet in length. No live-aboards are allowed. Water and electricity are provided, as well as a picnic area, clubhouse, restroom, shower, laundry, and café. Instructions are given; rental boats are available for military personnel. Also available are all such base facilities as swimming pool, basketball courts, and gymnasium.

No anchoring or mooring is allowed at the **Marine Corps. Recruit Depot Boathouse**, but there are fifty-six slips for boats ranging from twenty to forty feet in length. Boat rental facilities, water, electricity, and restrooms are all available. Slips are available for rent to active duty and retired military, but no live-aboards are permitted. Passing under the bridges allows you access to the estuary, which is dredged to fifteen feet in the center of the channel.

Marine Corps. Recruit Depot Boathouse (619) 524-5269

Naval Sailing Center, Point Loma (619) 524-6498

Marine Corps. Recruit Depot Boathouse

Facilities

Airport
Dock
Exercise room
Groceries
Hotel   Travel Lodge Point Loma (619) 223-8171
                         Holiday Inn San Diego Bayside (619) 224-3612
                         Vagabond Inn Point Loma (619) 224-3371
Laundry
Park
Parking
Pool
Restaurant   North China Restaurant (619) 224-3568
                         Pizza Nova (619) 226-0268
                         Point Loma Seafoods (619) 223-1109
Restrooms
Showers
Telephone
Tennis courts

Attractions and Transportation

Naval Sailing Center is rather isolated from stores and shopping. Walking north on Nimitz Boulevard two blocks will put you on Rosecrans Street, where fast food and shopping abound.

Public transportation, bus #28, runs along Rosecrans Street, stopping at a variety of stores along the main thoroughfare, or going to the Old Town Transfer Station to connect with transportation to all parts of San Diego County. Also, buses #22 and #23 run along Nimitz Boulevard and Harbor Drive, going to American Plaza Transfer Station to transfer to all areas of the county.

Attractions

Balboa Park (619) 239-0512
Belmont Park (619) 491-2988
Cabrillo National Monument (619) 557-5450

Flying Leatherneck Aviation Museum (858) 693-1723

Marine Corps. Recruit Depot Museum (619) 524-6038

Maritime Museum (619) 234-9153

Mission Bay Park (619) 221-8900

Mission Basilica San Diego de Alcalá (619) 281-8449

Old Town State Historical Park (619) 220-5422

Presidio Park Historical Site (619) 297-3258

Qualcomm Stadium (619) 641-3100

San Diego Chamber of Commerce (619) 232-0124

San Diego Maritime Museum (619) 234-9153

San Diego Sports Arena (619) 224-4176

San Diego Visitors Center (619) 276-8200

San Diego Zoo (619) 234-3153

Sea World (619) 226-3901

Seaport Village (619) 235-4014

Transportation

Amtrak (800) 872-7245

Becker Auto Rentals (619) 298-5990

Enterprise Rent-A-Car (619) 225-0848

San Diego Cab (619) 232-6566

San Diego Metropolitan Transit District (619) 322-3004

San Diego Trolley (619) 231-8549)

San Diego Water Taxi (619) 235-8294

Harbor Island (see chart page 98)

NOAA Charts #18773, #18765, #18766, #18772

Latitude 32°43.4' N, Longitude 117°12.9' W

(Off the entrance to the west basin)

Harbor Island is the second most popular boating area on San Diego Bay. Numerous private marinas, restaurants, and hotels abound in the area; however, jet noise from adjacent Lindbergh Field can be bothersome. The area is surrounded with parks, green grass, palm trees, and bike paths, with marinas close to popular downtown San Diego tourist sights. San Diego's Lindbergh Field is within walking distance of all the marinas.

West entrance to Harbor Island

The first European settlers arrived in 1769 with the Portolá party and Father Junípero Serra, intent on settling the area. They first lived within the walls of the presidio, or "fort," for protection and safety from the Indians. In time they slowly moved down Presidio Hill to an area presently called "Old Town." The frontier outpost was quiet for many years, but with Mexican independence in 1823, more settlers arrived. Richard Henry Dana, Jr., author of *Two Years Before the Mast*, wrote of his visit in 1835:

" . . . and jumping ashore, set out on our walk for the town which was nearly three miles off . . . . Our crew fell in with some who belonged to the other vessels, and, sailor-like steered for the first grog-shop. This was a small adobe building, of only one room, in which were liquors, dry goods, West India goods, shoes, bread, fruits and everything which is vendible in California . . . . The small settlement lay directly below the fort, composed of about forty dark-brown-looking huts, or houses, and three or four larger ones, whitewashed, which belonged to the *gente de razon*. This town is not more than half as large as Monterey, or Santa Barbara, and has little or no business."

The California Gold rush (1849) and statehood (1950) did little to attract settlers to the area. Finally, in 1867 with the arrival of Alonzo Horton, plans to develop "New Town" along the San Diego waterfront began. A fire in 1872 destroyed much of "Old Town," which insured success of the new bay development. Changes along the waterfront proceeded for decades.

With the success of Shelter Island in 1950, a similar project began in 1964 as a one and one-half million dollar bond issue was passed to develop Harbor Island. This sixty-nine-acre island was created by dredging San Diego Bay to increase the depth in the main channel and docking areas to forty-one feet, accommodating new aircraft carriers making San Diego their home port. Navy dredges created an island very similar in size to Shelter Island, 300 feet wide and 8,000 feet long, with a marked difference between the two islands in vertical building height allowed. Major construction took eight years to complete—from 1961 to 1969. Improvements to Lindbergh Field and Spanish Landing Park across from the Harbor Island were finished in 1967. The *Californian*, a 145-foot topsail schooner and replica of the *C.W. Lawrence Revenue Cutter* (1851), was built in 1983 in Spanish Landing Park. It now sails the seas as the State of California Official Tall Ship, acting as a good will ambassador as well as a classroom for training youth about a bygone era. Even today, minor development is being made to this central location on San Diego Bay.

Harbor Island is close to San Diego's Lindbergh Field

The original site of city development has been restored at Old Town San Diego State Historic Park, where a six-block area commemorates the founding of the first European settlement in California. Many of the original buildings are preserved, with nearby Presidio Park being the site of the first mission and military for-

San Diego's Old Town

Presidio Park, site of the oldest fort in California

tress. Along the waterfront is Harbor Island, home to six private marinas, hotels, restaurants, chandleries, yacht brokers, yacht clubs, and fuel docks. Docking facilities are surrounded by green grass, palm trees, and walking trails. It is an excellent place for the family to picnic and watch all harbor activities.

Harbor Island West Marina

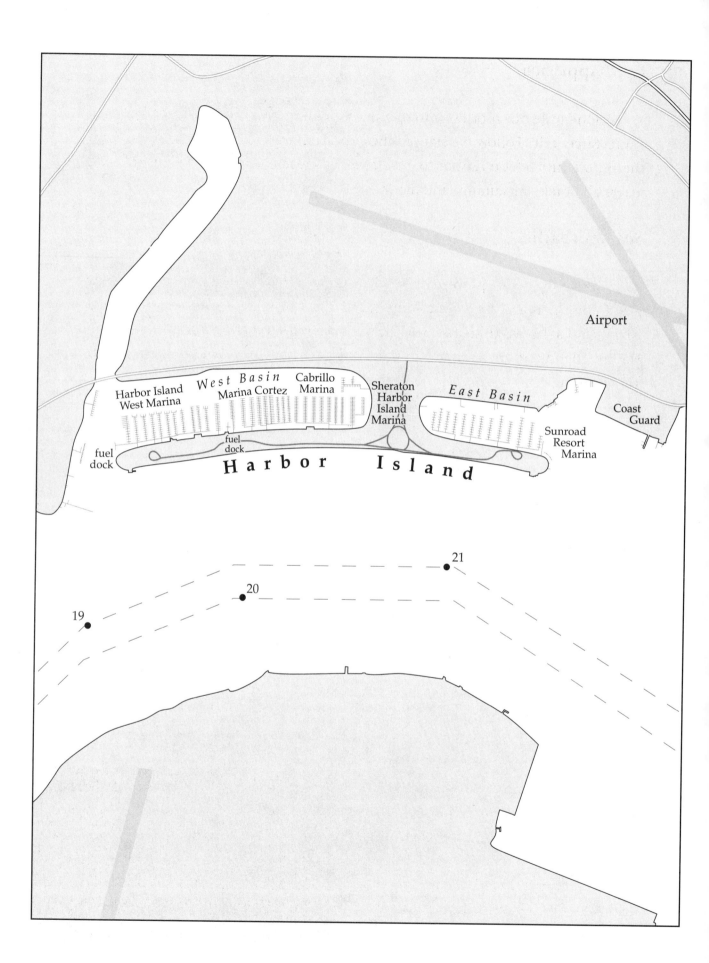

Harbor Island West Marina

West Basin

Marina Cortez

Cabrillo Marina

Sheraton Harbor Island Marina

East Basin

Coast Guard

Sunroad Resort Marina

fuel dock

fuel dock

Harbor Island

Airport

19

20

21

Land Approach

One mile north of downtown San Diego, exit Interstate 5 at the Airport, or Laurel Street exit. Follow the signs to the airport. Once you are directly across from the airport, turn left on Harbor Island Drive. This road circles around Harbor Island where all hotels, restaurants, and marinas are located.

Sea Approach

From the ocean, proceed down the main ship channel of San Diego Bay in the lee of Point Loma. Pass Ballast Point, the U.S. Naval Submarine Base, and Shelter Island, and at buoy "19" leave the channel and travel southeast to the western tip of Harbor Island and the entrance to the west basin (latitude 32°43.4' N, longitude 117°12.9' W).

Local Weather Service (858) 289-1212
San Diego Harbor Police (619) 223-1133
Sea Tow (888) 473-2869
Tow Boat U.S. (800) 493-7869
Vessel Assist (800) 399-1921

Anchorage and Berthing

No anchoring or mooring is allowed in Harbor Island. The closest anchorage is the Cruising Anchorage (Anchorage–A8) across from the east end of Harbor Island. Slips are available at five private marinas located in east and west basin of

Harbor Island. **Harbor Island West Marina**, at the west end of west basin, contains 620 slips with accommodation for boats from twenty-five to one hundred feet in length. Restrooms, showers, water, electricity, ice, restaurants, swimming pool, and spa are available. Two fuel docks are on Harbor Island—one on the west end of the island and one in the center of the west basin. **Marina Cortez** is the next marina, with 520 slips, accommodating boats from twenty-five to seventy feet in length. Swim-

Marina Cortez fuel dock

ming pool, spa, showers, restrooms, ice, phone, laundry, electricity, and water are all available. **Cabrillo Isle Marina** has 450 slips for boats twenty-six to eighty feet in length. Restrooms, swimming pool, spa, ice, showers, deli, electricity, and water are available. At the end of west basin are the forty-two slips of the Sheraton Harbor Island Marina. They have room for vessels thirty-five to seventy feet in length. Laundry, cable T.V., picnic area, and tennis courts are available at this facility. Harbor Island east basin contains the 610-slip **Sunroad Resort Marina**. They can accommodate boats from thirty to sixty-five feet in length with electricity, water, swimming pool, spa, and picnic area available to boaters. The local chandlery, Horizon Marine, is on the island to provide for all your boating needs. Harbor Island Park has tables and a grassy lawn on which to have a wonderful picnic lunch and watch all the activity on San Diego Bay.

Cabrillo Isle Marina

Sunroad Resort Marina in east basin

San Diego Water Taxi provides a unique service throughout San Diego Bay. For a nominal fee, they will pick you up at your boat or slip and deposit you anywhere on the bay.

Cabrillo Isle Marina (619) 297-6222
Harbor Island West Marina (619) 291-6440
Marina Cortez (619) 291-5985
Sheraton Harbor Island Marina (619) 692-2249
Sunroad Resort Marina (619) 574-0736

Facilities

Airport
Chandlery   Downwind Marine (619) 224-2733
Horizon Marine (619) 297-4312
San Diego Marine Exchange (619) 223-7159

West Marine (619) 225-8844
US Boat (619) 298-3020

Convenience store	
Dock	
Exercise room	
Fuel	Cortez Fuel Dock (619) 296-2331
	Harbor Island Fuel Dock (619) 291-6443
Hotels	Hilton San Diego Airport (619) 291-6700
	Sheraton Harbor Island (619) 291-2900
Ice	
Laundry	
Park	
Parking	
Restaurants	Boathouse (619) 291-8011
	Reuben's (619) 291-5030
	Tom Ham's Lighthouse (619) 291-9110
Shops	
Swimming	
Telephone	
Tennis court	
Yacht charters	San Diego Yacht Charters (800) 456-0222

Attractions and Transportation

All types of hotels and restaurants are within walking distance of the marinas on Harbor Island. Limited marine facilities are found here, so a trip to Shelter Island is necessary to access all marine facilities. Major tourist sites of San Diego are a distance from Harbor Island; some type of transportation is needed to visit them.

Public transportation—buses #22 and #23—runs along Harbor Drive, taking you to the America Plaza Transfer Station for connections to all parts of San Diego County.

Attractions

Balboa Park (619) 239-0512
Belmont Park (619) 491-2988
Cabrillo National Monument (619) 557-5450

Flying Leatherneck Aviation Museum (858) 693-1723

Marine Recruit Depot Museum (619)

Mission Bay Park (619) 221-8900

Mission Basilica San Diego de Alcalá (619) 281-8449

Old Town State Historical Park (619) 220-5422

Presidio Park Historical Site (619) 297-3258

Qualcomm Stadium (619) 641-3100

San Diego Chamber of Commerce (619) 232-0124

San Diego Maritime Museum (619) 234-9153

San Diego Sports Arena (619) 224-4176

San Diego Visitors Center (619) 276-8200

San Diego Zoo (619) 234-3153

Sea World (619) 226-3901

Seaport Village (619) 235-4014

Transportation

Amtrak (800) 872-7245

Becker Auto Rental (619) 298-5990

Enterprise Rent-A-Car (619) 225-0848

San Diego Cab (619) 232-6566

San Diego Metropolitan Transit District (619) 322-3004

San Diego Trolley (619) 231-8549)

San Diego Water Taxi (619) 235-8294

Fuel dock west end Harbor Island

Cruising Anchorage (Anchorage–A9) (see chart page 105)

NOAA Charts #18773, #18772, #18765

Latitude 32°43.6' N, Longitude 117°11.2' W (Center of Cruising Anchorage)

The Cruising Anchorage is a central, protected, inconvenient, and noisy anchorage. Although it is central to downtown San Diego tourist activities, the one-half-mile row to the dinghy dock and shore makes it inconvenient. The anchorage is off the beach in front of the U.S. Coast Guard Station and one-quarter mile from San Diego's Lindbergh Field flight path. Anchoring is by permit only, issued by the San Diego Unified Port District Mooring Office, limited to out-of-county residents only, for thirty days at a time.

Cruising Anchorage

The U.S. Coast Guard, founded in 1790 at the recommendation of Alexander Hamilton, the first Secretary of the Treasury of the United States, was formed to stamp out smuggling and piracy along the U.S. coast. It was originally called Revenue Marine, then the Revenue Cutter Service, and finally, in 1915, the U.S. Coast Guard. It is the oldest continuous sea-going force in the United States, commissioned with protecting life and property at sea and enforcing U.S. Maritime Law. In peacetime it operates under the jurisdiction of the Department of Transportation, but during war it is an active part of the U.S. Navy. U.S. Coast Guard Station, San Diego began service here in 1934 to prevent smuggling coming from Mexico. The station includes three helicopters, with each crew consisting of two pilots, one flight engineer, and a rescue swimmer. It also has two forty-one-foot utility boats and four 110-foot cutters patrolling a 200-mile Economic Exclusion Zone off the southern California coast.

The Cruising Anchorage (Anchorage–A9) is located at the southwest edge of the U.S. Coast Guard Air Station. No landing is allowed on government property, but rowing southeast along the Coast Guard property will place you at the dinghy dock along Harbor Drive.

Coast Guard Station adjacent to Cruising Anchorage

Land Approach

One mile north of downtown San Diego, exit Interstate 5 at Washington Street and drive west. Turn south on Pacific Coast Highway, drive one mile to Laurel Street, and turn west. At the end of Laurel Street is Harbor Drive; the dinghy dock is located just south of the Coast Guard Station on Harbor Drive. Row northwest around the U.S. Coast Guard Station to the Cruising Anchorage, off the north end of the station.

Sea Approach

From the ocean, proceed down the main ship channel of San Diego Bay in the lee of Point Loma, past Ballast Point, U.S. Naval Submarine Base, Shelter Island, and Harbor Island. At buoy #21, off Harbor Island, turn northeast out of the channel toward the south end of Harbor Island. A large, white, stern-wheeler paddleboat restaurant is at the east end of Harbor Island. Proceed north past the stern-wheeler, anchoring in the Cruising Anchorage (latitude 32°43.6' N, longitude 117°11.2' W) in Convair Lagoon, just north, off the beach of the U.S. Coast Guard Air Station.

Local Weather Service (858) 289-1212
Sea Tow (888) 473-2869
Tow Boat U.S. (800) 493-7869
Vessel Assist (800) 399-1921

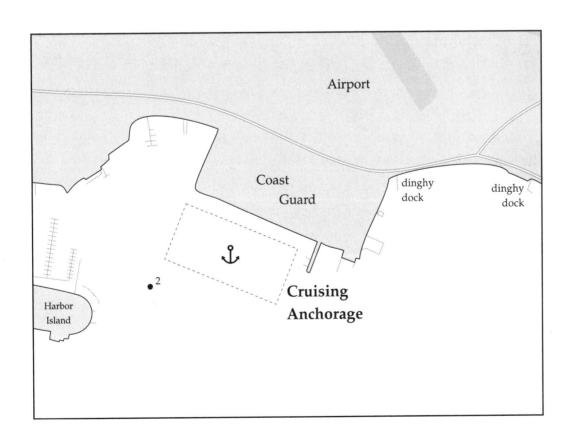

Anchorage and Berthing

There are no mooring buoys or slips in Cruising Anchorage (Anchorage–A9). The closest slips are on Harbor Island directly west of the anchorage. Anchor here in nine to twelve feet of water, where a soft sand and mud bottom makes excellent holding ground. Winds generally blow from the northwest; with the anchorage in the lee of Harbor Island, the water is generally smooth and calm. Strong winter storms occasionally arrive from the northwest from December to March; if inclement weather is expected, pay out plenty of scope to anchor. Pleasure boats up to sixty-five feet may anchor here for a maximum of ninety days in any given year. Free anchoring permits are controlled by the San Diego Unified Port District Mooring Office and are issued for thirty days at a time. Boats and owners must be from outside San Diego County, as this anchorage is intended for boats transiting the San Diego area. Persons interested in anchoring their vessel must obtain a permit from the San Diego Port District. During popular summer months such as August, September, October, and November, when everyone is traveling south to Mexico, there may be a waiting list; however, the port opens up additional anchorages to accommodate all boats. To apply, complete an application and submit your current vessel registration or documentation. To apply in person, make an appointment with the mooring office. To request an anchoring application for San Diego Bay, write:

San Diego Unified Port District Mooring Office

2890 Shelter Island Drive

San Diego, CA 92001

Please contact the mooring office with any questions. No landing is permitted on U.S. Coast Guard property, so rowing east to the dinghy docks of the Laurel Street Roadstead is imperative.

San Diego Unified Port District Mooring Office (619) 686-6227

San Diego Harbor Police (619) 223-1133

Facilities

Airport	
Dinghy dock	
Hotel	Holiday Inn on the Bay (619) 232-3861
	Pacific Inn Hotel (619) 232-6391
	Residence Inn by Marriott (619) 338-8200
Parking	

Restaurants	China Camp (619) 232-0686
	Anthony's Fish Grotto (619) 232-5103
	Anthony's Star of the Sea Room
	(619) 232-7408
Restrooms	
Telephone	

Attractions and Transportation

The anchorage is rather isolated and is affected by heavy automobile traffic around San Diego's Lindbergh Field. Some restaurants and hotels are within walking distance, but transportation will be needed to visit boating facilities and major tourist attractions.

San Diego Water Taxi provides a unique service throughout San Diego Bay. For a nominal fee, they will pick you up at your boat or slip and deposit you anywhere on the bay.

Buses #22 and #23 run along Harbor Drive to the American Plaza Transfer Station, where they connect with transportation to all parts of San Diego County.

Attractions

Balboa Park (619) 239-0512
Belmont Park (619) 491-2988
Cabrillo National Monument (619) 557-5450
Flying Leatherneck Aviation Museum (858) 693-1723
Marine Corps. Recruit Depot Museum (619) 524-6038
Maritime Museum (619) 234-9153
Mission Bay Park (619) 221-8900
Mission Basilica San Diego de Alcalá (619) 281-8449
Old Town State Historical Park (619) 220-5422
Presidio Park Historical Site (619) 297-3258
Qualcomm Stadium (619) 641-3100
San Diego Chamber of Commerce (619) 232-0124
San Diego Maritime Museum (619) 234-9153
San Diego Sports Arena (619) 224-4176
San Diego Visitors Center (619) 276-8200
San Diego Zoo (619) 234-3153

Sea World (619) 226-3901
Seaport Village (619) 235-4014

Transportation

Amtrak (800) 872-7245
Becker Auto Rental (619) 298-5990
Enterprise Rent-A-Car (619) 225-0848
San Diego Cab (619) 232-6566
San Diego Metropolitan Transit District (619) 322-3004
San Diego Trolley (619) 231-8549)
San Diego Water Taxi (619) 235-8294

Coast Guard is active in San Diego

Embarcadero (see chart page 112)

NOAA Charts #18773, #18765, #18766, #18772

Latitude 32°43.2' N, Longitude 117°10.5' W (Off the Embarcadero)

The Embarcadero, or "pier, wharf," is the marine area closest to downtown San Diego and its central city tourist sights. People have enjoyed this area since the founding of San Diego, and it continues to remain popular for its many attractions: the *Star of India*, the Maritime Museum, Anthony's Restaurants, Navy Pier, Broadway Pier, Cruiseship Terminal, and all the harbor cruise ships. The only pleasure-boating dock in the area is Anthony's Fish Grotto Restaurant guest dock.

Anthony's Fish Grotto and guest dock

Wharfs expand trade and commerce so, in 1850, William Davis built the first wharf in San Diego, at the corner of Market Street and Pacific Coast Highway. Soon, Pacific Mail steamers and other shipping firms shifted their business from the La Playa area to the new wharf in the central bay. Wharfs began to proliferate with the building of Horton Wharf (1868), Kimball Wharf (1871), and Babcock and Story Wharf (1886). Over the years, wharfs were bought, sold, and constructed by train, steamship, and trading companies as needs arose. In 1914, Broadway Pier was constructed, becoming the first reinforced concrete pier in San Diego.

Joe Brennan, a tugboat captain, was the first harbor master and port director of San Diego Bay. He began his tenure in 1918, holding the position until 1948. This was a time of large bay developments: piers were expanded, trade boomed, the bay was dredged, and Lindbergh Field was constructed. B-Street Pier was built in 1926, during Brennan's tenure.

In 1927, the *Star of India* was donated to a group of San Diego historians. The 1957 restoration of this iron barque made it the oldest seagoing square-rigged vessel in the world. It is tied along the quay with the ferryboat *Berkeley* and the steam yacht *Medina*, which serve as headquarters to the San Diego Maritime Museum, preserving the memory of our seafaring heritage.

Eleven blocks east, within walking distance of the Embarcadero, is the famous 1200-acre Balboa Park. In 1915, the California-Panama Exposition was held here, celebrating the opening of the Panama Canal. This successful exposition, which ran for two years, was attended by past and future presidents, vice-presidents, and movie stars.

Dr. Harry Wegeforth, while visiting the exposition, decided it would be a great site for a future zoo. So in 1916, the Zoological Society of San Diego was born, with Drs. Harry and Paul

Broadway Pier, first reinforced concrete pier in San Diego

Star of India, **oldest seagoing square-rigged vessel in the world**

Historic Berkley ferryboat houses San Diego Maritime Museum

1200-acre Balboa Park is eleven blocks from the waterfront

Wegeforth serving as its two directors. Belle Benchley, a temporary bookkeeper with no education in zoology or biology, was hired in 1925. By 1926, she was executive secretary of the Zoological Society. She expanded the zoo into one of the largest in the world, with more than 4,000 animals on exhibit.

In 1961, the zoo expanded to Escondido, where 2,200 acres were developed into The Wild Animal Park, which opened to the public in 1972. Here animals are not in cages, but roam the hills naturally, as visitors pass by in the safety of a monorail.

Today, Balboa Park and the San Diego Zoo are major tourist attractions in San Diego. The Embarcadero remains a bustling tourist center, as well, with close proximity to the San Diego Trolley, Amtrak, and the historic Santa Fe Train Station.

World-famous San Diego Zoo in Balboa Park

Land Approach

One mile north of downtown San Diego, exit Interstate 5 at the Airport, or Laurel Street exit. Follow signs to the airport and turn left on Harbor Drive. The square-rigged sailing ship, *Star of India*, will be on the right, in the center of the Embarcadero area. Parking meters direct visitors to parking stalls along the quay. Public parking is also found across the street in the City of San Diego parking lot.

Sea Approach

From the ocean, proceed down the main ship channel of San Diego Bay in the lee of Point Loma. Pass Ballast Point, the U.S. Naval Submarine Base, Shelter Island, and Harbor Island, and at buoy "21" leave the channel and travel 075°M (degrees magnetic), heading for the square-rigged sailing ship, *Star of India*, along the harbor front quay of the Embarcadero. Proceed with caution during times of limited visibility, as this course will pass through the Laurel Street Roadstead (Mooring–A3). The location off the Embarcadero is latitude 32°43.2' N, longitude 117°10.5' W.

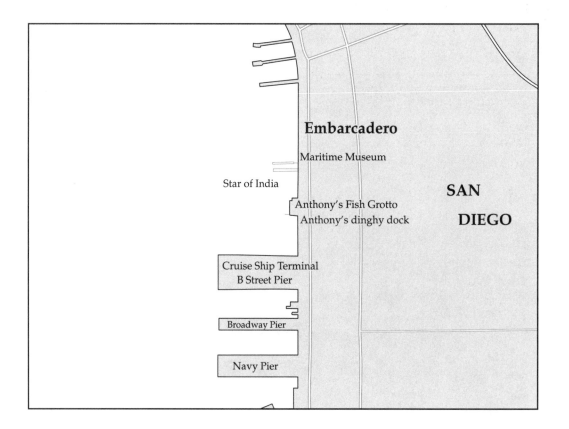

Local Weather Service (858) 289-1212

San Diego Harbor Police (619) 223-1133

Sea Tow (888) 473-2869

Tow Boat U.S. (800) 493-7869

Vessel Assist (800) 399-1921

Anchorage and Berthing

No anchoring or mooring is allowed off the Embarcadero. The closest anchorage is in the Cruisers Anchorage (Anchorage–A9) off the east end of Harbor Island. No public docks or private marinas are in the area. Anthony's Fish Grotto Restaurant has a seventy-five-foot guest dock on the south side of the building along the Embarcadero. Dining in the restaurant allows you temporary use of their dock. This is an excellent spot to load and unload passengers from the quay. Depths are dredged to twenty-five feet.

Anthony's Fish Grotto Restaurant (619) 232-5103

Facilities

Airport

Dinghy dock

Dock

Hotel   Holiday Inn on the Bay (619) 232-3861

                Pacific Inn Hotel (619) 232-6391

                Residence Inn by Marriott (619) 338-8200

Parking

Restaurants   Anthony's Fish Grotto (619) 232-5103

                Anthony's Star of the Sea Room (619) 232-7408

                Ruth Chris Steak House (619) 233-1422

                Mona Lisa (619) 234-4893

Restrooms

Telephone

Attractions and Transportation

All types of hotels and restaurants are within walking distance of the Embarcadero. No marine facilities are near; the closest is Shelter Island. Major tourist attractions along the Embarcadero are within walking distance, or public transportation is nearby.

Public transportation—buses #22, #23, and #992—runs along Harbor Drive, in front of the Embarcadero. Take any of these buses to transfer stations to connect with transportation to all parts of San Diego County. The America Plaza Transfer Station is within walking distance, as are the San Diego Trolley, Amtrak, and the Santa Fe Train Depot.

Embarcadero has excellent transportation

Attractions

Balboa Park (619) 239-0512
Belmont Park (619) 491-2988
Cabrillo National Monument (619) 557-5450
Flying Leatherneck Aviation Museum (858) 693-1723
Horton Plaza Shopping Center (619) 238-1596
Marine Corps. Recruit Depot Museum (619) 524-6038
Mission Bay Park (619) 221-8900

Mission Basilica San Diego de Alcalá (619) 281-8449
Old Town State Historical Park (619) 220-5422
Presidio Park Historical Site (619) 297-3258
Qualcomm Stadium (619) 641-3100
San Diego Chamber of Commerce (619) 232-0124
San Diego Maritime Museum (619) 234-9153
San Diego Sports Arena (619) 224-4176
San Diego Visitors Center (619) 276-8200
San Diego Wild Animal Park (619) 234-6541
San Diego Zoo (619) 234-3153
Sea World (619) 226-3901
Seaport Village (619) 235-4014

Transportation

Amtrak (800) 872-7245
Becker Auto Rental (619) 298-5990
Enterprise Rent-A-Car (619) 225-0848
San Diego Cab (619) 232-6566
San Diego Coronado Ferry (619) 234-4111
San Diego Metropolitan Transit District (619) 322-3004
San Diego Trolley (619) 231-8549)
San Diego Water Taxi (619) 235-8294

Laurel Street Roadstead (Mooring–A3) (see chart p. 118)
NOAA Charts #18773, #18765, #18766, #18772
Latitude 32°43.5' N, Longitude 117°10.7' W (Center of Roadstead)

Laurel Street Roadstead is an exposed, central mooring area close to downtown San Diego. It is near all central tourist activities and within walking distance of transportation that goes all over the county. Because this mooring area is exposed to the northwest wind, chop makes it rolling and uncomfortable in all weather. During strong winter storms, the roadstead can even become dangerous.

Laurel Street Roadstead

In the early years, San Diego Bay and the fishing industry developed simultaneously. Catches ranged from whales in 1840, to fur seals in 1880, and abalone in 1890. When Chinese fishermen left the bay, their jobs were filled by Portuguese (1880) and Italian (1900) fishermen. The Ghio family, which arrived in 1901, is still active in the Anthony's Restaurant chain. Tuna fishing and canning was a big industry in San Diego during the 1920's, but of this once grand industry, only the piers remain. "Little Italy" on India Street, a few blocks north of the roadstead, is an ethnic area that in its heyday housed 6,000 Italians, when San Diego was the center of the world's tuna industry. This is the oldest continuously operating neighborhood busi-

**Mediterranean mooring at
Laurel Street Roadstead**

ness district in San Diego, but today only a remnant of the Italian fishing families remain to run restaurants and shops, remembering a bygone era. The Waterfront, a bar and restaurant in this area, is the oldest bar in San Diego; in the olden days, mud flats extended from its back door to the bay. Stop by to look at historic photographs of old San Diego at Anthony's Fish Grotto, Mona Lisa, and The Waterfront for a trip back in time.

**Little Italy was center of
San Diego tuna fishing industry**

Row in from the mooring of the Laurel Street Roadstead and find palm trees and bike paths following the quay. Parking lots and restrooms line the shore, while busy traffic winds its way to downtown San Diego or Lindbergh field. Laurel Street Roadstead is near the center of all the downtown activity. The roadstead is filled with mooring buoys controlled by the San Diego Unified Port District Mooring Office.

Land Approach

One mile north of downtown San Diego, exit Interstate 5 at the Airport, or Laurel Street exit. Follow the signs to the airport and turn left on Harbor Drive. The Laurel Street Roadstead is at the west end of Laurel Street, with parking meters along the quayside.

Sea Approach

From the ocean, proceed down the main ship channel of San Diego Bay in the lee of Point Loma. Pass Ballast Point, the U.S. Naval Submarine Base, Shelter Island, and Harbor Island, and at buoy "21" leave the channel and travel northeast to the mooring east of the U.S. Coast Guard Station (latitude 32°43.5' N, longitude 117°10.7' W).

Local Weather Service (858) 289-1212
Sea Tow (888) 473-2869
Tow Boat U.S. (800) 493-7869
Vessel Assist (800) 399-1921

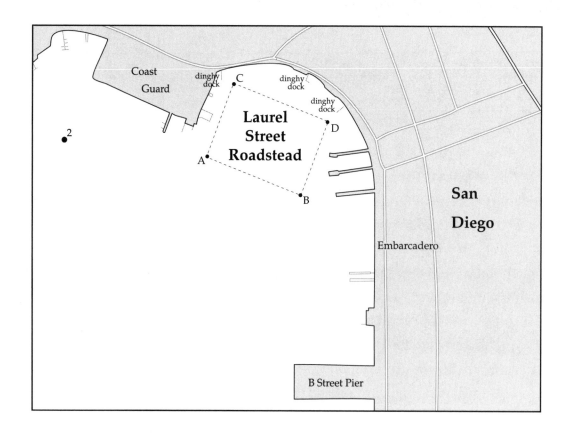

Anchorage and Berthing

No anchoring is allowed in the Laurel Street Roadstead (Mooring–A3). The closest anchorage is the Cruising Anchorage (Anchorage–A9) at the east end of Harbor Island. There are 130 single-point moorings for boats nineteen to sixty-five feet

Dinghy dock for Roadstead tenants

in length and twenty-four Mediterranean moorings against the center of the quay for boats nineteen to fifty feet in length. Moorings are by permit only. All persons interested in mooring their vessel to a port mooring must obtain a mooring permit from the San Diego Port District. Because of the high demand, each mooring area has a waiting list. To apply, complete an application and submit your current vessel registration or documentation along with an application fee.

Each applicant may submit only one application. To apply in person you must make an appointment with the mooring office. There is no separate waiting list for Mediterranean moorings. To request a mooring application for San Diego Bay, write:

San Diego Unified Port District Mooring Office

2890 Shelter Island Drive

San Diego, CA 92001

Prior to receiving a mooring permit all applicants must have their vessels inspected by the U.S. Coast Guard Auxiliary. The Courtesy Marine Examinations are conducted at the Auxiliary Inspection dock every Saturday between 8 A.M. and 4 P.M. The inspection dock is located along the quay at the north end of the Laurel Street Roadstead (Mooring–A9). The address is:

Vessel Inspection Dock

2320 N. Harbor Drive

San Diego, CA 92101

This inspection may be conducted no more than six months prior to the date of receiving a mooring permit. Please contact the mooring office should you have any questions.

San Diego Unified Port District Mooring Office (619) 686-6227
San Diego Harbor Police (619) 223-1133

Facilities

Airport
Dinghy dock
Hotel   Holiday Inn at the Embarcadero (619) 232-3861
                         Pacific Inn Hotel (619) 232-6391
                         Residence Inn by Marriott (619) 338-8200
Parking
Restaurants   Anthony's Fish Grotto (619) 232-5103
                         Mono Lisa (619) 234-4893
                         Shakespeare Pub and Grille (619) 299-0230
                         The Waterfront (619) 232-9656
Restrooms
Telephone

Attractions and Transportation

It's an easy walk from the Laurel Street Roadstead to all types of hotels and restaurants, major tourist attractions along the Embarcadero, and public transportation. No marine facilities are near; the closest is at Shelter Island.

Buses #22, #23, and #99 run along Harbor Drive in front of the Laurel Street Roadstead, while buses #40 and #70 run along Laurel Street. Take any of these buses to the transfer stations for transportation to all parts of San Diego County.

Attractions

Balboa Park (619) 239-0512
Belmont Park (619) 491-2988
Cabrillo National Monument (619) 557-5450
Flying Leatherneck Aviation Museum (858) 693-1723
Horton Plaza Shopping Center (619) 238-1596
Mission Bay Park (619) 221-8900
Mission Basilica San Diego de Alcalá (619) 281-8449
Old Town State Historical Park (619) 220-5422

Qualcomm Stadium (619) 641-3100
Presidio Park Historical Site (619) 297-3258
San Diego Chamber of Commerce (619) 232-0124
San Diego Maritime Museum (619) 234-9153
San Diego Sports Arena (619) 224-4176
San Diego Visitors Center (619) 276-8200
San Diego Zoo (619) 234-3153
Sea World (619) 226-3901
Seaport Village (619) 235-4014

Transportation

Amtrak (800) 872-7245
Becker Auto Rental (619) 298-5990
Enterprise Rent-A-Car (619) 225-0848
San Diego Cab (619) 232-6566
San Diego Metropolitan Transit District (619) 322-3004
San Diego Trolley (619) 231-8549)
San Diego Water Taxi (619) 235-8294

G Street Mole   (see chart page 124)

NOAA Charts #18773, #18772, #18765

Latitude 32°42.5' N, Longitude 117°10.4' W (Off Entrance to G Street Mole)

G Street Mole is a snug commercial basin close to downtown San Diego, where the San Diego commercial fishing boats and the tuna fleet dock. The United States Tuna Association is at the north corner of the harbor, and the San Diego Water Taxi dock is on the south corner, just north of Seaport Village.

Entrance to the G Street Mole

Alonzo Horton, a merchant from San Francisco, arrived in 1867 when San Diego's "Old Town" was a collection of flea-bitten buildings at the base of Presidio Hill. Thinking that the bayfront was the proper place to build a city, he bought 960 acres on the water south of Old Town, to develop his "New Town." In 1872 a fire in Old Town destroyed much of the established business district, thereby assuring the success of "New Town." By 1869, it supported 3,000 inhabitants, with every steamer from San Francisco bringing more settlers. The startling discovery of gold in Julian, fifty miles to the east, brought more growth in 1870, and by 1908 New Town sprawled

Alonzo Horton
"Father of San Diego"

Horton Plaza Shopping Center
Downtown San Diego

far beyond Horton's map, with 40,000 people calling San Diego home. A growing military population in the 1920's brought expansion of North Island Naval Air Station, with the construction of Navy Hospital.

In 1925, Ryan Airlines offered the first regularly scheduled commercial airplane flight in the United States, marking the beginning of the aviation industry in San Diego. Ryan soon built the plane *Spirit of St. Louis*, which took Charles Lindbergh on his historic 1927 transatlantic flight from New York to Paris. With World War II, San Diego expanded into a vast network of war industries, which brought thousands of people to the area. Alonzo Horton's grand visions for San Diego were realized, and his name was memorialized in the Horton-Grand Hotel and Horton Plaza.

Today, just a few blocks east of G Street Mole is Horton Plaza, one of the premier shopping areas in San Diego County. This five-level shopping center contains three major department stores, 140 specialty shops, a fourteen-screened cinema, a theater, and numerous restaurants. It is a wonderful place to shop for anything under the sun. South of the plaza is the historic Gaslamp Quarter, containing a sixteen-block, thirty-eight-acre area where old downtown San Diego has been recreated. Beautiful Victorian architecture is found in restored buildings that house coffee shops, galleries, antique shops, and restaurants. It is an exciting area in which to stroll, shop, or eat after dark, enjoying the ambiance of San Diego.

Land Approach

From the center of downtown San Diego, exit Interstate 5 at Broadway, continuing west until it ends at Marina Drive. Turn south until you reach Tuna Way, then turn right into the parking area for G Street Mole.

Sea Approach

From the ocean, proceed down the main ship channel of San Diego Bay, in the lee of Point Loma. Pass Ballast Point, the U.S. Naval Submarine Base, Shelter Island, Harbor Island, and the Embarcadero, and at buoy "22" leave the channel, traveling east to the entrance of G Street Mole (latitude 32°42.5' N, longitude 117°10.4' W).

Local Weather Service (858) 289-1212
Sea Tow (888) 473-2869
Tow Boat U.S. (800) 493-7869
Vessel Assist (800) 399-1921

Anchorage and Berthing

No anchoring or mooring is allowed in the G Street Mole. The nearest anchorage is the Cruising Anchorage (Anchorage–A9) east of Harbor Island. The port of San Diego has reserved these docks and slips for commercial fishing boats exclusively. The 129-slip marina caters to commercial boats, accommodating boats eighteen to eighty feet in length. Commercial boats may use this as a transient dock, as well. If you plan to stay here, make sure you have the following:

- ❑ California State Registration or U.S. Documentation
- ❑ California State Fish and Game License
- ❑ San Diego County Vessel Assessment Tags
- ❑ Fish Sales License

If you have any questions, you can call the phone numbers below or write:

San Diego Port District
G Street Mole Commercial Wharf
1140 N. Harbor Drive
San Diego, CA 92101

The inner harbor is dredged to fourteen feet. Restrooms, telephone, water, electricity, and parking are available for commercial operators. A few blocks east on Market Street is the famous restaurant, Kansas City Barbeque, where the movie *Top Gun* was filmed. Stop in for some good food and enjoy all the movie memorabilia on the walls.

G Street Mole (619) 683-8966 (working hours)
(619) 686-6346 (after hours/weekends)
San Diego Harbor Police (619) 223-1133

Facilities

Bank
Convenience store
Dinghy dock
Dock
Hotels   Embassy Suites San Diego (619) 239-2400
                Holiday Inn on the Bay (619) 232-3861
                U.S. Grant Hotel (619) 232-3121
                Westgate (619) 238-1818
Ice

Laundry
Library
Park
Parking
Restaurants   Anthony's Fish Grotto (619) 232-5103
                     Fish Market (619) 233-3474
                     Kansas City Barbeque (619) 231-9680

Restrooms
Shops
Telephone

Attractions and Transportation

All types of hotels and restaurants are within walking distance of the G Street Mole. It is close to many major tourist sites in San Diego, with easy access to public transportation. North of the mole, Broadway Pier is the dock for the San Diego-Coronado Ferry; south is Seaport Village, where shopping abounds in a quaint village atmosphere. A few blocks east is the Historic Gaslamp Quarter with restaurants, hotels, theaters, and shows, as well as Horton Plaza Shopping Mall. This location is also central to the train, trolley, and city buses.

Public transportation, bus #7, runs along Harbor Drive to a variety of stores along the main thoroughfare; it also goes to American Plaza Transfer Station for transfers to all parts of San Diego County.

Slips at G Street Mole are close to downtown

Attractions

Balboa Park (619) 239-0512
Belmont Park (619) 491-2988
Cabrillo National Monument (619) 557-5450
Flying Leatherneck Aviation Museum (858) 693-1723

Horton Plaza (619) 238-1596
Marine Corps. Recruit Depot Museum (619) 524-6038
Mission Bay Park (619) 221-8900
Mission Basilica San Diego de Alcalá (619) 281-8449
Old Town State Historical Park (619) 220-5422
Presidio Park Historical Site (619) 297-3258
Qualcomm Stadium (619) 641-3100
San Diego Chamber of Commerce (619) 232-0124
San Diego Maritime Museum (619) 234-9153
San Diego Sports Arena (619) 224-4176
San Diego Visitors Center (619) 276-8200
San Diego Zoo (619) 234-3153
Sea World (619) 226-3901
Seaport Village (619) 235-4014

Transportation

Amtrak (800) 872-7245
Becker Auto Rental (619) 298-5990
Enterprise Rent-A-Car (619) 225-0848
San Diego Cab (619) 232-6566
San Diego-Coronado Ferry (619) 234-4111
San Diego Metropolitan Transit District (619) 322-3004
San Diego Trolley (619) 231-8549)
San Diego Water Taxi (619) 235-8294

Marriott Marina   (see chart page 130)
NOAA Charts #18773, #18765, #18766, #18772
Latitude 32°42.5' N, Longitude 117°10.1' W
(Off Marriott Marina Entrance)

The Marriott Marina is a small, compact central harbor close to all activities in downtown San Diego. It is directly in front of the San Diego Convention Center and the twin Marriott Towers Hotel, which make excellent landmarks to find the marina. Adjacent to Seaport Village and the Historic Gaslamp District of San Diego, it is close to all transportation, making this one of the most popular marinas in the bay.

Entrance to Marriott Marina

A lively area along the waterfront between First and Fifth Street was known as "Stingaree" in 1870. Here one could find brothels, gambling halls, beer joints, and opium dens. Marshall Wyatt Earp, of Tombstone, Arizona fame, owned three establishments in the area.

A large Chinese population lived here, and their industrious efforts contributed to economic growth of the city. Laws prohibited Chinese women from coming to America; therefore, men came intending to work hard, make their fortune, and return rich to their families and native land. The greatest number came during the California Gold Rush, but stayed to build the railroads and California levees and to work in the agriculture and fishing industries. By the 1880s the primary export from San Diego was dried fish, with Chinese fishermen leading the industry. When the 1890s brought a stagnant economy and Chinese exclusion laws were passed, forcing men out of their jobs, the once-prosperous Chinese community declined and disappeared. The few remaining Chinese were employed as market gardeners, launderers, domestic servants, cooks, clerks, hotel employees, and restaurateurs.

Today, this historic area is known as the Gaslamp Quarter. It contains a sixteen-block, thirty-eight acre area where old downtown San Diego buildings are being restored. Beautiful Victorian architecture is renewed, where buildings containing coffee shops, galleries, antique shops, and restaurants line the streets. It is a wonderful area to stroll and window shop.

Restored Victorian Gaslamp Quarter

North along the bayfront is Seaport Village, a re-created 18th century whaling village, with over fourteen acres of landscaped park accompanying harborside shops and restaurants. Gaslamp Quarter and Seaport Village are both popular tourist areas in downtown San Diego. Changes abound with the San Diego Convention Center expanding, a ballpark being constructed, and the Historic Gaslamp Quarter being renewed. Excitement is everywhere, making this a fun place to explore.

Land Approach

From the center of downtown San Diego, exit Interstate 5 at Broadway, continue west until Fifth Street, and turn south. Continue on Fifth Street across Harbor Drive, coming to the San Diego Convention Center. Once you are on the west side of the convention center, turn north into the marina parking lot. Be especially careful with traffic when a convention is in progress, as the area becomes very congested.

Sea Approach

From the ocean, proceed down the main ship channel of San Diego Bay in the lee of Point Loma. Pass Ballast Point, the U.S. Naval Submarine Base, Shelter Island, Harbor Island, and the Embarcadero, and at buoy "23" leave the channel and travel northeast to the entrance of the Marriott Marina (latitude 32°42.5' N, longitude 117°10.1' W).

Local Weather Service (858) 289-1212
San Diego Harbor Police (619) 223-1133
Sea Tow (888) 473-2869
Tow Boat U.S. (800) 493-7869
Vessel Assist (800) 399-1921

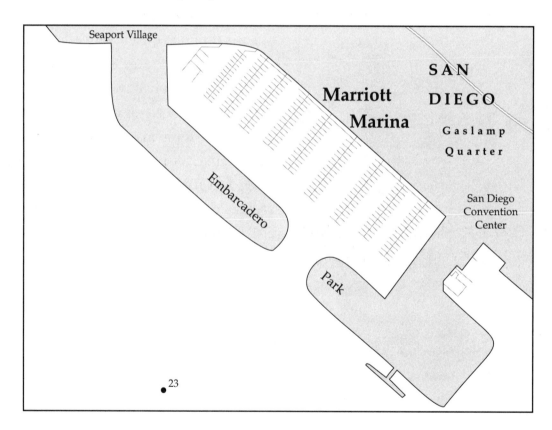

Anchoring and Berthing

No anchoring or mooring is allowed in the Marriott Marina. The closest anchorage is the Cruising Anchorage (Anchorage–A9) off the east end of Harbor Island; the nearest mooring area is the Laurel Street Roadstead (Mooring–A3) off the Embarcadero. The **Marriott Marina** has 445 slips for boats twenty-five to eighty-

Slips at the Marriott Marina

Historic San Diego Rowing Club

three feet in length, with end ties available for boats up to 130 feet. Pool, spa, workout room, and tennis courts are available, in addition to such regular services as laundry, showers, restrooms, T.V., telephone, electricity, and water. The basin is dredged to thirteen feet, but shoal areas exist south of the marina entrance; therefore, stay in the center of the channel.

The palm trees and grassy knolls of Embarcadero Marina Park surround the marina with a public fishing pier at the south end of the park. This is a great place for a picnic lunch on a warm Sunday afternoon. The Chart House Restaurant, in the historic boathouse of the San Diego Rowing Club, has pictures of old San Diego adorning the walls, making a treat for young and old alike. Visit the former mayor of San Diego and national talk show host Roger Hedgecock in his restaurant, Roger's on Fifth, a few blocks east in the Historic Gaslamp Quarter.
Marriott Marina (619) 230-8955

Facilities

Bank
Convenience store
Dinghy dock
Dock
Exercise room
Grocery store
Hotel   Clarion Hotel Bay View (619) 696-0234
                               Hyatt Regency San Diego (619) 232-1234
                               San Diego Marriott Hotel (619) 234-1500
Ice

Laundry
Park
Parking
Pool/Spa
Rental concessions   Downtown Boat Rental (619) 239-BOAT
Restaurants   Chart House (619) 233-7391
                             Harbor House Restaurant (619) 232-1141
                             Roger's on Fifth (619) 702-0444
                             The Field (619) 232-9840
                             The Old Spaghetti Factory (619) 233-4323
Restrooms
Shops
Showers
Telephone
Tennis courts

Attractions and Transportation

All types of hotels, restaurants, and major tourist attractions along the Embarcadero are within walking distance of the Marriott Marina. It is a short walk to all transportation including the trolley, train, bus, and the historic Santa Fe train depot. The San Diego Trolley runs along Harbor Drive in front of the San Diego Convention Center and the Marriott Hotel. Take the trolley north to the American Plaza Transfer Station to transportation to all parts of San Diego County.

Shops and restaurants of Seaport Village

No marine facilities are near. Shelter Island is the closest location to access all marine facilities.

Attractions

Balboa Park (619) 239-0512
Belmont Park (619) 491-2988
Cabrillo National Monument (619) 557-5450
Flying Leatherneck Aviation Museum (858) 693-1723
Horton Plaza (619) 238-1596
Marine Corps. Recruit Depot Museum (619) 524-6038
Mission Bay Park (619) 221-8900
Mission Basilica San Diego de Alcalá (619) 281-8449
Old Town State Historical Park (619) 220-5422
Presidio Park Historical Site (619) 297-3258
Qualcomm Stadium (619) 641-3100
San Diego Chamber of Commerce (619) 232-0124
San Diego Maritime Museum (619) 234-9153
San Diego Sports Arena (619) 224-4176
San Diego Visitors Center (619) 276-8200
San Diego Wild Animal Park (619) 234-6541
San Diego Zoo (619) 234-3153
Sea World (619) 226-3901
Seaport Village (619) 235-4014

Transportation

Amtrak (800) 872-7245
Becker Auto Rental (619) 298-5990
Enterprise Rent-A-Car (619) 225-0848
San Diego Cab (619) 232-6566
San Diego-Coronado Ferry (619) 234-4111
San Diego Metropolitan Transit District (619) 322-3004
San Diego Trolley (619) 231-8549)
San Diego Water Taxi (619) 235-8294

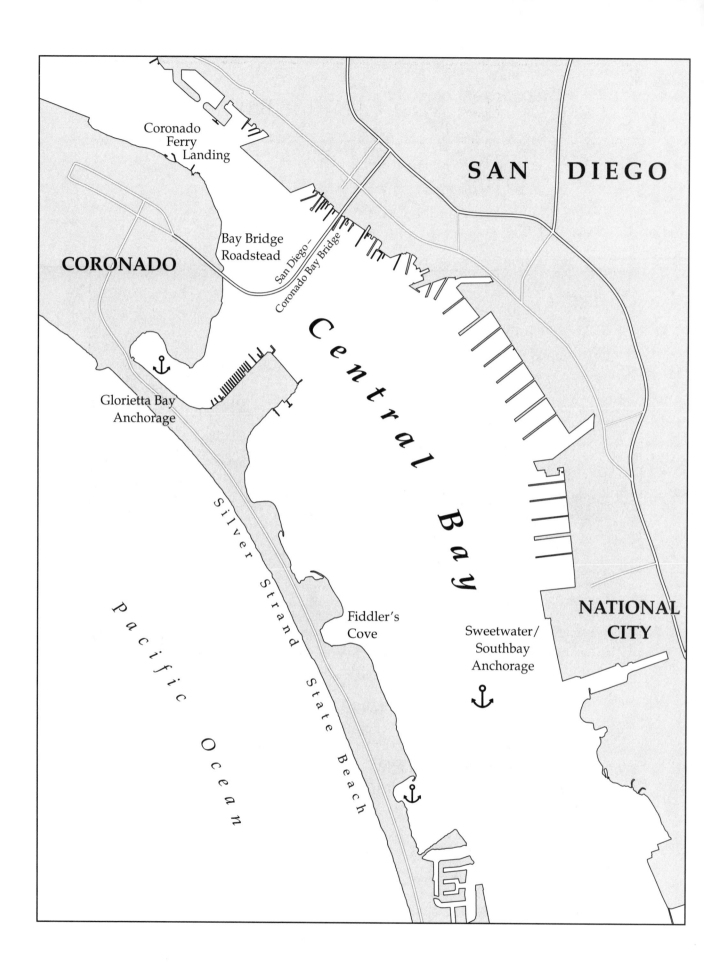

Coronado
Ferry
Landing

SAN DIEGO

CORONADO

Bay Bridge
Roadstead

San Diego–
Coronado Bay Bridge

Central Bay

Glorietta Bay
Anchorage

Silver Strand State Beach

Pacific Ocean

Fiddler's
Cove

Sweetwater/
Southbay
Anchorage

NATIONAL
CITY

10 THE CENTRAL BAY

"The Pacific well deserves its name, for except in the southern part, at Cape Horn, and in a few western parts, near China and the Indian Ocean, it has few storms and is never either extremely hot or cold."

Richard Henry Dana, Jr., *Two Years Before the Mast* (1835)

Coronado Ferry Landing (see chart page 138)

NOAA Charts #18773, #18772, #18765

Latitude 32°42.1' N, Longitude 117°10.3' W (Off Ferry Landing)

Coronado Ferry Landing is an excellent place to dock, eat lunch in the fine waterside restaurants, and watch spectacular views of the bay and the San Diego skyline. Here you can walk or stroll in a park-type setting and visit all the shops in the Ferry Landing.

210-foot guest dock at Coronado Ferry Landing

The barren sand "island" Coronado was undeveloped until 1885 when Gruendike, Babcock, and Story began to promote the area. They visualized a fine resort and a planned community on this sandy peninsula. The plan involved ferryboats, ferry landings, trains, land sales, and a hotel. They formed the Coronado Beach Company, Coronado Water Company, San Diego and Coronado Ferry Company, Coronado Brick Company, and Coronado Beach Railroad. The first "ferry" arrived at the foot of Orange Avenue in December, 1885 in the form of the steam yacht *Della* towing a barge carrying forty Chinese laborers to begin development. They built a ferry landing, planted orange trees down Orange Avenue to the site of the Hotel del Coronado, and constructed a railway connecting the ferry terminal with the hotel. They also built a railroad, the Belt Line Railroad, around the south end of the bay through Imperial Beach and National City to bring heavy supplies and passengers from San Diego. Over the years, the ferry landing would have a hotel, a boatyard, a railway station, and various shops surrounding the docks. Numerous ferries plied the waters of San Diego Bay: *Coronado* (1886), *Benicia* (1888), *Ramona* (1903), and *Coronado* (1929). They took passengers and cars not only to downtown, but also to Ballast Point and La Playa. The longest and last auto ferry was *Crown City* (1954); it was 242 feet long and carried sixty automobiles across the bay. In 1969, completion of the Coronado Bay Bridge brought an end to eighty-four years of ferry crossings.

Coronado Ferry Landing is south of carrier docks at North Island Naval Air Station

Today the Coronado Ferry Landing is home to 40,000 square feet of shops and restaurants. A fishing pier, ferry landing, and 210-foot public boat dock invite visitors from all over the country to enjoy this beautiful area. A new passenger ferry crosses the bay hourly to take sightseers to Broadway Pier on the San Diego waterfront.

Land Approach

Two miles south of downtown San Diego, exit Interstate 5 at the Coronado, or State Highway 75 exit. Cross over the Coronado Bay Bridge and turn north on Orange Avenue. One-half mile north on Orange Avenue will be Centennial Park and the Coronado Ferry Landing.

Sea Approach

Continue south down the main ship channel and pass Shelter Island, Harbor Island, the Embarcadero, and Broadway Pier. At buoy "23" turn west and approach the Coronado Ferry Landing (latitude 32°42.1' N, longitude 117°10.3' W). Tie up at the 210-foot public dock in front of the restaurants and enjoy the area.

Local Weather Service (858) 289-1212
Sea Tow (888) 473-2869
Tow Boat U.S. (800) 493-7869
Vessel Assist (800) 399-1912

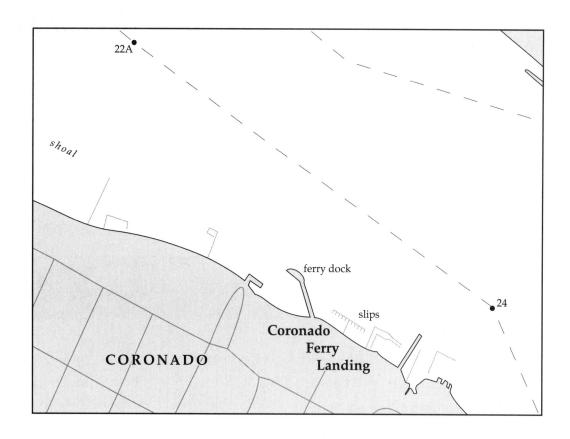

Anchorage and Berthing

No anchoring is allowed off the Coronado Ferry Landing. The closest anchorage is Glorietta Bay (Anchorage–A5). Coronado Ferry Landing has ten public slips to accommodate boats to thirty-five feet and an end tie for boats up to 210 feet in length. The main ship channel is dredged to forty-two feet; the water is twenty feet deep under the public docking area.

San Diego Harbor Police
(619) 223-1133

Facilities

Bank
Convenience store
Dock
Ferry landing
Grocery store
Fishing
Laundry
Park
Parking
Restaurants   Bay Beach Café (619) 435-4900
                       Il Fornaio (619) 437-4911
                       Peohe's (619) 437-4474
Restrooms
Shops
Telephone

Aircraft Carrier Memorial

Attractions and Transportation

The Coronado Ferry Landing is a great place to tie up your boat and enjoy a great meal and visit local shops. Here you will find over thirty restaurants and shops in a park-like setting with fountains and pools. The docks offer magnificent views of the San Diego skyline. Occasionally, local military installations of North Island Naval Air Station and the Naval Amphibious Base have events open to the public, so call for schedules. Biking and walking trails emanate from the landing to all parts of Coronado.

Public transportation, bus #904, runs along First Street. Take it south to downtown Coronado to transfer to buses that travel to all parts of San Diego County. A new passenger ferry crosses the bay between Coronado Ferry Landing and Broadway Pier near downtown San Diego; this is a pleasant way to see the sights of San Diego Bay.

Attractions

Coronado Chamber of Commerce (619) 435-9260
Coronado Golf Course (619) 435-3121
Coronado Playhouse (619) 435-4856
Coronado Visitors Bureau (619) 437-8788
Lamb's Players Theatre (619) 437-0600
Hotel del Coronado (619) 435-6611
Navy Amphibious Base Coronado (619) 437-2011
North Island Naval Air Station (619) 545-1011

Transportation

Becker Auto Rental (619) 298-5990
Coronado Cab (619) 435-6310
Coronado Transit Information (619) 233-3004
Enterprise Rent-a-Car (619) 522-6111
San Diego-Coronado Ferry (619) 234-4111
San Diego Trolley (619) 231-8549
San Diego Water Taxi (619) 235-8294

Bay Bridge Roadstead (Mooring–A4)
NOAA Charts #18773, #18772, #18765
Latitude 32°41.4' N, Longitude 117°09.7' W (Bay Bridge Moorings)

The Bay Bridge Roadstead is a quiet, isolated mooring area in the shadow of the Coronado Bay Bridge. Moderate chop from bay traffic and wind make the mooring area uncomfortable at times. Surrounded by Tidelands Park and a garden-like setting you can moor for an unlimited time period and explore all the environs of Coronado and the surrounding area.

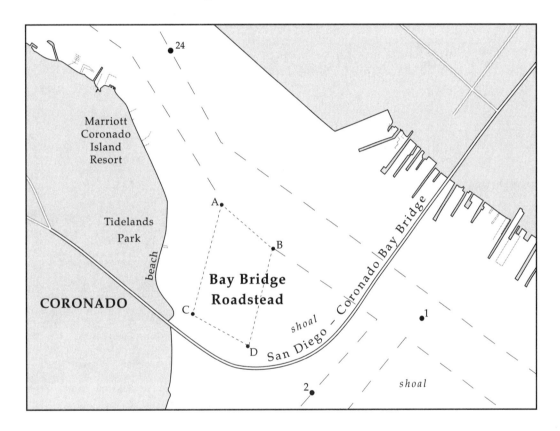

Ever since people crossed the bay in boats to the windswept, sandy island to picnic, hunt rabbits, or just explore, they thought there must be a better way to transit the bay. By 1912, people grumbled about the slow ferry service, and a Spreckel's company proposed a drawbridge from Market Street in San Diego to First Street in Coronado, but dropped the project in 1929. As early as 1926, committees formed to discuss a "tube" or tunnel vs. a bridge. Serious discussion about building a bridge began in 1935, but opposition from the navy halted debate. In 1957 the city council seriously considered the possibility of a bridge or tunnel crossing the bay, while citizens and the navy continued to oppose the idea. Finally in 1965, objections and fighting ceased and construction of the San Diego-Coronado Bay Bridge was approved.

On August 2, 1969 the curved, 200-foot high, five-laned, two-and-one-quarter-mile bridge officially opened. California Governor Edmund (Pat) Brown pushed hard for the bridge, but the ribbon-cutting ceremony was performed by Governor Ronald Reagan. The bay ferries crossed the bay for the last time and ceased operation. In 1984 the twenty-two acre Tidelands Park was dedicated, with its grass, trees, and playground equipment. Park, bike trails, and beaches are located immediately in front of the anchorage, and dinghies can be taken up on the beach. Immediately to the north is the sixteen-acre, 300-room Marriott Coronado Island Resort. It is a convenient place for friends to stay and visit in Coronado.

Mooring area at the west end of the bridge

Land Approach

Two miles south of downtown San Diego, exit Interstate 5 at the Coronado, or State Highway 75 exit. Cross over the Coronado Bay Bridge and turn right on the first street, Glorietta Boulevard, and then right on Millinix Drive to enter Tidelands Park. The mooring area is just off the beach of Tidelands Park.

Sea Approach

Continue south down the main ship channel and pass Shelter Island, Harbor Island, the Embarcadero, and Broadway Pier. Past buoy "24" begin to turn west; there will be numerous boats swinging from mooring buoys (latitude 32°41.4' N, longitude 117°09.7' W) off the Tidelands Park north of the bridge. Be watchful of shoal areas between the moorings and the bridge piers "12" through "14," where depths drop to five feet and below at low tide. If you pass under the bridge, you have gone too far.

Local Weather Service (858) 289-1212

Sea Tow (888) 473-2869

Tow Boat U.S. (800) 493-7869

Vessel Assist (800) 399-1912

Anchorage and Berthing

If you go south past the bridge, you have gone too far

There are no slips in the Bay Bridge Roadstead. There are sixty-nine single-point mooring buoys for boats nineteen to sixty-five feet in length. Water depth of sixteen feet exists among the buoys and twenty yards off-shore. Stay within the mooring area and there should be no chance of going aground. A sandy beach at the south end of Tidelands Park directly under the bridge provides space to tie your dinghy, as there is no dinghy dock. All moorings are controlled by the San Diego Unified Port District.

Persons interested in mooring their vessel to a port mooring must obtain a mooring permit from the San Diego Port District. Because of the high demand, each mooring area may have a waiting list. To apply, complete an application and submit your current vessel registration or documentation along with an application fee. Each applicant may submit only one application. To apply in person, make an appointment with the mooring office. To request a mooring application for San Diego Bay, write:

San Diego Unified Port District Mooring Office
2890 Shelter Island Drive
San Diego, CA 92001

Prior to receiving a mooring permit all applicants must have their vessels inspected by the U. S. Coast Guard Auxiliary. Courtesy marine examinations (CMEs) are conducted every Saturday at the Auxiliary inspection dock between 8 a.m. and 4 p.m. The inspection dock is located along the quay at the north end of the Laurel Street Roadstead (Mooring–A9). The address is:

Vessel Inspection Dock
2320 N. Harbor Drive
San Diego, CA 92101

This inspection may be conducted no more than six months prior to the date of receiving a mooring permit. Please contact the mooring office with any questions.

San Diego Harbor Police (619) 223-1133
San Diego Unified Port District Mooring Office (619) 686-6227

Facilities

Hotel	Coronado Marriott Resort (619) 435-3000
	Crown City Inn (619) 435-3116
Park	
Parking	
Restaurant	La Escale (619) 522-3039
Restrooms	
Swimming	
Telephone	

Attractions and Transportation

This is a rather isolated location. If you walk and use public transportation, you can visit all the sights of Coronado, such as Hotel del Coronado, Coronado Ferry Landing, the theater, shops, and restaurants. Occasionally, local military installations of North Island Naval Air Station and the Naval Amphibious Base will have events open to the public, so call for schedules. An exciting time to visit is the Fourth of July, when there is a parade down Orange Avenue and the "Over the Bay Run," where runners cross the Coronado Bay Bridge and visitors come from all over the country to participate.

Public transportation, Coronado bus #904, runs along First Street to the Coronado Hospital. These are within one or two blocks of Tidelands Park, an easy walk. Transfer to bus #901 or #902 to cross the bridge to San Diego and American Plaza Transfer Station, where connections can be made to all parts of San Diego County.

Attractions

Coronado Chamber of Commerce (619) 435-9260
Coronado Golf Course (619) 435-3121
Coronado Playhouse (619) 435-4856
Coronado Visitors Bureau (619) 437-8788
Hotel del Coronado (619) 435-6611
Lamb's Players Theatre (619) 437-0600
Navy Amphibious Base Coronado (619) 437-2011
North Island Naval Air Station (619) 545-1011

Transportation

Becker Auto Rental (619) 298-5990
Coronado Cab (619) 435-6310
Coronado Transit Information (619) 233-3004
Enterprise Rent-a-Car (619) 522-6111
San Diego-Coronado Ferry (619) 234-4111
San Diego Trolley (619) 231-8549
San Diego Water Taxi (619) 235-8294

Glorietta Bay (Anchorage–A5) (see chart page 149)
NOAA Charts #18773, #18772, #18765
Latitude 32°40.7' N, Longitude 117°10.1' W (Anchorage Glorietta Bay)

Glorietta Bay, or "Circle Bay," is a quiet, secluded anchorage in which to spend an afternoon, a day, or three days. This tranquil bay is central to the small, quaint, navy town of Coronado and its numerous shops, sights, and restaurants.

Glorietta Bay Anchorage

Grumwald, Babcock, and Story were the primary early developers of this barren sand "island" across the bay from San Diego in 1885. John D. Spreckels, son of the Hawaiian sugar baron, joined this group in 1887 when he bought major shares in the Coronado Beach Company. They envisioned and built the luxurious Hotel del Coronado and boathouse and offered real estate to private buyers. The Coronado Boathouse, with the same distinctive Victorian style as Hotel del Coronado, was built in 1887. William Ritter, a U.C. Berkeley biologist, used it in 1903 for marine research before he moved to a more permanent home later to become known as the Scripps Institute of Oceanography, in La Jolla. In 1900 Spreckels established "Tent City" just

Historic John D. Spreckels mansion at the head of the bay

south of the Hotel del Coronado, across from Glorietta Bay. It was a campground that provided tents for rent, with the added attractions of a large bathhouse, plunge, dance hall, and restaurants. During the summer season people would escape the heat of the inland valleys to the cool sea breezes of the beach, and each year it grew to attract more visitors. In 1911 John D. Spreckels built a family mansion overlooking Glorietta Bay; his one-time home is known today as the Glorietta Bay Inn. In 1936 the gambling ship *Monte Carlo*, anchored three miles off Coronado, broke her mooring and grounded on the beach. No one claimed her, and disputes raged regarding responsibility and liability. Remains of her hull can be seen today south of the condominiums at low tide. Completion of the Coronado Bay Bridge in 1969 brought a building frenzy to Coronado, including the thirty-six-acre waterfront real estate development known as Shore Towers Condominiums, which was completed in 1971.

Today Glorietta Bay is the ideal place for a transient vessel to anchor and visit this tranquil and historic area of San Diego. The Coronado Boathouse, Glorietta Bay Inn, and famous Hotel del Coronado, where heads of state, foreign dignitaries, and presidents stay, contain all types of memorabilia of a bygone era. Continue north on Orange Avenue to find fascinating shops, restaurants, and boutiques. The Coronado Golf Course is just north of Gloretta Bay.

Town is a short walk from the bay

Land Approach

Two miles south of downtown San Diego, exit Interstate 5 at Coronado, or State Highway 75. Cross over the Coronado Bay Bridge and turn south on Orange Avenue. One mile south on Orange Avenue lie Hotel del Coronado (locals call it "The Del") and downtown Coronado. Across from the hotel is the Coronado Boathouse Restaurant and Glorietta Bay. The dinghy dock located one-half mile south of the boathouse is on the left in Glorietta Bay Park.

Pass under the San Diego-Coronado Bay Bridge

Sea Approach

Continue south down the main ship channel and pass under the Coronado Bay Bridge between piers "18" and "20." Shoal areas exist under other pier areas. Immediately past the bridge turn west and proceed between buoys "1" and "2," following the range (218° magnetic) into Glorietta Bay. Stay within the marked channel; water south of the channel is home to the Naval Amphibious Base and is restricted to U.S. Navy only. Buoy "8" (latitude 32°40.7' N, longitude 117°10.1' W) marks the southeast end of the

Entrance to Glorietta Bay

Glorietta Bay Anchorage (Anchorage–A5). North of this anchorage are the distinctive Coronado Boathouse, Glorietta Bay Marina, and Coronado Yacht Club.

Local Weather Service (858) 289-1212
San Diego Harbor Police (619) 223-1133
Sea Tow (888) 473-2869
Tow Boat U.S. (800) 493-7869
Vessel Assist (800) 399-1921

Anchorage and Berthing

There are no mooring buoys in Glorietta Bay. Docks and slips can be found at **Glorietta Bay Marina** and the **Coronado Yacht Club**; however, to use the yacht club you must be a yacht club member and you must have secured their permission. Anchor within the marked area in fifteen feet of water, soft mud, and sand bottom. This is excellent holding ground where you can swing at anchor in the fifteen-knot afternoon sea breezes with ease. Anchoring is allowed for a maximum of seventy-two hours; no permit is required. Row southwest to the dinghy dock south of the launch ramp and north of Glorietta Bay Park.

San Diego Water Taxi provides a unique service throughout San Diego Bay. For a nominal fee, they will pick you up at your boat or slip and deposit you anywhere on the bay.

Coronado Yacht Club (619) 455-1848

Glorietta Bay Marina (619) 435-5203

San Diego Unified Port District Mooring Office (619) 686-6227

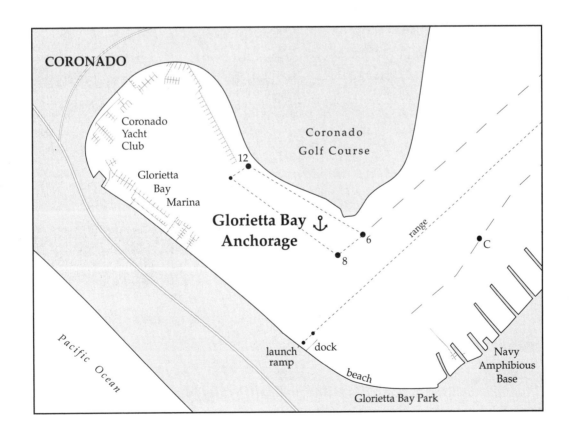

Facilities

Bank
Boat dock
Dinghy dock
Fishing
Golf
Grocery store
Hotels   Glorietta Bay Inn (619) 435-3101
                                 Hotel del Coronado (619) 435-3101
                                 La Avenida Inn (619) 435-3191

Ice
Launch ramp
Laundry
Library
Park
Parking
Post office
Rental Concession   Seaforth Coronado (619) 437-1590
Restaurants   Brigantine (619) 435-4166
                                 Coronado Boathouse (619) 435-4237
                                 Miguel's Cocina (619) 437-4237

Restrooms
Showers
Slips
Surfing
Swimming
Telephone
Tennis courts
Theater

Attractions and Transportation

Glorietta Bay Anchorage is rather isolated; a dinghy and the ability to walk are necessary. However, after a short distance all varieties of entertainment await you. The historic Hotel del Coronado, Coronado Boathouse, Spreckels Mansion, shops, and restaurants are all nearby. Coronado supports two theater groups--the Lamb's

Players and the Coronado Playhouse—that provide excellent entertainment. Public events at the local military installations are held occasionally, so call for a schedule.

Public transportation buses #901 and #904 pass by on Silver Strand Boulevard, traveling north to Coronado and south to Imperial Beach. Here you can transfer to buses that travel to all parts of San Diego County.

Attractions

Coronado Chamber of Commerce (619) 435-9260
Coronado Golf Course (619) 435-3121
Coronado Playhouse (619) 435-4856
Coronado Visitors Bureau (619) 437-8788
Hotel del Coronado (619) 435-6611
Lamb's Players Theatre (619) 437-0600
Navy Amphibious Base Coronado (619) 437-2011
North Island Naval Air Station (619) 545-1011

Transportation

Becker Auto Rental (619) 298-5990
Coronado Cab (619) 435-6211
Coronado Transit Information (619) 233-3004
Enterprise Rent-A-Car (619) 522-6111
San Diego Trolley (619) 231-8549
San Diego Water Taxi (619) 235-8294

Coronado (see chart page 155)

NOAA Charts #18773, #18772, #18765

Latitude 32°40.8' N, Longitude 117°10.4' W (Center of Glorietta Bay)

Coronado, or "The Crowned One," is a small town whose numerous sights and attractions lure visitors from all over the world. The famous Hotel del Coronado, with its charming Victorian architecture, is a recognized landmark. The city has the charm of a small navy town, yet just a short ride over the Coronado Bay Bridge is the bustling metropolis of downtown San Diego.

Coronado Yacht Club

Juan Cabrillo arrived in 1542, making little mention of the small sand peninsula south of the harbor. No trees were present; it was covered with reeds and grasses. Here a fresh water spring, "The Russian Spring," allowed sailing vessels to fill their water casks for long ocean voyages.

Coronado was originally two islands. Directly across from Ballast Point lay North Island, with a small cove called "Whaler's Bight," where ship captains would careen their vessels to repair and maintain the bottoms of their ships. Today North Island Naval Air Station is located in this area. A large bay called "Spanish Bight" separated North Island from South Island, where the 5.2-square-mile city of Coronado is today.

Just before the Mexican-American War, in 1846, Mexican Governor Pío Pico granted the land to Pedro Carillo as a wedding gift. The island's ownership changed several times, until finally in 1885 Gruendike, Babcock, and Story bought it to build a hotel and develop the area. Construction of the famous hotel began in 1886 and Hotel del Coronado, "The Queen of the Beach," was completed in 1888. John D. Spreckles, son of the Hawaiian sugar baron, bought shares of the project in 1889. In 1887 the Coronado Railroad went down Orange Avenue from the Ferry Landing to the Hotel Del Coronado. In 1890 the city of Coronado was founded with 450 full-time residents. Ten years later, a tent city was built south of the hotel for summer visitors to escape the summer heat of El Centro, Yuma, and San Diego counties. The U.S. Navy has been in the area since the early 1900s; its presence remains strong today.

The city, served by ferries between 1886 and 1969, experienced slow growth due to limited access. Today, the Coronado Bay Bridge provides a quick avenue to downtown San Diego for the 26,000 Coronado residents. However, even with the increased growth, Coronado maintains small-town charm. The center of town con-

World famous Hotel del Coronado is across the street from the bay

tains boutiques, restaurants, theaters, movies, and ice cream parlors. Tourists still descend on this area in the summer months, though it is quiet in the winter months. Royalty, presidents, and heads of state from all over the world come to the Hotel del Coronado (locals calls it "the Del") for rest and relaxation. It is close to Mexico with horse racing, bull fighting, and the busy border town Tijuana.

The harbor is located in Glorietta Bay across from the Hotel del Coronado and one block south of downtown. Here are the Glorietta Bay Marina and the Coronado Yacht Club.

Glorietta Bay Marina

Land Approach

Two miles south of downtown San Diego, exit Interstate 5 at Coronado, or State Highway 75. Cross over the Coronado Bay Bridge and turn south on Orange Avenue. One mile south on Orange Avenue lie downtown Coronado and Hotel del Coronado. The marina and yacht club are in Glorietta Bay, across from the hotel.

Sea Approach

Continue south down the main ship channel and under the Coronado Bay Bridge. Pass between piers "18" and "20"—shoal areas exist under other piers. Immediately past the bridge, turn west and proceed between buoys "1" and "2" following the range (218° magnetic) into

Beach and golf course in Coronado

Glorietta Bay. Stay within the marked channel, as water south of the channel is restricted to U.S. Navy and Naval Amphibious Base use only The bay is dredged to a minimum depth of fifteen feet. Once past buoy "8," turn north into the inner basin of Glorietta Bay (latitude 32°40.8' N, longitude 117°10.4' W), with its distinctive Coronado Boat House and Coronado Yacht Club.

Local Weather Service (858) 289-1212

San Diego Harbor Police (619) 223-1133

Sea Tow (888) 473-2869

Tow Boat U.S. (800) 493-7869

Vessel Assist (800) 399-1921

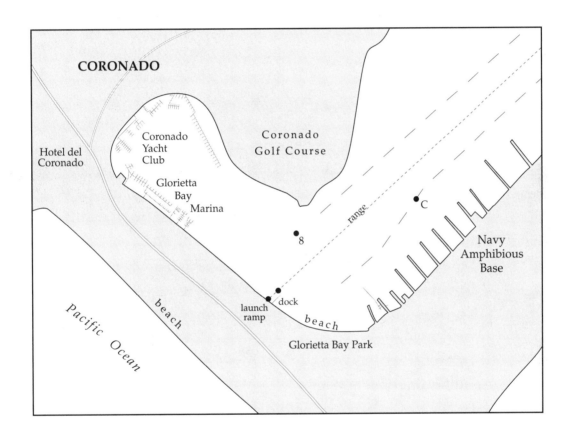

Anchorage and Berthing

No mooring buoys are present in Glorietta Bay. Anchoring is allowed for seventy-two hours within the marked area (Anchorage–A5) in Glorietta Bay; no permit is required. The **Glorietta Bay Marina** on the west side of the bay has 125 slips for boats ranging from twenty to sixty feet. Water, electricity, restrooms, and showers are provided to tenants. **Coronado Yacht Club** at the north end of the bay has 150 slips, and if you are a yacht club member and your club has reciprocal privileges, they may have room on their guest dock for a transient boat. This area is within walking distance of the quaint village of Coronado. Golf, tennis, shopping, and restaurants are all in close proximity.

Coronado Yacht Club (619) 435-1848

Glorietta Bay Marina (619) 435-5203

Facilities

Bank

Boat dock

Boat rentals — Seaforth Coronado (619) 437-1590

Fishing

Golf

Dinghy dock

Grocery store

Hotel — Glorietta Bay Inn (619) 435-3101

Hotel del Coronado (619) 435-6611

La Avenida Inn (619) 435-3191

Ice

Launch ramp

Laundry

Library

Park

Parking

Post office

Public transportation

Restaurants — Brigantine (619) 435-4166

Coronado Boathouse (619) 435-4237

Miguel's Cocina (619) 437-4237

Restrooms

Shops

Swimming

Surfing

Telephone

Tennis courts

Theater

Attractions and Transportation

Coronado is a wonderful place to visit. Hotel del Coronado is alive with history, and long, wide, white sandy beaches lie just west of the hotel. The movie *Some Like It Hot*, starring Marilyn Monroe and Tony Curtis, was one of many movies filmed here; numerous commemorative pictures and plaques surround the hotel and grounds. The Lamb's Players Theatre and the Coronado Playhouse put on excellent performances year around in historic theaters. Occasionally, the local military installations—North Island Naval Air Station and the Naval Amphibious Base—will have events open to the public, so call for schedules. A good time to visit is the Fourth of July, when there is a parade down Orange Avenue and fireworks in Glorietta Bay.

Public transportation, buses #901, #902, and #904, travel down Silver Strand Boulevard and Orange Avenue, connecting to Imperial Beach and downtown San Diego. Transfer here to transportation to all parts of San Diego County.

Attractions

Coronado Chamber of Commerce (619) 435-9260
Coronado Golf Course (619) 435-3121
Coronado Playhouse (619) 435-4856
Coronado Visitors Bureau (619) 437-8788
Hotel del Coronado (619) 435-6611
Lamb's Players Theatre (619) 437-0600
Navy Amphibious Base Coronado (619) 437-2011
North Island Naval Air Station (619) 545-1011

Transportation

Becker Auto Rental (619) 298-5990
Coronado Cab (619) 435-6310
Coronado Transit Information (619) 233-3004
Enterprise Rent-a-Car (619) 522-6111
San Diego Trolley Information (619) 231-4549
San Diego Water Taxi (619) 235-8294

Fiddler's Cove   (see chart page 161)
NOAA Charts #18773, #18772, #18765
Latitude 32°38.3' N, Longitude 117°08.7' W (Entrance to Fiddler's Cove)

Fiddler's Cove, containing Fiddler's Cove Marina and R.V. Park, is U.S. government property limited to active duty, retired, military, and Department of Defense personnel and their families only. One of three military marinas in San Diego Bay, it is located in a small, isolated area along the Silver Strand Beach south of the city of Coronado. Quiet waters, sandy beaches, surfing, docks, moorings, boat rentals, a yacht club, and a small convenience store make this area popular with the military family.

Entrance to Fiddler's Cove

The U.S. government has always been interested in Coronado's North Island. In 1890 they authorized the navy to build Zuñiga Jetty at the north end of the island to protect San Diego's large natural harbor. The army located Rockwell Field on North Island in the early 1900's. In 1917, at the beginning of World War I, the U.S. Congress divided North Island between the U.S. Army and Navy, authorizing each to operate half of the 1,232 acres. Both army and navy pilots trained here, their leaders squabbling over rights to the whole island, until a 1935 visit from President Franklin D. Roosevelt decided the matter in favor of the navy. By 1938 the Army Air Corps had vacated the island for their March Air Base in Sunnyvale, California, where the "lighter than air" program was being operated. In 1936 the navy filled in "Whaler's Bight," where many years earlier the great sailing ships had been careened to care for their bottoms. In 1943 The U.S. Naval Amphibious Base was established on 290 acres of reclaimed land south of the city of Coronado on the Silver Strand Beach. This is the home of the Navy Frogmen, Underwater Demolition Team (UDT), and today's Navy SEALS. In 1945 the navy filled in "Spanish Bight" to further increase land holdings on Coronado's North Island.

Today Fiddler's Cove Marina and R.V. Park is one of the exclusive recreation sites on the bay used by the military and their dependents. In 1998 a one million dollar redevelopment of the area greatly improved the facilities. Large new block buildings contain friendly marina staff, while a volunteer group operates and manages the Fiddler's Cove Yacht Club.

Fiddler's Cove Marina

Land Approach

Two miles south of downtown San Diego, exit Interstate 5 at Coronado, or State Highway 75. Cross over the Coronado Bay Bridge and turn south on Orange Avenue. Two miles south of Hotel del Coronado, turn left across Silver Strand Boulevard and enter Fiddler's Cove Marina and R.V. Park.

Sea Approach

Continue south under the Coronado Bay Bridge in the main ship channel, passing the National Steel and Shipbuilding Company (NASSCO) and U.S. Naval Base. At buoy "32," across from National City pier #12, turn southwest. As you approach the Silver Strand Peninsula, Fiddler's Cove Marina and R.V. Park will be at the north end of the naval housing (latitude 32°38.3' N, longitude 117°08.7' W). Fiddler's Cove is protected by a floating tire breakwater; the entrance to the cove is on the south end of this breakwater. Red and green lights mark the entrance between the tires. The cove is dredged to twelve feet at low tide; however, some of the boats near shore rest on the bottom at low tide. Water depths north and south of the cove maintain an eight to ten foot depth for thirty yards off the beach.

Tire breakwater off the marina

Local Weather Service (858) 289-1212
San Diego Harbor Police (619) 223-1133
SeaTow (888) 473-2869
Tow Boat U.S. (800) 493-7869
Vessel Assist (800) 399-1921

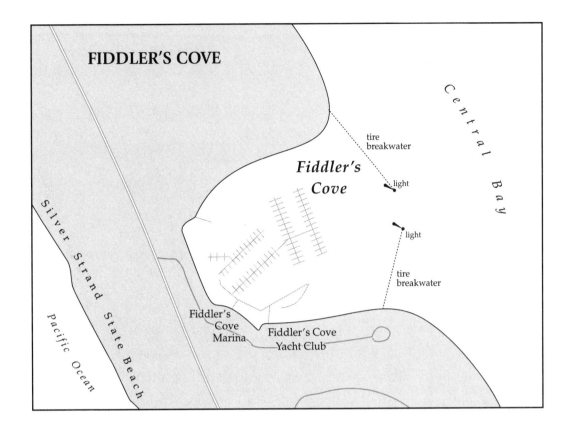

FIDDLER'S COVE

Silver Strand State Beach

Pacific Ocean

Fiddler's Cove

Central Bay

tire breakwater

light

light

tire breakwater

Fiddler's Cove Marina

Fiddler's Cove Yacht Club

Anchorage and Berthing

No anchoring is allowed in Fiddler's Cove. The nearest anchorage is Sweetwater/ Southbay Anchorage (Anchorage–A8). **Fiddler's Cove Marina** has 308 slips for boats ranging from nineteen to sixty feet in length. Outside the docking area are buoys for 120 boats. Laundry, pumpout, showers, restrooms, community room, yacht club, picnic tables, store, and boat rental facility are enjoyed by all active and retired military personnel.

> Fiddler's Cove Marina (619) 522-8680
> Fiddler's Cove Marina and R.V. Park (619) 522-8681
> Fiddler's Cove Yacht Club (619) 437-0320

Facilities

> Boat dock
> Convenience store
> Fishing
> Ice
> Laundry

Park

Parking

Pumpout

Rental Concessions

Restrooms

R.V. Park

Showers

Surfing

Swimming

Telephone

Attractions and Transportation

Fiddler's Cove Marina is located in a relatively isolated area of San Diego County where services are minimal. Within walking distance is Silver Strand State Beach, whose numerous beach activities include swimming, surfing, and fishing. The Tijuana River Nature Estuary, a naturalist's paradise, is located two miles south of the state beach. Border Field State Park, the most southwestern corner of the continental United States, is just south of the estuary. Excellent bike paths and walking trails are found along Silver Strand State Beach. Occasionally, local military installations of North Island Naval Air Station and the Naval Amphibious Base will have events open to the public, so call for schedules.

Public transportation, buses #901 and #904, run along Silver Strand Boulevard, with #904 stopping at the Coronado Cays to transport passengers north to Coronado and south to Imperial Beach. From these stations you can transfer to buses that access all areas of the county.

Attractions

Border Field State Park (619) 428-3034

Coronado Chamber of Commerce (619) 435-9260

Coronado Visitors Bureau (619) 437-8788

Navy Amphibious Base Coronado (619) 437-2011

North Island Naval Air Station (619) 545-1011

Silver Strand State Beach (619) 435-5184

Tijuana River Nature Estuary (619) 575-3613

Transportation

Becker Auto Rental (619) 298-5990

Coronado Cab (619) 435-6211

Coronado Transit Information (619) 233-3004

Enterprise Rent-a-Car (619) 522-6111

San Diego Trolley (619) 231-8549

San Diego Water Taxi (619) 235-8294

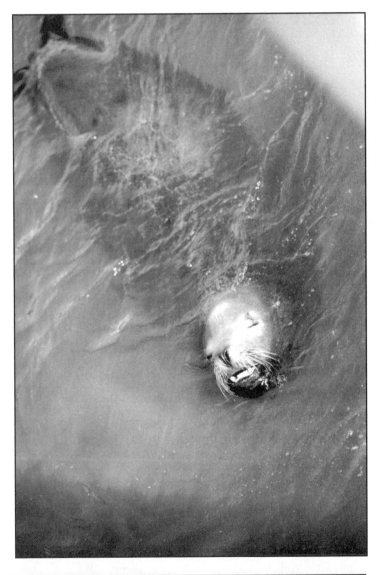

Harbor seal

Silver Strand State Beach
NOAA Charts # 18773, #18772, #18765
Latitude 32°38.1' N, Longitude 117°08.0' W (Outside Crown Cove)

Silver Strand State Beach is an isolated, quiet anchorage. Anchor during daylight park hours and participate in all types of water sport activities, such as swimming, sailing, surfing, water skiing, and jet skiing. Ashore, fire rings, picnic areas, play equipment, and an RV Park make this an excellent area for the family to spend a leisurely day on the water.

Silver Strand State Beach from San Diego Bay

In 1888 the Coronado Railroad Company laid tracks for a steam train (The Belt Train) from the Coronado Ferry Landing to Hotel del Coronado, Imperial Beach (Coronado Heights), National City, and San Diego. Passengers and freight could circle the bay from San Diego to Coronado. In 1931, Spreckel's holding companies (formerly Babcock and Story's "Coronado Beach Company") turned over land along the Silver Strand Beach to the California State Park Commission; this was the beginning of the Silver Strand State Beach. The U.S. Civilian Conservation Corps (CCC

Camps were created by President Franklin D. Roosevelt to get America back to work after the depression) from Cuyamaca Rancho constructed major improvements—restrooms, shelters, and parking—in 1936. The State Beach was officially dedicated in 1937. The park owes its name to the silver seashells mixed with the sand that sparkle in the sunlight on the beach year around. It has been a popular recreation sight since the early 1900's when "Tent City" was established south of the Hotel del Coronado.

The last run of the "Belt Train" along the Silver Strand State Beach was in 1971. Today Silver Strand State Beach provides one of the most scenic and natural settings along the Southern California coast. Recreational activities include swimming, sunbathing, surfing, picnicking, bike riding, hiking, and fishing. Overnight camping is allowed for self-contained vehicles only.

Land Approach

Two miles south of downtown San Diego, exit Interstate 5 at the Coronado, or State Highway 75 exit. Cross over the Coronado Bay Bridge and turn south on Orange Avenue. Four miles south of downtown Coronado, exit Silver Strand Boulevard at Coronado Cays or Silver Strand State Beach and follow the signs to the beach.

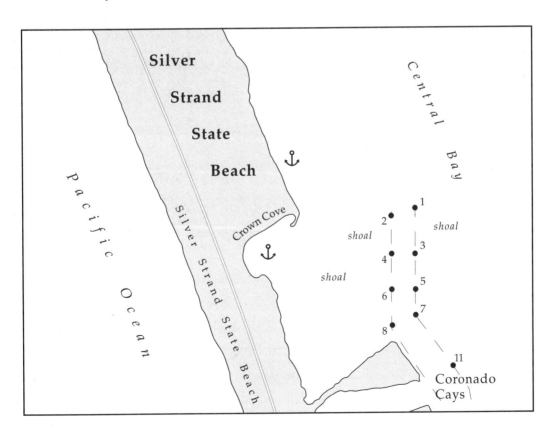

Sea Approach

Continue south past the Coronado Bay Bridge in the main ship channel. Pass the National Steel and Shipbuilding Company (NASSCO), U.S. Naval Base, and the National City Marine Terminal. At buoy "40," across from Sweetwater River Channel, turn southwest. As you approach the Silver Strand State Beach, day markers "1" and "2" appear on poles marking the entrance to the Coronado Cays Channel (Latitude 32°38.1' N, Longitude 117°08.0' W). Continue west into Crown Cove and the surrounding Silver Strand State Beach. The cove is dredged to twelve feet at low tide. Line up channel entrance markers "1" and "2" and use as range markers to enter Crown Cove. Straying south of this range will put you immediately aground in soft mud. Water depths north of the cove maintain eight to ten feet for thirty yards off the beach.

Crown Cove boathouse on the bay

Local Weather Service (858) 289-1212

San Diego Harbor Police (619) 223-1133

SeaTow (888) 473-2869

Tow Boat U.S. (800) 493-7869

Vessel Assist (800) 399-1921

Anchorage and Berthing

No docks or mooring buoys exist in Silver Strand State Beach. The nearest docks are south in Coronado Cays or Chula Vista. The state beach allows day anchoring only in **Crown Cove** and 1,000 yards off state beach property. A special events permit can be obtained from the State Beach Rangers to extend use of the facilities. The white sandy beaches surrounding the cove allow five or six boats to anchor comfortably in twelve feet of water. The sand and mud bottom is an excellent holding ground when the fifteen-knot wind from the northwest comes up in the early afternoon. The beach offers park benches, fire rings, tables, and paved walking and riding trails. Tunnels give access to the ocean side of the state park, where surfing is available. Fishing in the bay will provide perch, cobina, bass, and croaker year around. This South Bay state beach offers breathtaking views of the San Diego sky-line. Camping is allowed for 133 self-contained vehicles. No reservations are taken; maximum stay is seven days. However, additional days can be approved, depending on campsite availability. Gates open year around at eight A.M. and close at sundown. No traffic is allowed in or out when the gates are closed.

Silver Strand State Beach (619) 435-5184

Silver Strand Lifeguards (619) 435-0126

Facilities

Fishing

Park

Parking

Rental concessions (summer only)

Restrooms

R.V. park

Showers

Snack bar (summer only)

Surfing

Swimming

Telephone

Crown Cove

Attractions and Transportation

Silver Strand State Beach is located in a relatively isolated area of San Diego County; services are minimal. Within walking distance is Silver Strand Beach, where beach activities including swimming, surfing, and fishing. The Tijuana River Nature Estuary, a naturalist's paradise, is located a mile south of the state park. Excellent bike paths and walking trails are found along Silver Strand State Beach. Border Field State Park contains a monument commemorating the peace treaty and the international border between Mexico and the United States. It also marks the furthest southwest corner of the continental United States.

Public transportation, bus #904, runs along Silver Strand Boulevard, stopping at the Coronado Cays to transport passengers north to Coronado and south to Imperial Beach. From these stations you can transfer to buses that access all areas of the county.

Attractions

Border Field State Park (619) 428-3034
Coronado Chamber of Commerce (619) 435-9260
Coronado Visitors Bureau (619) 437-8788
Silver Strand State Beach (619) 435-5184
Tijuana River Nature Estuary (619) 575-3613

Transportation

Becker Auto Rental (619) 298-5990
Coronado Cab (619) 435-6310
Coronado Transit Information (619) 233-3004
Enterprise Rent-a-Car (619) 522-6111
San Diego Trolley (619) 231-8549
San Diego Water Taxi (619) 235-8294

Sweetwater/South Bay Anchorage (Anchorage–A8) (see p. 170)

NOAA Charts #18773, #18772, #18766

Latitude 32°38.9' N, Longitude 117∞07.6' W (Center of anchorage)

Sweetwater/South Bay is a large, isolated, exposed anchorage in south San Diego Bay. It is the only anchorage where you can stay at no charge for an unlimited amount of time.

Sweetwater/South Bay Anchorage

Sweetwater/South Bay anchorage has long been a backwater site forgotten by the San Diego Port District. Here the government, U.S. Navy, private companies, and individuals would store derelict "boats." Anchored in years past were platforms, barely above the water; barges; tugs; restaurants; castles; yachts; catamarans; work boats; trimarans; fishing boats; houseboats; dredges; tankers; and large power boats. Many of these are still floating; a number of them are resting on the bottom. Legends tell of floating casinos and brothels that operated in this area years ago. Currently the port district is trying to clean up the area, taking the derelicts out to sea and finding owners to salvage their boats. As part of this cleanup effort, the post district requires a yearly inspection to insure that vessels are functioning properly. Today

Sweetwater/South Bay is the only place to anchor long term, but be careful transiting this area—the abandoned vessels create many underwater obstructions.

The dinghy dock is located in Sweetwater Channel at the National City boat ramp. It is approximately a one-mile row, so a tender with an outboard engine makes the trip easier. Once you reach the National City boat ramp a car is nice, since it is another mile's walk to public transportation. All repair and maintenance can be done at Knight and Carver Boatyard, a short row across the ship channel. The Sweetwater Marsh Refuge, south of the Sweetwater Channel, is an excellent place to view wildlife.

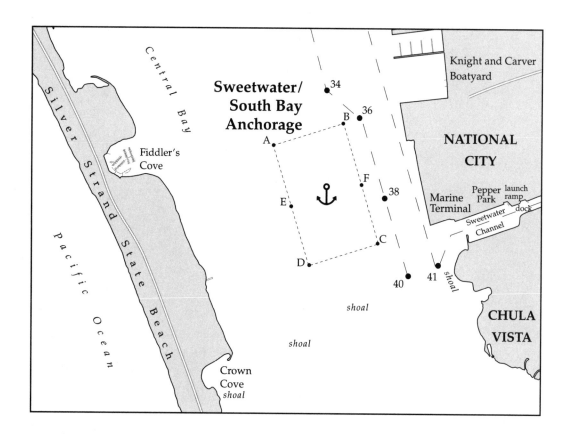

Land Approach

Six miles south of downtown San Diego, exit Interstate 5 on Bay Marina Drive. Travel west to Tidelands Avenue and turn left. Continue through the industrialized area until you reach Pepper Park. The National City boat ramp and docking facility are on the south edge of the park. This is the closest dock to the Sweetwater/South Bay anchorage. Leave the dinghy dock and go west out the Sweetwater Channel past the National City Marine Terminal. Cross the main shipping channel; the anchorage is just to the northwest of buoy "40."

Sea Approach

Continue south down the main shipping channel under the Coronado Bay Bridge. Pass by National Steel and Ship Building (NASSCO), U.S. Naval Station. and National City Marine Terminal. On the west side of the channel between buoys "36" to "40" and directly west of National City Marine Terminal is the Sweetwater/South Bay anchorage (latitude 32°38.9' N, longitude 117°07.6' W). Stay within the channel, which is dredged to thirty-five feet, since south of the bridge and in the anchorage it becomes shallow to ten feet. If you pass the Sweetwater River Channel you have gone too far.

Local Weather Service (858) 289-1212
San Diego Harbor Police (619) 223-1133
SeaTow (888) 473-2869
Tow Boat U.S. (800) 493-7869
Vessel Assist (800) 399-1921

Continue south past NASSCO and the U. S. Naval Station

Anchorage and Berthing

There are no slips or mooring buoys in the Sweetwater/South Bay anchorage. The closest slips are in Coronado Cays or Chula Vista. For years this area has been used for boat storage; boats of any size may anchor here. However, now vessels need yearly permits for an extended stay. Each year anchored vessels must go to the inspection dock under their own power to prove their seaworthiness and be inspected by the port district. This new requirement is an attempt by the port district to rid the anchorage of derelicts.

Anchoring in ten to fifteen feet of water with a sand and mud bottom provides good holding ground when the wind increases in the afternoon. Swell and heavy chop come into this unpro-

The anchorage is across from the National City Marine Terminal

tected anchorage, making it uncomfortable in high winds. Care should be taken when anchoring, as debris and obstructions on the sea floor may prevent the anchor from being properly set. Once at anchor you are still isolated. The closest dinghy dock is one mile away down the Sweetwater Channel at the National City boat ramp.

San Diego Unified Port District Marine Office   (619) 686-6340
San Diego Unified Port District Mooring Office (619) 686-6227
San Diego Harbor Police   (619) 223-1133

Facilities

Boatyard   Knight and Carver (619) 336-4141
Dinghy dock
Fishing
Launch ramp
Park
Parking

Restrooms
Telephone

Attractions and Transportation

Sweetwater/South Bay anchorage is in a secluded area of San Diego Bay. The National City Railroad Museum is a short walk down Tidelands Avenue at the end of Pepper Park adjacent to National City launch ramp and dinghy dock. A good time to visit National City is May as marching bands from all over the country compete in the famous Maytime Band Review.

Public transportation—San Diego Trolley, buses #601 and #602—is a one and one-half mile walk down Tideland Avenue to Bay Marina Drive and the 24th Street Transportation Center. The San Diego Trolley and connections to San Diego County are accessible here.

Attractions

National City Chamber of Commerce	(619) 477-9339
National City Railroad Museum	(619) 474-4400

Transportation

Amtrak	(800) USA-RAIL
Becker Auto Rental	(619) 298-5990
Enterprise Rent-a-Car	(619) 477-7699
Fiesta Taxi	(888) 549-5900
National City Transportation Center	(619) 474-7505
San Diego Trolley	(619) 233-3004
San Diego Water Taxi	(619) 285-8294

National City

NOAA Charts #18773, #18772, #18766

Latitude 32∞38.9' N, Longitude 117∞06.6' W (Off Launch Ramp)

National City boat ramp and dinghy dock is in a small, quiet, isolated area adjacent to the Sweetwater Marsh National Wildlife Refuge. It is located in a park setting on the Sweetwater channel at the extreme south end of Central San Diego Bay and has limited facilities.

Enter the Sweetwater River channel

The Kumeyaay Indians occupied this area before the Spanish arrived in 1769. The Kumeyaay migrated with the seasons between the Jamul Mountains and San Diego Bay. Present-day National Avenue follows the ancient Indian migratory trail. After Mexican Independence, church lands were divided, one large tract becoming known as Rancho de la Nación, or "National Ranch." National City, one of the oldest cities in San Diego County, grew out of this rancho. A map of 1863 showed six populated areas around San Diego Bay: La Playa, Roseville, Old Town, Middle Town, New Town, and National City. Frank Kimball, the father of National City and owner of the California Southern Railroad, wanted his city to be the western terminus of the

Transcontinental Railway. In 1885 National City became the "Gateway to the Orient" as the final link of the railway was completed. This began a boom that slowly faded as more and more trade went through ports in Los Angeles. Today, the city is highly industrial and home to over 55,000 people. The largest employer is the U.S. Navy; the active waterfront contains the National City Marine Terminal, which receives cars from all over the world.

The docking and boat launching facility is located in Pepper Park on the north side of the Sweetwater River Channel. This major industrial area of the city is adjacent to the National City Marine Terminal. The full service boatyard of Knight and Carver is just north of the marine terminal. The Sweetwater Marsh Refuge, which lies south across the channel, is an excellent place to view wildlife.

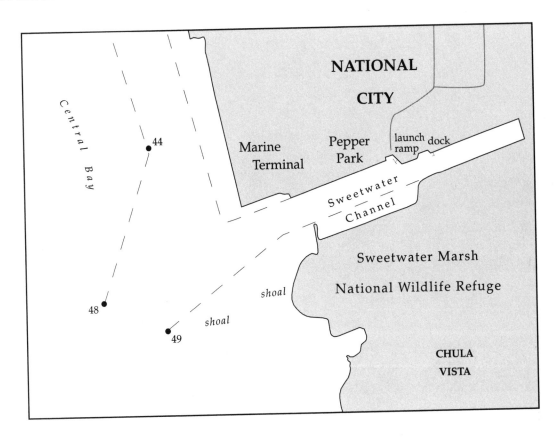

Land Approach

Six miles south of downtown San Diego, exit Interstate 5 on Bay Marina Drive. Travel west to Tidelands Avenue and turn left. Continue through the industrialized area until you reach Pepper Park. The boat ramp and docking facility are on the south edge of the park.

Sea Approach

Continue south down the main shipping channel under the Coronado Bridge. Pass by National Steel and Ship Building, U.S. Naval Station, and National City Marine Terminal. Sweetwater channel enters from the east just south of the marine terminal. Turn east at buoy "39" (latitude 32°38.2' N, longitude 117°07.2' W) and enter the Sweetwater River channel, which is dredged to thirty-five feet the length of the marine terminal. Past the terminal the controlling depth is ten feet. Always stay within the channel markers, since the channel shoals rapidly on the south.

Pass by the National City Marine Terminal

Local Weather Service (858) 289-1212
SeaTow (888) 473-2869
Tow Boat U.S. (800) 493-7869
Vessel Assist (800) 399-1921

Anchorage and Berthing

No anchoring or mooring is allowed in National City Boat Basin. The nearest anchorage is the Sweetwater/South Bay Anchorage (Anchorage–A8). Facilities here are very limited, with only a boat ramp, dinghy dock, fishing pier, bathrooms, telephone, and park. National City and the San Diego Port District are planning a full service marina in this area, but at present it is a quiet, isolated spot to have lunch, pick up passengers, stroll in the park, or go fishing.

San Diego Port District Marine Office	(619) 686-6340
San Diego Harbor Police	(619) 223-1133

National City launch ramp and dock

Facilities

Boat dock
Boatyard   Knight and Carver   (619) 336-4141
Dinghy dock
Fishing
Launch ramp
Park
Parking

Restrooms

Telephone

Attractions and Transportation

The National City Railroad Museum is a short walk down Tidelands Avenue. A good time to visit the city is May as marching bands from all over the country compete in the famous Maytime Band Review.

The National City launch ramp and dinghy dock is isolated. The nearest public transportation is a one and one-half mile walk down Tideland Avenue to Bay Marina Drive and the Twenty-fourth Street Transportation Center. The San Diego Trolley and connections to San Diego County are accessible here.

Attractions

National City Chamber of Commerce	(619) 477-9339
National City Railroad Museum	(619) 474-4400

Transportation

Amtrak	(800) USA-RAIL
Becker Auto Rental	(619) 298-5990
Enterprise Rent-a-Car	(619) 477-7699
Fiesta Taxi	(888) 549-5900
National City Transportation Center	(619) 474-7505
San Diego Trolley	(619) 233-3004
San Diego Water Taxi	(619) 235-8294

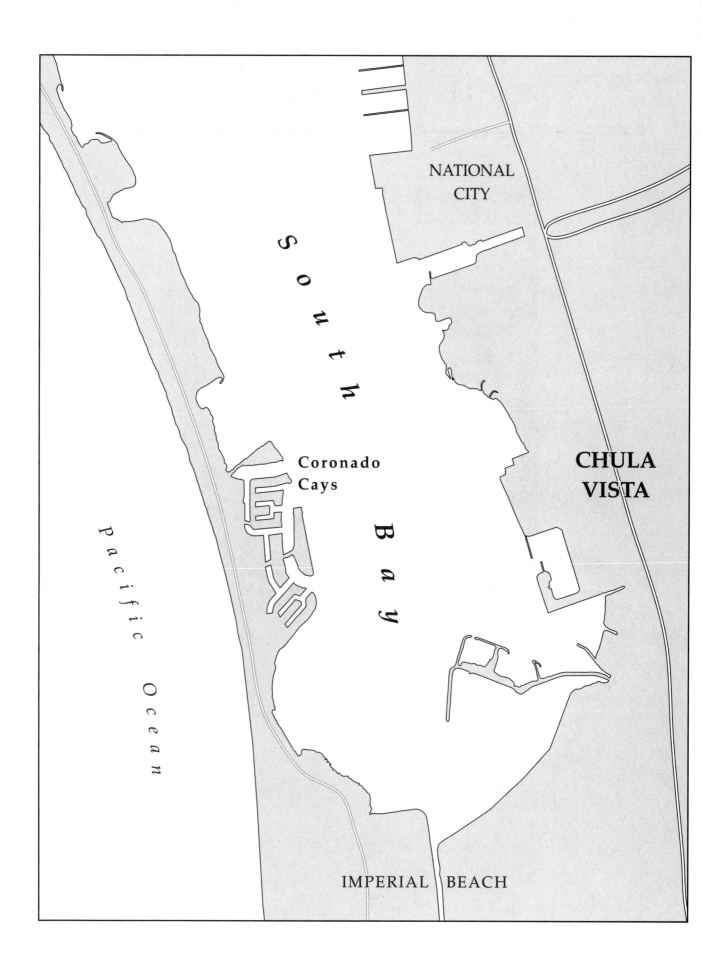

NATIONAL
CITY

CHULA
VISTA

South

Bay

Coronado
Cays

Pacific

Ocean

IMPERIAL   BEACH

"The *California* had finished discharging her cargo and was to get under way at the same time as us. Having washed down the decks and got breakfast, the two vessels lay side by side, in complete readiness for sea, our ensigns hanging from the peaks and our tall spars reflected in the glassy surface of the river, which since sunrise, had been unbroken by a ripple. At light a few whiffs came across the water, and by eleven o'clock a regular northwest wind set steadily in."

Richard Henry Dana, Jr., *Two Years Before the Mast* (1835)

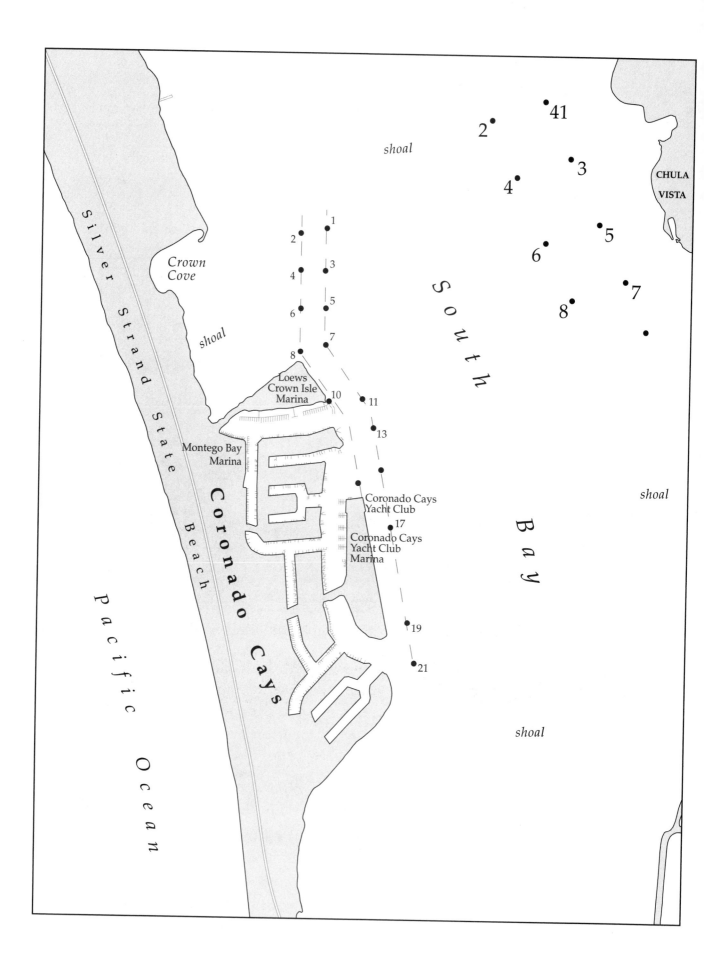

Crown Cove

Silver Strand State Beach

Pacific Ocean

Coronado Cays

shoal

shoal

2

41

3

4

5

6

7

8

CHULA VISTA

South Bay

shoal

shoal

shoal

1

2

3

4

5

6

7

8

10

11

13

17

19

21

Loews Crown Isle Marina

Montego Bay Marina

Coronado Cays Yacht Club

Coronado Cays Yacht Club Marina

Coronado Cays

NOAA Charts #18773, #18772, #18765

Latitude 32°38.1' N, Longitude 117°08.0' W (Channel entrance to Coronado Cays)

Coronado Cays, or "Crown Islands," is a small, quiet, isolated, upscale harbor community four miles south of the City of Coronado. This planned community with multi-million dollar bayfront homes and a world-class resort hotel is an excellent place to rest and relax from an ocean passage.

Coronado Cays Channel entrance

When Cabrillo discovered San Diego in 1542, the sand "islands" across from Point Loma were covered with sagebrush, reeds, grasses, and wildflowers. People went over to "Coronado Island" to hunt rabbit and to picnic. The last Mexican governor, Pío Pico, gave a land grant including Coronado to Pedro Carillo for a wedding gift in 1846. Development began in 1886 when Babcock and Story started construction of the Hotel del Coronado.

After Coronado became a city in 1890, unprecedented growth occurred. Concerned with the increasing amount of trash, the city created a trash dump in 1911, four miles south of the city, on a wide beach area along Silver Strand Beach. This was later developed into a 200-acre "hog ranch" called Rancho Carrillo. In 1968, Atlantic Richfield Company bought the land for four million dollars, and in conjunction with the city, dredged and filled these southern tidelands to create the modern, gated, marina community of Coronado Cays. ("Cay," or "key," is a seventeenth-century term that comes from the Spanish word *cayos* and describes a small, low island.) Coronado Cays contains private residences, condominiums, and town homes, with many homes having their own dock.

The surrounding area contains the world-class Lowe's Coronado Bay Resort Hotel, Port Royal Swim and Tennis Club, Loews Crown Isle Marina, Coronado Cays Yacht Club, Coronado Cays Yacht Club Marina, and Montego Bay Marina. Across the highway are the broad Pacific Ocean and Silver Strand State Park. A short distance south are the Tijuana River Estuary Nature Reserve and Border Field State Park.

Land Approach

Two miles south of downtown San Diego, exit Interstate 5 at Coronado, or State Highway 75. Cross over the Coronado Bay Bridge and turn south on Orange Avenue. Four miles south of downtown Coronado, exit Silver Strand Boulevard at Coronado Cays.

Loews Crown Isle Marina

Montego Bay Marina
at the end of the waterway

Coronado Cays Yacht Club Marina

Sea Approach

Continue south under the Coronado Bay Bridge in the main ship channel. Pass the National Steel and Shipbuilding Company (NASSCO), U.S. Naval Base, and the National City Marine Terminal. At buoy "40," across from Sweetwater River Channel, turn southwest. Approaching the Silver Strand Beach, you will see day markers "1" and "2" on poles marking the entrance to the Coronado Cays Channel (latitude 32°38.1' N, longitude 117°08.0' W). Enter the channel and follow the channel markers. The channel and boat basin are dredged to eight feet or deeper at low tide. Straying out of the channel will put you immediately aground in soft mud.

Local Weather Service	(858) 289-1212
San Diego Harbor Police	(619) 223-1133
SeaTow	(888) 473-2869
Tow Boat U.S.	(800) 493-7869
Vessel Assist	(800) 399-1921

Anchorage and Berthing

There is no anchoring or mooring allowed in the Coronado Cays. The nearest anchorage is Sweetwater/Southbay Anchorage (Anchorage–A8). The first marina upon entering the Cays, the **Loews Crown Isle Marina**, is directly west of marker "11." It has eighty-one slips accommodating boats thirty to 140 feet in length. The marina fronts the Lowe's Coronado Resort; tenants have use of all resort facilities including gym, spa, swimming pool, restaurants, restrooms, laundry, and shower. Rental concessions are at the end of the dock. This is an excellent place to visit with friends and family, as there are numerous activities along the dock and in the hotel.

Down the channel from the Loews Crown Isle Marina are the slips of the **Montego Bay Marina**. These boat slips, intended for residents and guests of Coronado Cays, range from twenty-four to fifty-six feet in length, with water and electricity available. Further south down the main channel are the large clubhouse, dining room, and guest dock of the **Coronado Cays Yacht Club** at the north end of Grand Caribe Island. This friendly group welcomes other yacht club members with reciprocal privileges to enjoy the swimming pool, spa, and guest dock on a space-available basis. Adjacent to the yacht club is the **Coronado Cays Yacht Club Marina**. It has fifty-six slips with showers and restrooms. Be sure to call ahead to determine if space is available in any of these facilities.

Coronado Cays Yacht Club Marina (619) 429-0133

Coronado Cays Yacht Club (619) 429-0133
Loews Crown Isle Marina (619) 424-4455
Montego Bay Marina (619) 224-2471

Facilities

Boat docks	
Exercise room	
Hotel	Loews Coronado Resort (619) 424-4000
Ice	
Laundry	
Parking	
Pool/Spa	
Rental concession	
Restaurant	Azzura Point (619) 424-4000
Showers	
Surfing	
Telephone	
Tennis courts	

Attractions and Transportation

Coronado Cays is in a relatively isolated area of San Diego County where services are minimal. Sights within walking distance are Silver Strand Beach and Silver Strand State Beach, where numerous beach activities, including swimming and surfing, are available. The Tijuana River Nature Estuary is a naturalist's paradise. One of four California marine sanctuaries along the coast, Tijuana River Nature Estuary is considered the most pristine estuary south of San Francisco and one of the few remaining natural estuaries in the United States. Just south of the estuary is Border Field State Park, the most southwest corner of the continental United States. Excellent bike paths and walking trails are found along Silver Strand Beach.

Public transportation, bus #904, runs along Silver Strand Boulevard, stopping at the Coronado Cays to transport passengers north to Coronado and south to Imperial Beach. From transfer stations you can change to buses that access all areas of San Diego county.

Attractions

Border Field State Park	(619) 428-3034
Coronado Chamber of Commerce	(619) 435-9260
Coronado Visitors Bureau	(619) 437-8788
Silver Strand State Beach	(619) 435-5184
Tijuana River Nature Estuary	(619) 575-3613

Transportation

Becker Auto Rental	(619) 298-5990
Coronado Cab	(619) 435-6211
Coronado Transit System	(619) 233-3004
Enterprise Rent-a-Car	(619) 522-6111
San Diego Trolley Information	(619) 231-4549
San Diego Water Taxi	(619) 235-8294

Coronado Cays Yacht Club and guest dock

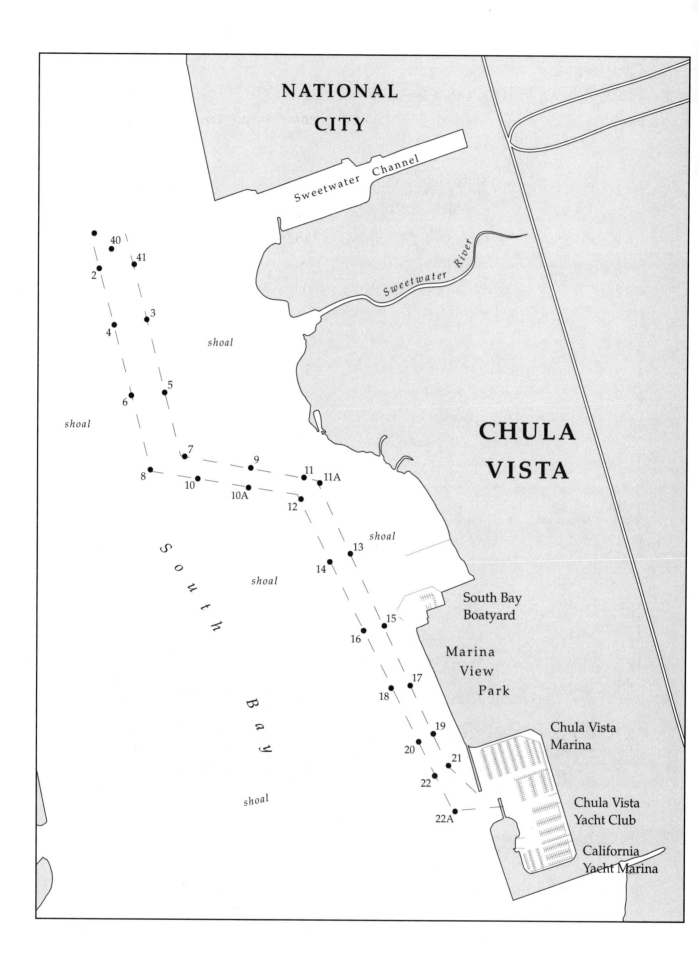

NATIONAL
CITY

Sweetwater Channel

Sweetwater River

CHULA
VISTA

shoal

shoal

shoal

South

Bay

shoal

shoal

shoal

40
41
2
3
4
5
6
7
8
9
10
10A
11
11A
12
13
14
15
16
17
18
19
20
21
22
22A

South Bay
Boatyard

Marina
View
Park

Chula Vista
Marina

Chula Vista
Yacht Club

California
Yacht Marina

Chula Vista

Charts #18773, #18772, #18765

Latitude 32°37.4' N, Longitude 117°06.3' W (Center Harbor Entrance)

Chula Vista, which means "Beautiful View," contains the southernmost marinas in San Diego Bay and the closest U.S. marinas to Mexico. It is a small, quiet harbor in a park-like setting, with a boatyard, a chandlery, and convenient transportation nearby. Chula Vista's less expensive marinas are often missed by boaters because of their fifteen-nautical-mile distance to open ocean, but reduced slip fees and excellent access to public transportation make them attractive for long-term stays.

**Chula Vista harbor entrance
one mile south of marker "12"**

The Jamacha Indians were the original inhabitants of Chula Vista when the Spanish soldiers and Catholic missionaries arrived in San Diego in 1769. Father Junípero Serra established a series of twenty-one missions from San Diego to San Francisco. These missions were connected by "El Camino Real," or "The Royal Road." After Mexican independence the church lands were given to friends and family of the leaders of the new country. The large southern landholdings of the church known as

"Rancho del Rey" became "Rancho de la Nación."

Ultimately, after the U.S.-Mexican war 27,000 acres were bought and developed by the Kimball family. Frank Kimball, originally from New Hampshire, made his fortune in the San Francisco construction industry. A contemporary and competitor of Alonzo Horton (a prominent San Diego developer), Kimball developed a transportation system that linked south county and points east to San Diego. He owned the California Southern Railroad, San Diego Land and Town Company, and the National City and Otay Railroad.

**Chula Vista Marina
north of the entrance**

Land changed from grazing to citrus orchards and finally to a thriving city of nearly 200,000 people. Today, Broadway Street through the center of town follows the original path of the famous "El Camino Real." Chula Vista is the second-fastest-growing city in San Diego County. One of the large employers in the area is Goodrich (formerly Rohr Industries), a leader in the aerospace industry.

The harbor area fronts the city of Chula Vista. Protected by a cement and rock breakwater, it contains Chula Vista Marina, Chula Vista Yacht Club, and California Yacht Marina. The harbor is surrounded by parks–Bayside Park to the north and Marina View Park to the south. Bayside Park is home to active windsurfing and parasailing groups. During low tide a sandy beach gives easy access to the shallow, flat waters of the south San Diego Bay. The northwest wind blows unobstructed, making this the windiest area

**California Yacht Marina
south of the harbor entrance**

in the bay. A public launch ramp is on the peninsula west of the harbor. This area provides excellent access to public transportation. Directly across the marina parking lot a bus connects to the Chula Vista Transportation Center and the San Diego Trolley. Here you can travel to all areas in San Diego and to the Mexican border. Adjacent to the dock is a small marine supply store, and within close walking distance is a large chandlery. South Bay Boatyard is just north of Bayside Park. Various restaurants in the area provide harbor-view dining.

Land Approach

Chula Vista is located eight miles south of downtown San Diego and eight miles north of the international border. Approaching from the north or south on Interstate Highway 5, exit the freeway at "J" Street and Marina Parkway. Drive a short quarter-mile west to the harbor.

Sea Approach

Continue south down the main shipping channel under the Coronado Bridge. Pass by National Ship Building, U.S. Naval Station, and the National City Marine Terminal. Sweetwater Channel, just south of the National City Marine Terminal, marks the beginning of South San Diego Bay. Here the coastal bay front rises slowly to rolling inland hills that end on the southeast horizon with the Jamul Mountains. San Miguel peak rises to 2685 feet on the horizon, serving as a landmark to all south bay boaters.

Across from the Sweetwater Channel, begin looking for buoys "40" and "41." Enter between the markers (latitude 32°38.7' N, longitude 117°07.4' W), and proceed south about half a mile to marker "7." At marker "7" turn east a quarter mile to marker "12." At marker "12" turn south and follow the markers one mile to the harbor entrance (latitude 32°37.4' N, longitude 117°06.3' W) on the east side of the channel. You will see a public fishing pier on the north side of the entrance and a rock breakwater on the south side. The channel is dredged to a depth of sixteen feet. Across from marker "16" is the entrance to South Bay Boatyard.

Caution must be exercised when entering the harbor at night, since background lights from the city obscure channel lights, and channel lights are only illuminated on every other channel marker. South Bay is riddled with shoals, so deep-keeled vessels need to be sure to stay within the channel. Even a slight deviation from the channel will put your boat aground.

Key landmarks in this area are the large power generating plant one-half mile south of the harbor and the white salt mounds of the Western Salt Company. Evaporation ponds extend all around the southern rim of the bay.

Local Weather Service (858) 289-1212
San Diego Harbor Police (619) 223-1133
SeaTow (888) 473-2869
Tow Boat U.S. (800) 493-7869
Vessel Assist (800) 399-1921

Anchorage and Berthing

No overnight anchoring or mooring is allowed in Chula Vista Harbor. The nearest anchorage is Sweetwater/South Bay Anchorage (Anchorage–A8). The **Chula Vista Marina**, with 555 slips, is the first marina you encounter when entering the harbor. Located on the northeast side of the harbor, it extends to the Marina Parkway Pier. The marina is operated in conjunction with Chula Vista R.V. Resort. Facilities are shared by both. In addition to typical marina amenities they have a pool and spa. The 352 slips south of the harbor entrance and Marina Parkway Pier belong to **California Yacht Marina**. **Chula Vista Yacht Club**, on marina property, is the second-oldest yacht club on the bay, having been founded in 1889. It has moved location from the base of "F" Street to "G" Street and finally, in 1987, to its present location. The club has a guest dock for cruising boaters if space is available.

All these facilities are remote from the main boating areas in San Diego, and their reduced slip fees reflect that fact. Chula Vista is an excellent harbor to stay long term away from the hustle and bustle of the main port. There is excellent access to public transportation to all of San Diego and Mexico.

California Yacht Marina	(619) 442-2595
Chula Vista Marina	(619) 691-1860
Chula Vista Yacht Club	(619) 442-7888

Facilities

Bait and Tackle Shop	Bay View Nautical (619) 442-9028
Boat Dock	
Boatyard	South Bay Boatyard (619) 427-6767
Chandlery	Bay View Nautical (619) 442-9028
	West Marine (619) 422-1904
Convenience Store	
Dinghy Dock	
Exercise Room	
Fishing	
Haulout	
Ice	
Launch Ramp	
Laundry	
Park	

Parking
Pool/Spa
Propane
Public Transportation
Pumpout
Restaurants   Galley Restaurant (619) 422-5714
                               Bob's By the Bay (619) 476-0400

Restroom
Showers
Telephone

Chula Vista Yacht Club is the second-oldest on the bay

Attractions and Transportation

The marina is quiet, but its proximity to public transportation makes it an ideal base for visits to such local sights as Coor's Amphitheater, Knott's "Soak City" water park, ARCO Olympic Training Center, and Tijuana. Chula Vista Nature Center, a mile north of the harbor, makes an interesting day of sightseeing.

San Diego Water Taxi provides a unique service throughout San Diego Bay. For a nominal fee, they will pick you up at your boat or slip and deposit you anywhere on the bay.

This is an excellent location for ham radio operators to pick up their Mexican Amateur Radio Operator's Permit before setting off for Mexican waters. Called an SCT permit, it can be obtained at:

> SCT
> Calle 16, # 1071
> Colonia Libertad Parte Baja
> Tijuana, Baja California, Mexico
> (0115266) 82-9500 Phone

The office is located less than thirty minutes from the border via taxi. You will need the following: 1) two copies of your U.S. passport; 2) stamped tourist visa, plus two copies; 3) $90.00 U.S. in exact change; and 4) your original amateur radio license, plus two copies. They will provide you with a Mexican radio permit good for 180 days.

Directly across the marina parking lot, public transportation, Chula Vista Bus Route #706A, takes you to the Chula Vista Transit Center. From the center you can travel all over the county and to the international border.

Attractions

ARCO Olympic Training Center	(619) 482-6103
Chula Vista Nature Center	(619) 422-2473
Chula Vista Visitors Center	(619) 425-4444
Knott's Soak City	(619) 661-7373
Mexican Consulate	(619) 231-8414
Tijuana/Mexico Visitors Center	(619) 425-2088

Transportation

Becker Auto Rental	(619) 298-5990
Chula Vista Cab	(619) 421-4466
Chula Vista Transit System	(619) 233-3004
Enterprise Rent-A-Car	(619) 427-1414

| San Diego Trolley | (619) 233-3004 |
| San Diego Water Taxi | (619) 235-8294 |

Chula Vista has wonderful transportation

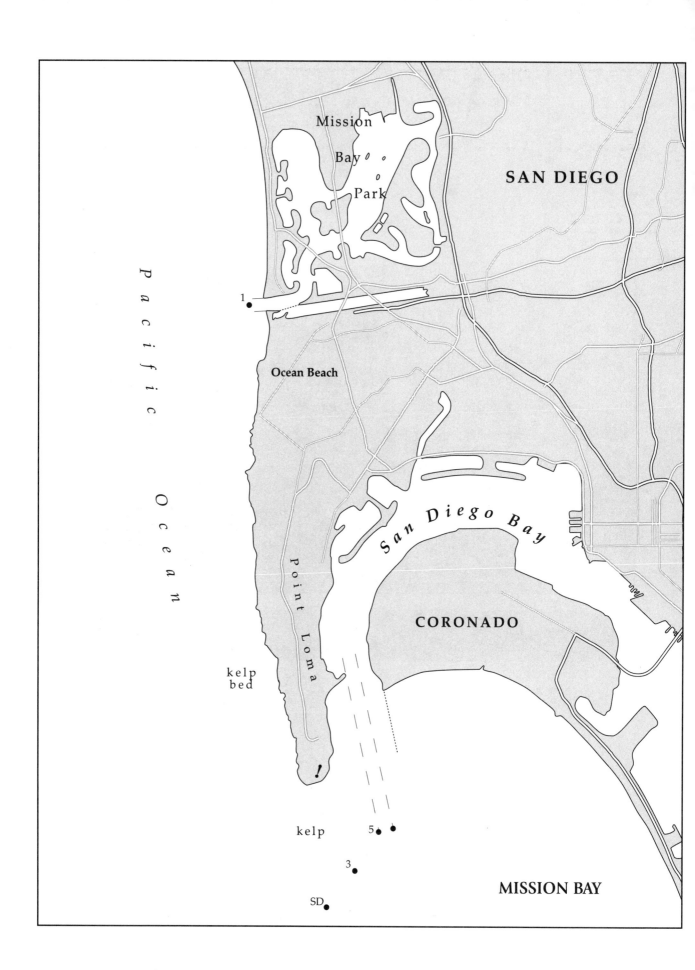

Mission

Bay

Park

SAN DIEGO

1

Ocean Beach

P a c i f i c   O c e a n

S a n   D i e g o   B a y

CORONADO

kelp
bed

Point Loma

!

kelp

5

3

SD

MISSION BAY

12   MISSION BAY

"Those who go down to the sea in ships,
Who do business on great waters;
They have seen the works of the Lord
And his wonders in the deep."

Psalms 107: 23-24

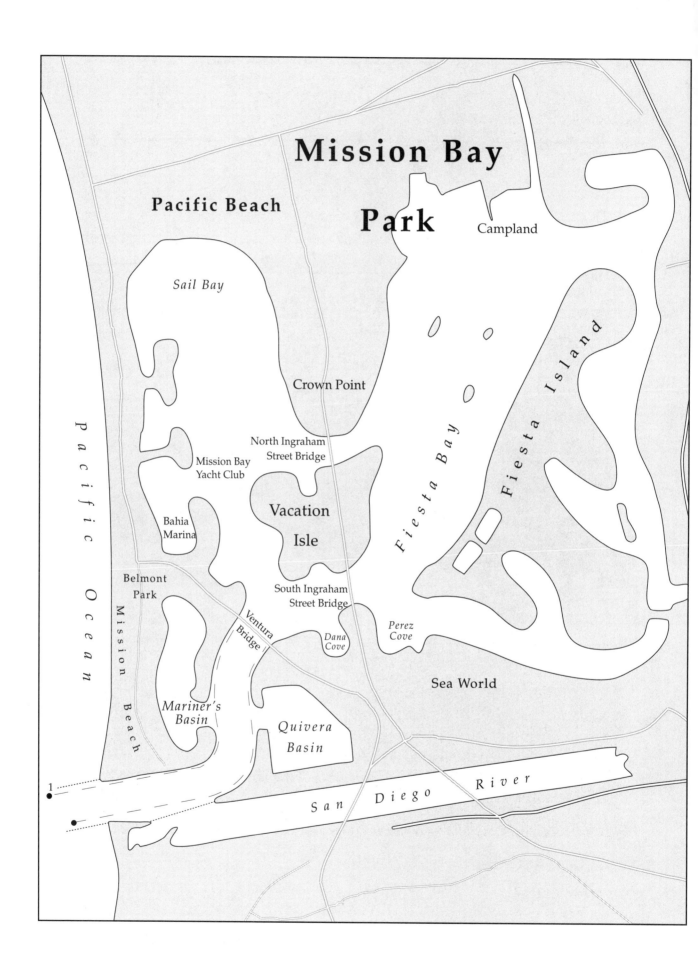

Mission Bay

Park

Pacific Beach

Campland

Sail Bay

Crown Point

P a c i f i c

North Ingraham
Street Bridge

Mission Bay
Yacht Club

Vacation Isle

O c e a n

Bahia
Marina

Belmont
Park

South Ingraham
Street Bridge

*Perez
Cove*

*Dana
Cove*

Sea World

F i e s t a   B a y

F i e s t a   I s l a n d

M i s s i o n   B e a c h

Ventura
Bridge

*Mariner's
Basin*

*Quivera
Basin*

1

S a n   D i e g o   R i v e r

Mission Bay

NOAA Chart #18765
Latitude 32°45.5' N, Longitude 117°15.8' W (North jetty light)
Latitude 32°45.4' N, Longitude 117°15.5' W (South jetty light)

Mission Bay, located five and one-half miles north of Point Loma and thirty miles south of Oceanside Harbor, is "the world's finest aquatic playground." The 4,600-acre park is split equally between land and water, with twenty-seven miles of shoreline, nineteen miles of sandy beaches, and two miles of designated swimming areas. The largest natural tourist attraction in southern California, Mission Bay has sailing, windsurfing, water skiing, personal watercraft, and all types of water activities. Within the park are five unique harbor areas: Quivera Basin, Mariner's Basin, Dana Cove, Perez Cove, and Campland Marina

Entrance to Mission Bay Harbor

Thousands of years ago snow fell on the Cuyamaca Mountains far to the east of where San Diego now stands. Spring came, snows melted, and water formed streams that passed through the mountains to the valleys below. The small streams merged together and grew into the San Diego River. The river passed through areas now called Santee, Mission de Alcalá, Mission Valley, San Diego estuary, and eventually into the sea. For years the estuary stood as wild marshland between Point Loma and La Jolla where the first recorded Indians, the La Jollans, gathered shells and years later the Kumeyaay Indians traveled with the seasons. When Juan Rodriguez Cabrillo arrived in 1542, the estuary was named "False Bay." The Indians and the European settlers likely fished and hunted in this game-rich area; towns grew around choice lands and the estuary was left alone. Cities grew and tidelands became dump sites and sanitary land fill until 1929, when Mission Bay became part of the California State Park System. A plan to develop the area started in 1930; however, it wasn't begun until 1945, when assistant city manager Glenn Rick supervised planning, development, and construction of Mission Bay Park as we know it today. The state park was deeded back to the city of San Diego, and through the efforts of the state government, city government, and a two million dollar bond issue the park was begun. Since its inception the unique plan was to keep twenty-five percent of the land for commercial use and the remaining seventy-five percent for public park.

Planned development included: flood control channel, dredging, filling, hotels, restaurants, boat slips, launch ramps, boatyard, fishing, bait docks, boat rental concessions, recreational fishing and diving boats, Sea World, golf course, and wildlife sanctuary. Today, 2200 acres of navigable waterways in the park are enjoyed by thousands of residents and tourists.

Main channel into Mission Bay

Sea Approach

Approaching from the west, Mission Bay lies in the lowlands between Point Loma on the south and La Jolla on the north. A municipal fishing pier at Ocean Beach, three-tenths of a mile south of the entrance, is a prominent feature as well as the 338-foot Sea World tower two miles east of the channel entrance. The sixteen-story Hyatt Islandia Resort Tower just east of the channel entrance is another landmark. The south jetty light (latitude 32°45.4' N, longitude 117°15.5' W) and north jetty light (latitude 32°45.5' N, longitude 117°15.8' W) mark the outer entrance. The controlling depth in the center of the channel is twenty feet; however, shoaling is reported on the south side of the channel. Stay in mid channel to avoid these shallows. South of the south jetty is a 1,200-foot weir separating the San Diego River from the entrance channel. During high tides it appears to be open water across this bar. In heavy west swells, breaking seas can be expected at the entrance. Seas tend to break on the south jetty, so stay in the north quarter of the channel. Ventura Bridge, one and three-tenths miles from the channel entrance, has a vertical clearance of thirty-eight feet and controls traffic into the inner waters of Mission Bay.

Local Weather Service	(858) 298-1212
Mission Bay Park	(619) 221-8899
San Diego Lifeguards	(619) 221-8899
	(619) 221-8800 (after hours/weekends)
Sea Tow	(888) 473-2869
Tow Boat U.S.	(800) 493-7869
Vessel Assist	(800) 399-1921

San Diego River flood channel

Attractions and Transportation

San Diego is called "America's Finest City," and Mission Bay Park is certainly a contributing factor. Attractions nearby include Belmont Park; Old Town San Diego State Historical Park; Cabrillo National Monument; Birch Aquarium at Scripps Institution of Oceanography; Museum of Contemporary Art, San Diego; Salk Institute for Biological Studies; and the San Diego Sports Arena. Thousands of spectators come to the bay in June for the "Over-The-Line Tournament" and in September for the "Thunder Boat Races."

Public transportation is near each one of the marinas. Other transportation around Mission Bay Park includes taxis, rental cars, trains, and trolleys.

Attractions

Balboa Park (619) 239-0512
Belmont Park (858) 488-1549
Birch Aquarium at Scripps Institution of Oceanography (858) 534-3474
Cabrillo National Monument (619) 557-5450
Maritime Museum (619) 234-9153
Mission Basilica San Diego de Alcalá (619) 281-8449
Mission Bay Golf Course (858) 490-3370
Mission Bay Park (619) 221-8900
Museum of Contemporary Art San Diego (858) 454-3541
Old Town San Diego State Historical Park (619) 220-5422
Qualcom Stadium (619) 641-3100
Salk Institute for Biological Studies (858) 453-4100
San Diego Chamber of Commerce (619) 232-0124
San Diego Sports Arena (619) 224-4176
San Diego Visitors Center (619) 276-8200
San Diego Zoo (619) 234-3153
Sea World Park (619) 226-3901

Transportation

Amtrak (800) 872-7245
Becker Auto Rental (619) 298-5990
Enterprise Rent-A-Car (858) 483-3800

San Diego Cab (619) 232-6566
San Diego Metropolitan Transit System (619) 233-3004
San Diego Trolley (619) 231-8549

San Diego River

Quivera Basin (see chart page 206)
NOAA Chart # 18765
Latitude 32°45.8' N, Longitude 117°14.4' W (Center of Quivera Basin)

Ocean-close, Quivera Basin is the primary marina in Mission Bay. It is outside Ventura Bridge and not limited by the thirty-eight foot bridge clearance. Quivera Basin, in a park-like setting, has the most boating facilities of any of the Mission Bay harbors. Hotels, marinas, fuel, pumpout, boatyard, chandlery, shops, fishing, bait and tackle are located here in compact surroundings.

Entrance to Quivera Basin

Land Approach

Quivera Basin is located on the southwest side of Mission Bay Park. Two miles north of downtown San Diego, exit Interstate 5 at Sea World Drive. Proceed west past Sea World and follow signs to West Mission Bay Drive. From West Mission Bay Drive turn left on Quivera Road, which runs all around Quivera Basin.

Sea Approach

From the ocean continue east down Mission Bay Channel. Shoal areas exist on the south side of the channel, so stay within the center. Once you are past the breakwater the channel turns north; the entrance to Quivera Basin is immediately on the east, protected by a stone jetty. Enter the basin (latitude 32°45.8' N, longitude 117°14.4' W) and reduce speed to comply with the no-wake zone enforced in the tight harbor. The average depth in Quivera Basin and Mission Bay Channel is twenty feet.

Local Weather Service (858) 289-1212
Mission Bay Park (619) 221-8900
San Diego Lifeguards (619) 221-8899
(619) 221-8800 (after hours/weekends)
SeaTow (888) 473-2869
Tow Boat U.S. (800) 493-7869
Vessel Assist (800) 399-1921

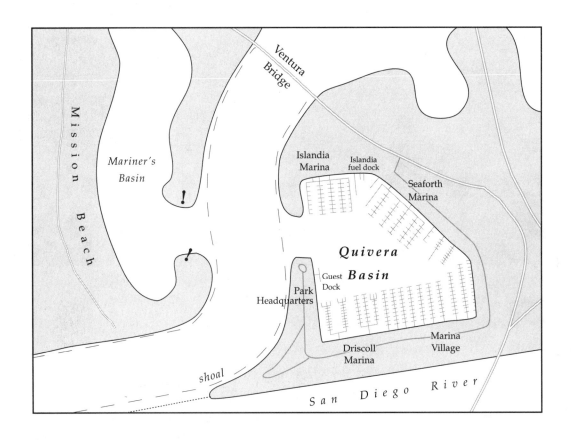

Anchorage and Berthing

No anchoring or mooring is allowed in Quivera Basin. The nearest anchorage is west across Mission Bay Channel in Mariner's Basin. South of the entrance to Quivera Basin are the public dock and Mission Bay Park Headquarters. Stop here to determine slip, mooring, and anchoring availability in the park. After regular business hours, the Lifeguard Services Division next door should be able to help.

The 250-slip **Islandia Marina** is the first marina north of Quivera Basin entrance. This marina is operated in conjunction with the Hyatt Hotel, and slip holders have access to all such hotel amenities as swimming pool, spa, sauna, and exercise room. The fuel dock and pumpout for Quivera Basin is located here.

Next is **Seaforth Marina**, with 230 slips for boats from twenty-five to thirty-five feet in length and a large fishing boat and boat rental concession.

Marina Village Marina at the southeast edge of the basin is the largest marina, with 640 slips accommodating boats twenty to fifty feet in length. Restaurants, shops, laundry, showers, and pumpout are all handy.

Driscoll Mission Bay Marina on the south side of Quivera Basin has 250 slips for boats from twenty to ninety feet in length. It is associated with a full service boatyard that includes a 100-ton hoist and chandlery. The harbor is surrounded by bike paths, walking trails, trees, and green

Islandia Marina

Islandia fuel dock

Seaforth Marina

grass. Expect heavy surge inside the harbor, especially in strong westerly swells.

Driscoll Mission Bay Marina (619) 221-8456

Islandia Marina (619) 224-1234

Marina Village Marina (619) 224-3125

Seaforth Marina (619) 224-6807

Marina Village

Driscoll's Mission Bay Marina

Facilities

Bait and tackle	Seaforth Bait and Tackle (619) 224-5447
Boat dock	
Boatyard	Driscoll Mission Bay (619) 221-8456
Chandlery	Boat/US Marine Center (619) 298-3020
	Driscoll Mission Bay (619) 221-8456
	West Marine (619) 225-8867
Convenience store	
Exercise room	
Fishing	
Fuel	Islandia Fuel Dock (619) 222-1164
Hotel	Hyatt Islandia Resort (619) 224-1234
Ice	
Laundry	
Park	
Parking	
Pool/Spa	

Public Transportation
Rental concessions   Seaforth Boat Rentals (619) 223-1681
Restaurants   Hyatt Islandia Restaraunt (619) 224-1234
Restrooms
Showers
Telephone

Attractions and Transportation

Quivera Basin in Mission Bay Park features a tranquil setting among green grass, trees, and trails. All sorts of water sports are available, as well as the world famous Sea World Park, with its associated shows and exhibits. A short walk takes you to Liberty Carousel, shops, restaurants, and Belmont Park, a beachside amusement park featuring the classic 1925 wooden roller coaster "The Giant Dipper."

Public transportation, buses #27 and #34, run along West Mission Bay Drive. Either of these buses takes you to a public transit center where you can transfer to transportation to all parts of San Diego county.

Attractions

Belmont Park (858) 488-1549
Mission Bay Park (619) 221-8900
San Diego Chamber of Commerce (619) 232-0124
San Diego Visitors Center (619) 276-8200
Sea World Park (619) 226-3901

Transportation

Amtrak (800) 872-7245
Becker Auto Rental (619) 298-5990
Enterprise Rent-A-Car (858) 483-3800
San Diego Cab (619) 232-6566
San Diego Metropolitan Transit System (619) 233-3004
San Diego Trolley (619) 231-8549

Mariner's Basin

NOAA Chart #18765

Latitude 32°45.8' N, Longitude 117°14.9' W (Center of Mariner's Basin)

Mariner's Basin is the only anchorage in Mission Bay available for overnight anchoring. The time limit is seventy-two hours in any seven-day period and an adult must remain on board overnight. Mariner's Basin, outside Ventura Bridge, is not limited by the thirty-eight foot bridge clearance. The well-protected, calm anchorage is close to the ocean in a park setting; a short row to shore puts you on white sandy beaches among green grass, trees, and jogging and walking trails. This is an excellent spot for quiet solitude away from frenzied city life.

Entrance to Mariner's Basin

Land Approach

Mariner's Basin is located on the southwest side of Mission Bay Park. Two miles north of downtown San Diego, exit Interstate 5 at Sea World Drive. Proceed west past Sea World and follow signs to West Mission Bay Drive. Drive west past the

Hyatt Islandia Resort over the bridge and turn left onto Mariner's Way—Mariner's Way circles Mariner's Basin. Ample parking is found all around the anchorage.

Sea Approach

From the ocean, continue east down Mission Bay Channel. Shoal areas exist on the south side of the channel, so stay in the center. Past the breakwater the channel turns north; the entrance to Mariner's Basin (latitude 32°45.8' N, longitude 117°14.9' W) is immediately on the west. Mission Bay Channel and Mariner's Basin are dredged in mid channel to twenty feet. Depths become shallower along the shore.

Local Weather Service (858) 289-1212

SeaTow (888) 473-2869

Tow Boat U.S. (800) 493-7869

Vessel Assist (800) 399-1921

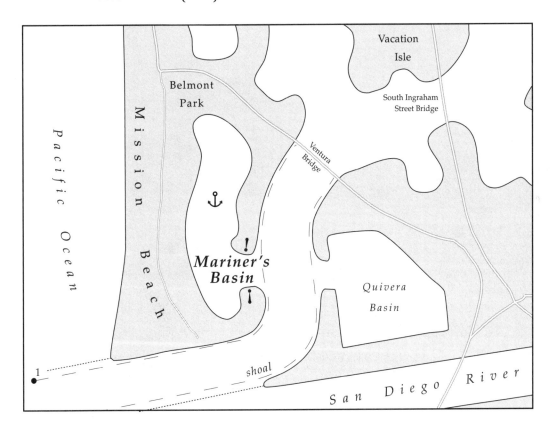

Anchorage and Berthing

No slips are present in Mariner's Basin. The nearest slips available are east across Mission Bay Channel in Quivera Basin. There are mooring buoys in the basin, but they are privately owned and controlled by the Lifeguard Service Division. Anchor anywhere in the basin out of the main channel. The holding ground is good; depths range from ten to twenty feet in sand and mud. The breeze is usually from the northwest at ten to fifteen knots in the afternoon. The anchoring time limit is seventy-two hours in any seven-day period, and an adult must remain on board overnight.

Anchorage in Mariner's Basin

This great anchorage is well protected, out of the wind, waves, and surge; you will spend a quiet night. Public restrooms and outdoor showers are located on shore north, south, and east of the anchorage. A short row to the sandy shore will put you in the center of the park with grass, trees, and walking trails. West across Mission Boulevard you will find surfing at Mission Beach. Take the family boating and spend a tranquil few days here.

Lifeguard Services Division (619) 221-8899 (business hours)
(619) 221-8800 (after hours/weekends)
Mission Bay Park   (619) 221-8900

Facilities

Convenience store
Hotel   Hyatt Islandia Resort (619) 224-1234
Park
Parking
Restaurants   Hyatt Islandia Resort (619) 224-1234
Restrooms
Surfing
Swimming
Telephone

Attractions and Transportation

Activities at Mariner's Basin include running, walking, volleyball, and swimming. Belmont Park, a beachside amusement park with the classic 1925 wooden roller coaster "The Giant Dipper," the Liberty Carousel, shops, and restaurants are a short walk. World-famous Sea World Park is one mile east on West Mission Bay Drive.

Buses #27 and #34 run along West Mission Bay Drive. Take either of these buses to the transfer station and travel to all parts of San Diego county.

**Mission Bay Park
has great beach activities**

Attractions

Belmont Park (858) 488-1549
Mission Bay Park (619) 221-8900
San Diego Chamber of Commerce (619) 232-0124
San Diego Visitors Center (619) 276-8200
Sea World Park (619) 226-3901

Transportation

Amtrak (800) 872-7245
Becker Auto Rental (619) 298-5990
Enterprise Rent-A-Car (858) 483-3800
San Diego Cab (619) 232-6566
San Diego Metropolitan Transit System (619) 233-3004
San Diego Trolley (619) 231-8549

MISSION BAY: INSIDE VENTURA BRIDGE

Dana Cove and West Mission Bay

NOAA Chart #18765

Latitude 32º46.1' N, Longitude 117º14.2' W (Center of Dana Basin)

Dana Cove and West Mission Bay in beautiful Mission Bay Park contain the first marinas inside Ventura Bridge near hotels, restaurants, and yacht clubs. They are close to the ocean, but the Ventura Bridge, with thirty-eight foot clearance, may prevent taller boats from using the area.

Entrance to Dana Cove

Land Approach

Dana Cove is located on the southwest side of Mission Bay Park. Two miles north of downtown San Diego, exit Interstate 5 at Sea World Drive. Proceed west past Sea World and follow signs to West Mission Bay Drive. From West Mission Bay Drive turn right on Dana Landing Road; the marinas will be along the road. For West Mission Bay, continue on West Mission Bay Drive and turn north on Mission Boulevard.

Sea Approach

From the ocean, continue east down Mission Bay Channel. Shoal areas exist on the south side of the channel, so stay within the center. Once you are past the breakwater the channel turns north and passes under Ventura Bridge (vertical clearance thirty-eight feet). Turn east, and Dana Cove (latitude 32°46.1' N, longitude 117°14.2' W) will be the first cove on the right side. If you continue north after passing under the bridge, West Mission Bay and all its facilities will be on the left side. All waterways outside Ventura Bridge are dredged to twenty feet at low tide, while all waterways inside Ventura Bridge are dredged to a depth of eight feet. Stay in the center of the channels and bays, as the water becomes shallower close to shore.

Local Weather Service	(858) 289-1212
Mission Bay Park	(619) 221-8900
San Diego Lifeguards	(619) 221-8899
	(619) 221-8800 (after hours/weekends)
SeaTow	(888) 473-2869
Tow Boat U.S.	(800) 493-7869
Vessel Assist	(800) 399-1921

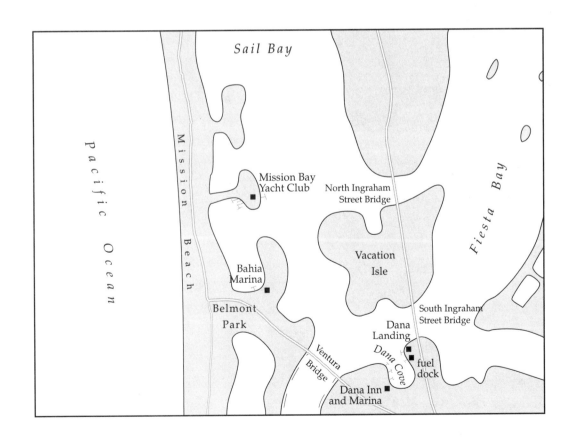

Slips at Dana Marina

Slips at Dana Landing

Bahía Motel and Marina

No overnight anchoring or mooring is allowed in Dana Cove. The nearest anchorage is in Mariner's Basin outside Ventura Bridge. Anchoring during the day is allowed anywhere in Mission Bay except in swimming areas, waterskiing areas, and designated channels.

The marina on the east side of the basin is **Dana Landing Marina**, with 165 slips for boats ranging from twenty to forty feet. Fuel, restrooms, showers, bait and tackle, and marine hardware are all available.

Dana Inn Marina, on the west side of the basin, has 145 slips for boats twenty-five to thirty feet in length. Slip holders have access to all the hotel amenities, such as pool, spa, tennis, restroom, showers, laundry, and restaurant.

North of Ventura Bridge on west Mission Bay is the **Bahia Hotel** with seventy-one slips for boats twenty-four to seventy feet in length. Slip holders have use of all hotel facilities including pool, spa, and tennis courts.

The **Mission Bay Yacht Club** may have guest slips available for members of reciprocating yacht clubs. Always call ahead to determine slip availability.

Bahia Hotel (858) 539-7695
Dana Inn and Marina (619) 222-6440
Dana Landing Marina (619) 224-2513
Mission Bay Yacht Club (858) 488-0501

Facilities

Boat dock

Exercise room
Fuel   Dana Landing Fuel Dock (619) 226-2929
Hotel   Bahia Hotel (858) 488-0511
              Dana Inn and Marina (619) 222-6440
              Catamaran Resort Hotel (858) 488-1081

Ice
Laundry
Park
Parking
Restaurant   Bahia Hotel (858) 488-0551
              Dana Inn and Marina (619) 222-6440
              Catamaran Resort Hotel (858) 488-1081

Restrooms
Showers
Surfing
Swimming
Tennis courts

Mission Bay Yacht Club

Attractions and Transportation

Dana Cove and West Mission Bay are both surrounded by the park setting of Mission Bay Park. Green grass, white sandy beaches, trees, walking trails, and bike paths envelope each area. Play volleyball, walk, fly a kite, swim, waterski, fish, or just relax. Famous Sea World Park is just east of Dana Basin and Belmont Park, a beachside amusement park with the classic 1925 wooden roller coaster "The Giant Dipper." The Liberty Carousel, shops, and restaurants are a short walk. You can surf at Mission Beach, just west across Mission Boulevard.

Public transportation, buses #27 and #34, run along West Mission Bay Drive and Mission Boulevard, headed to the transportation center, from which you can transfer to buses which access all areas of San Diego county.

Attractions

Belmont Park (858) 488-1549
Mission Bay Park (619) 221-8900
San Diego Chamber of Commerce (619) 232-0124
San Diego Visitors Center (619) 276-8200
Sea World Park (619) 226-3901

Transportation

Amtrak (800) 872-7245
Becker Auto Rental (619) 298-5990
Enterprise Rent-A-Car (858) 483-3800
San Diego Cab (619) 232-6566
San Diego Metropolitan Transit System (619) 233-3004
San Diego Trolley (619) 231-8549

Perez Cove   (see chart page 222)

NOAA Chart #18765

Latitude 32°46.1' N, Longitude 117°13.9' W (Center of Perez Cove)

Perez Cove, containing Sea World Marina, provides close access to Sea World Park and Mission Bay Park, with all their activities. Sea World Marina is one of two marinas east of the Ingraham Street bridges and their limiting clearances of thirty-six and thirty-one feet.

Entrance to Perez Cove

Land Access

Perez Cove is on the south side of Mission Bay Park. Two miles north of downtown San Diego, exit Interstate 5 at Sea World Drive. Proceed west past Sea World and follow the signs to West Mission Bay Drive. Turn right on Dana Landing Road, then drive east. The road will go under the Ingraham Street Bridge; Sea World Marina in Perez Cove will be on the left.

Sea Access

From the ocean, continue east down Mission Bay Channel. Shoal areas exist on the south side of the channel, so stay within the center. Past the breakwater the channel turns north and passes under Ventura Bridge (vertical clearance thirty-eight feet). Once you have passed Ventura Bridge, turn east and pass under the South Ingraham Street Bridge (vertical clearance thirty-six feet). Perez Cove (latitude 32°46.1' N, longitude 117°13.9' W) and Sea World Marina will be on your starboard side. The bays, basins, and channels on the ocean side of Ventura Bridge are dredged to twenty feet, while the bay inside Ventura Bridge is maintained to a depth of eight feet at low tide.

Local Weather Service	(858) 289-1212
Mission Bay Park	(619) 221-8899
San Diego Lifeguards	(619) 221-8899
	(619) 221-8800 (after hours/weekends)
Sea Tow	(888) 473-2869
Tow Boat U.S.	(800) 493-7869
Vessel Assist	(800) 399-1921

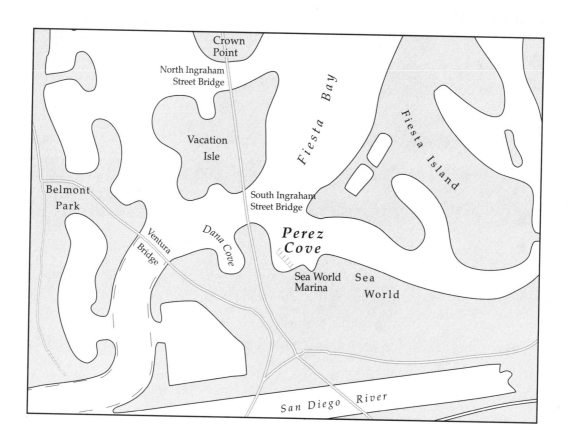

Anchorage and Berthing

No overnight anchoring or mooring is allowed in Perez Cove. The nearest overnight anchorage is in Mariner's Basin west of Ventura Bridge. Daytime anchoring is allowed anywhere in Mission Bay except swimming areas, water skiing areas, and main channels. **Sea World Marina**, in Perez Cove, has 200 slips and can accommodate boats from twenty-four to fifty-five feet in length.

In 1982 Sea World bought, improved, and changed the name of Perez Cove Marina. The refurbished marina includes restrooms, showers, ice, dry storage, and a two-ton hoist. Trees, grass, trails, private parking, and Sea World Park surround this new marina.

Sea World Marina (619) 226-3915

Sea World Marina in Perez Cove

Facilities

Boat dock
Ice

Park
Parking
Restrooms
Showers
Telephone

Attractions and Transportation

World-famous Sea World Park is a short walk from Sea World Marina. This 150-acre adventure park has shows, rides, aquariums, and marine life attractions. Star performers are killer whales, dolphins, sea lions, otters, walruses and sharks. The family can spend days viewing marine life attractions.

Buses #9 and #27 run along Sea World Drive to the transit center, where you can transfer to transportation to all parts of San Diego County.

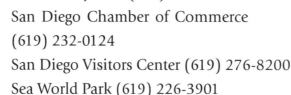

**World-famous Sea World
adjacent to Sea World Marina**

Attractions

Belmont Park (858) 488-1549
Mission Bay Park (619) 221-8900
San Diego Chamber of Commerce
(619) 232-0124
San Diego Visitors Center (619) 276-8200
Sea World Park (619) 226-3901

Transportation

Amtrak (800) 872-7245
Becker Auto Rental (619) 298-5990
Enterprise Rent-A-Car (858) 483-3800
San Diego Cab (619) 232-6566
San Diego Metropolitan Transit System (619) 233-3004
San Diego Trolley (619) 231-8549

Campland Marina   (see chart page 226)

NOAA Chart #18765

Latitude 32°47.6' N, Longitude 117°13.3' W (Outside Campland Marina)

Campland Marina, located on the north side of Mission Bay Park, is adjacent to Fiesta Bay water ski area. Ventura Bridge (vertical clearance thirty-eight feet), North Ingraham Street Bridge (vertical clearance thirty-one feet) and South Ingraham Street Bridge (vertical clearance thirty-six feet) limit access to this fine area. Campland Marina is associated with Campland On The Bay, a recreational vehicle park with campsites. Stay in the marina among the green grass, trees, and trails and spend days exploring all the sights in Mission Bay Park.

Entrance to Campland Marina

Land Access

Campland Marina is located on the northeast side of Mission Bay Park. Three miles north of downtown San Diego, exit Interstate 5 at Grand Avenue or Garnet Avenue. Drive west about one mile and turn left on Olney Street; continue three or four blocks. Turn left on Pacific Beach Drive and enter Campland On The Bay.

Sea Access

From the ocean, continue down Mission Bay Channel. Shoal areas exist on the south side of the channel, so stay within the center. Once you are past the break-water the channel turns north to pass under Ventura Bridge (vertical clearance thirty-eight feet). Past the bridge turn east and pass under the South Ingraham Street Bridge (vertical clearance thirty-six feet). Once past this second bridge, turn north into Fiesta Bay; Campland Marina (latitude 32°47.6' N, longitude 117°13.3' W) will be at the north end of Fiesta Bay next to Rose Inlet. The bays and channels east of Ventura Bridge are dredged to eight feet in the center of the channel, while outside the bridge the controlling depth is twenty feet.

Local Weather Service	(858) 289-1212
Mission Bay Park	(619) 221-8900
San Diego Lifeguards	(619) 221-8899
	(619) 221-8800 (after hours/weekends)
SeaTow	(888) 473-2869
Tow Boat U.S.	(800) 493-7869
Vessel Assist	(800) 399-1921

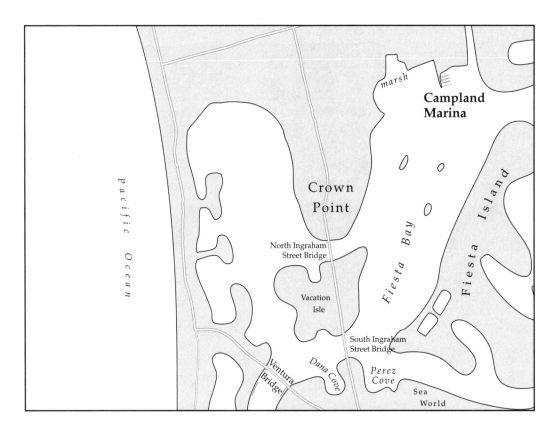

Anchorage and Berthing

No overnight anchoring or mooring is allowed in Campland Marina. The nearest overnight anchorage is in Mariner's Basin west of Ventura Bridge. Daytime anchoring is allowed in all areas of Mission Bay except swimming areas, water skiing areas, and designated channels. **Campland Marina** has 155 slips accommodating boats from twenty to fifty feet in length. Slip holders have use of all Campland On The Bay facilities, including swimming pools, playground, recreation room, boat rentals, restaurant, showers, restrooms, laundry, hoist, groceries, bait and tackle, and marine supplies.

Slips at Campland Marina

Campland Marina (858) 581-4224
Campland On The Bay (858) 581-4200

Facilities

Bait and tackle	Campland On The Bay (858) 581-4224
Boat docks	
Convenience store	
Ice	
Launch Ramp	
Laundry	
Park	
Parking	
Pool	
Restaurant	Campland On The Bay (858) 490-3389
Restroom	
R.V. Park	Campland On The Bay (858) 581-4200
Showers	
Swimming	
Telephone	

Attractions and Transportation

Campland Marina is close to all activities in Mission Bay Park. The Fiesta Bay water ski area is just outside the marina. Mission Bay Golf Course, an eighteen-hole course with driving range, is a short walk north on North Mission Bay Drive. Watch egrets and great blue herons search for dinner in the Kendall Frost Wildlife Preserve just to the west of the marina.

Beautiful beaches surround Mission Bay Park

Public transportation buses #30 and #27 run along Grand Avenue and Garnet Avenue to transit stations where you can transfer to transportation to all areas of San Diego County.

Attractions

Belmont Park (858) 488-1549
Mission Bay Golf Course (858) 490-3370
Mission Bay Park (619) 221-8900
San Diego Chamber of Commerce (619) 232-0124
San Diego Visitors Center (619) 276-8200
Sea World Park (619) 226-3901

Transportation

Amtrak (800) 872-7245
Becker Auto Rental (619) 298-5990
Enterprise Rent-A-Car (858) 483-3800
San Diego Cab (619) 232-6566
San Diego Metropolitan Transit System (619) 233-3004
San Diego Trolley (619) 231-8549

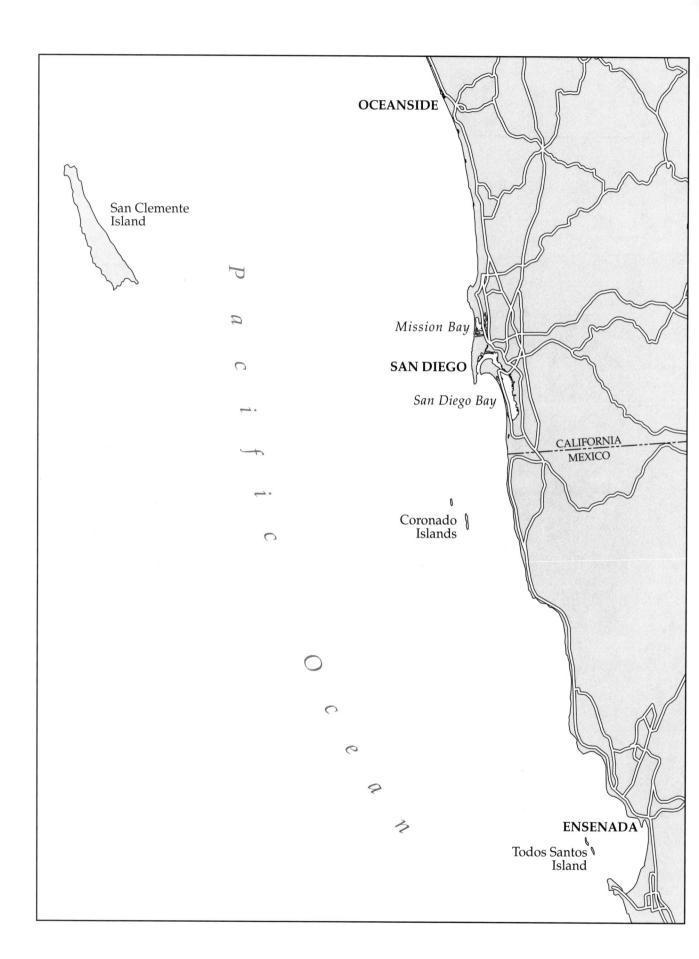

OCEANSIDE

San Clemente
Island

Pacific

Mission Bay

SAN DIEGO

San Diego Bay

CALIFORNIA
MEXICO

Ocean

Coronado
Islands

ENSENADA

Todos Santos
Island

13 OUTSIDE THE BAY

"A regulation of the port forbids any ballast to be thrown overboard; accordingly, our long boat was lined inside with rough boards and brought alongside the gangway, but where there one tubful went into the boat twenty went overboard. This is done by every vessel, as it saves more than a week of labor, which would be spent in loading the boats, rowing them to the point, and unloading them. When any people from the presidio were onboard, the boat was hauled up and the ballast thrown in; but when the coast was clear, she was dropped astern again, and the ballast fell overboard."

Richard Henry Dana, Jr., *Two Years Before the Mast* (1835)

Coronado Islands   (see chart page 234)

NOAA Charts #18765, #18766

Latitude 32°24.0' N, Longitude 117°14.0' W (South Coronado Island south light)

Latitude 32°24.8' N, Longitude 117°14.7' W (South Coronado Island north light)

The Coronado, or "Crown," Islands are four prominent, barren rock islands easily seen from San Diego. These Mexican islands—four miles south of the international border, seven miles off the coast of Baja California, and fifteen miles south of Point Loma—make a nice day's trip away from the hectic activity of the city. Excellent fishing and diving are found in the area, but make sure you have a Mexican fishing license.

Coronado Islands are fourteen miles from Point Loma

On September 26, 1542, after two months at sea, Juan Rodriguez Cabrillo sighted the Coronado Islands. The expedition log noted: "They sailed along the coast about eight leagues, passing by some three islands completely denuded of soil. One of them is larger than the others. They are three leagues from the mainland. They called them 'desert islands.'" (A league is a unit of distance varying at different periods of time and in different countries; in English- and Spanish-speaking countries it is roughly three miles.) Two days later Cabrillo landed in San Diego. Fifty years later, on November 8, 1602, Sebastian Vizcaino sailed past these four rocky islands and named them "Las Islas Coronados."

Not much has happened in the 400 years since these barren islands were first discovered. In recent times Mexican fishermen have built an occasional shelter for protection from the weather. Today the islands are a Mexican wildlife refuge where going ashore is prohibited. A small Mexican naval detachment housed on the south island enforces this law. These islands have no harbors, bays, or well-protected anchorages; all holding grounds are marginal, with surge and swell on even the calmest days. Excellent fishing and diving are the primary recreation attraction on these islands.

North Coronado Island (Coronado del Norte)

North Coronado Island, the closest of the islands to San Diego, is the second largest of the four islands. Rising to a height of 467 feet, it is surrounded by cliffs. The water depth drops off steeply close to shore, making anchoring difficult: Depths over 100 feet are encountered within fifty yards of shore.

Middle Coronado Island and Middle Ground Rock (Coronado del Medio)

Middle Coronado Island and Middle Ground Rock lie between the two major islands and the smallest of the four islands.

Lobster Cove
on North Coronado Island

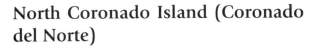

Moonlight Cove
on Middle Coronado Island

Puerto Cueva Cove
on South Coronado Island

They rise to a height of 251 feet and are surrounded by strong dangerous currents. Again, the bottom drops steeply close to shore; fishing and diving are the main attractions. These small islands are an important seal refuge area.

South Coronado Island (Coronado del Sur)

South Coronado Island is the largest and the furthest island from San Diego. Two miles long and a half mile wide at its widest point, it houses two lights, one at the southern tip (latitude 32°24.0' N, longitude 117°14.0' W) and the other on the eastern side one-quarter way down from the northern tip of the island (latitude 32°24.8' N, longitude 117°14.7' W). The island is primarily barren and rises to a height of 672 feet. The bottom drops off sharply close to shore, making anchoring difficult. Thick kelp extending for three miles off the southern end of South Coronado Island can be hazardous to boating.

Land Approach

None

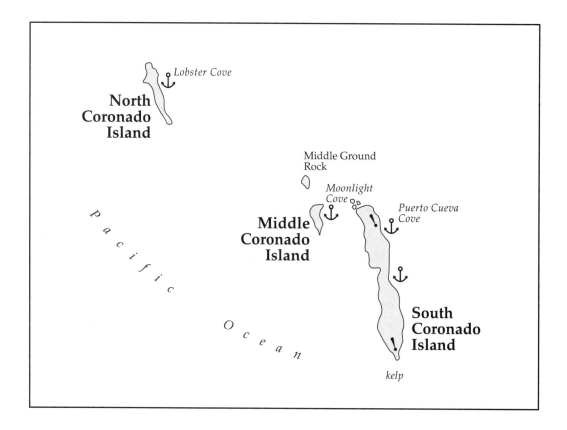

Sea Approach

Leave sea buoy "SD" and voyage twelve miles south on a course of 164° Magnetic, which will put you one-half mile east of South Coronado Island. The islands will be readily apparent on radar from any direction. Use caution approaching from the south, for the kelp extends three miles south of South Coronado Island. The trip south will be aided by the prevailing wind, waves, and 0.2-knot south-flowing California current. Allow extra time returning to San Diego Bay, as the wind, waves, and current will hinder your progress.

Local Weather Service (858) 289-1212

SeaTow (888) 473-2869

Tow Boat U.S. (800) 493-7869

Vessel Assist (800) 399-1921

Anchoring and Berthing

There are neither mooring buoys nor docks on the Coronado Islands. Around each island the bottom drops off rapidly near shore. On the four Coronado Islands only four possible anchorages exist, and these are marginal. No protected coves or harbors exist; swell and surge enter all anchorages even in still weather.

North Coronado Island has a marginal anchorage in **Lobster Cove** on the east side of the island. Anchor in fifty feet of water with a sand and rock bottom. The surge and swell make it uncomfortable even in smooth weather.

Middle Coronado Island has a small protected cove, **Moonlight Cove**, on the east side of the island. Anchor in thirty feet of water with a sand and rock bottom.

South Coronado Island has an anchorage just south of the north light on the east side of the island. This small cove, called "**Puerto Cueva**," has fair holding ground in twenty-four feet of water with a sand bottom. Again, swell and surge make it uncomfortable even in calm weather.

South Coronado Island has a second marginal anchorage off the east side of the island just south of the midpoint. Anchor here in forty feet of water on a sand bottom. Swell and surge enter here in all weather. If you anchor, let out plenty of scope even on quiet days. All these anchorages are unsafe in Santa Ana conditions, when the islands become "lee shores."

Facilities

> Diving
> Fishing
> Nature watching
> Underwater photography

Attractions and Transportation

Excellent fishing and diving are found around the Coronado Islands. Divers find underwater visibility of one hundred feet or greater, with lobster and abalone plentiful during the season. Fishermen find yellowtail, bass, bonito, albacore, rock cod, halibut, and barracuda. Numerous sport-fishing boats descend on the area during the seasons. A Mexican fishing license is needed to fish in Mexican waters; this is easily obtained at most San Diego area fish and tackle stores.

Anchorage at middle of South Coronado Island

> Fisherman's Landing (619) 221-8500
> Mexican Consulate (619) 231-8414
> Mission Bay Deep Sea Fishing (619) 224-3439
> San Diego Divers Supply Discount Outlet (619) 224-3439
> Tijuana/Mexico Visitors Center (619) 425-2088

San Clemente Island (see chart page 239)

NOAA Charts #18762, #18763, #18764, #18766

Latitude 32°49.2' N, Longitude 118°21.2' W (Pyramid Head light)

Latitude 33°00.2' N, Longitude 118°33.2' W (Wilson Cove light)

San Clemente Island is a military reservation off limits to the public. It may be dangerous because of naval activities, including gunfire, bombing, and rocket fire. However, when the navy isn't practicing maneuvers, excellent fishing, diving, and sightseeing from a boat are found all around the island.

Wilson Cove on east side of San Clemente Island

San Clemente Island is the fourth-largest and most southern of the Channel Islands. It was formed during volcanic eruptions from the ocean floor. Gas bubbles from the molten rock formed many caves around the island. Some naturalists believe this island was never part of the California mainland.

Excavations show that the Canalino Indians on the island went through centuries without change. These seafaring people depended heavily on the sea for survival. Using driftwood, they built large, flexible, planked boats that could hold up to twenty people. They lived in circular homes with six to a house and twenty-five people in a village. Total population on the island before foreign explorers arrived was 1,000 to 2,000.

On October 7, 1542 Juan Cabrillo sighted two islands he named La Victoria and San Salvador. Historians believe this was the first European sighting of San Clemente and Santa Catalina Islands. Years later, Spanish explorer Sebastian Vizcaino renamed the island San Clemente in honor of the saint on whose day—November 23—it was sighted.

Between 1820 and 1830 the native Indians were removed to work at mainland missions. In 1868 the government began leasing the island to sheep ranchers, the first of whom, a Mr. Gallagher, built a rock house there in 1868. Later, Charles Howland ran 10,000 to 15,000 sheep on the island. From 1890 to 1910, Chinese fisherman came out from San Diego Bay to gather abalones. Ultimately, in 1937 San Clemente was turned over to the U.S. Navy.

Today, most of the native vegetation has been destroyed by overgrazing of sheep and goats. Goats were introduced by mariners in the seventeenth and eighteenth centuries; the navy has tried to relocate them to allow the endemic flora and fauna to increase. More endemic plants are present on San Clemente than on any other Channel Island.

The fifty-six-square-mile island is eighteen miles long and four miles wide at its widest point. Located fifty-seven miles northwest of Point Loma, its highlands rise to a height of 1965 feet; its east side features bold, rocky cliffs. Here water is generally deep inshore, with kelp growing close to the beach. The west side of the island is lower, sloping and irregular. Giant brown kelp surrounds the island, extending several hundred yards offshore with many rocks inshore. Navigational buoys around the island, maintained by the U.S. Navy, are changed regularly. Check the *Local Notice to Mariners* for altered positions.

Land Approach

None

Sea Approach

Always contact the U.S. Navy or the San Diego Harbor Police regarding naval activities before setting off for the island. When naval operations are planned, announcements are usually broadcast over VHF radio Channel 16.

San Clemente Island is fifty-seven miles northwest of Point Loma. The top of the island appears as a tableland from a distance. A white radar dome on the highest part of the island is visible from both the east and the west side of the island.

From San Diego buoy "SD," turn northwest to course 350° M (magnetic) and you are on course for the island. From Mission Bay, set a course of 320° M. The outward passage from the mainland is more difficult because it is directly into the wind and waves. The California current moves south at a velocity of two-tenths of a knot, so course corrections will need to be made for wind, waves, and current for correct landfall. Direct passage to the island will traverse commonly traveled shipping lanes, so maintain a sharp lookout and make sure a good radar reflector is on board. The island is an excellent radar target from all directions..

Local Weather Service	(858) 289-1212
San Diego Harbor Police	(619) 223-1133
Sea Tow	(888) 473-2869
Tow Boat U.S.	(800) 493-7869
U.S. Naval Activities San Clemente Island	(619) 524-9214
Vessel Assist	(800) 399-1921

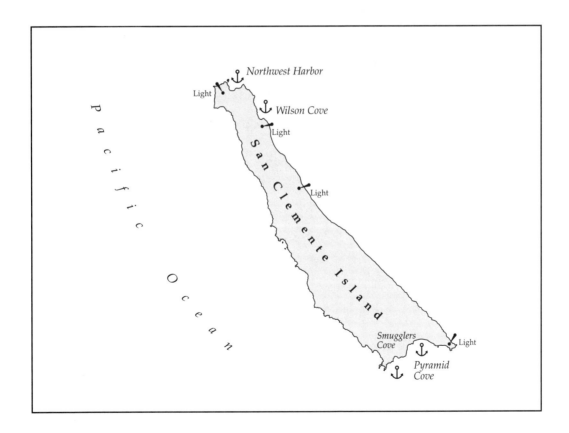

Anchorage and Berthing

There is no public landing on this U.S. Navy-controlled island. The pier and buoys in Wilson Cove are for exclusive Navy use. No well-protected harbors or coves exist around San Clemente Island; all anchorages are marginal, with swells and surge making for uncomfortable and rocky visits in any weather. However, anchoring under protected headlands is possible.

Navy piers in Wilson Cove

Wilson Cove (latitude 33°00.2' N, longitude 118°33.2' W) is a fair anchorage. Anchor in the lee of the kelp in twenty-five feet of water one mile northwest of the navy pier. Holding ground is fair in sand and rock bottom, but surge and swells come into the cove around the point. Strong winds blow down off the hills in the afternoon.

Northwest Harbor is a good anchorage in mild northwest and south wind. but becomes unsafe in strong northwest winds. Anchor in the lee of the large rock and kelp in twenty-five feet of water with a sand bottom.

Pyramid Cove (latitude 32°49.2' N, longitude 118°21.2' W) is a fair anchorage in northwest weather. Anchor in sixty feet of water, but do not enter the heavy kelp, as there are underwater dangers. The San Diego fishing boats commonly anchor here.

Smugglers Cove, west of Pyramid Cove, has one of the largest caves on the island. Local tales tell of pirate gold, Chinese smuggling, and rum running here in days gone by. If you anchor, always let out plenty of scope even on quiet days and be aware all these anchorages are unsafe in Santa Ana conditions, as the island becomes a "lee shore." In Santa Ana conditions the wind blows from the east, so the west side of the island offers protection.

Facilities

> Diving
> Fishing
> Nature watching
> Underwater photography

Attractions and Transportation

The public is not allowed on San Clemente. However, access to the bays and coves around the island is permitted. Diving, fishing, and sightseeing opportunities abound all around the island. Diving is excellent about the island, with clear water and visibility up to 100 feet or greater. Lobster and abalone are found in abundance during the season. Fishermen catch barracuda, halibut, bass, bonito, rockfish, sheephead, yellowtail, skipjack, and dorado on all sides of the island. Naturalists observe sea otters and elephant seals at Mail Point on the west side of the island. Sport diving and fishing boats regularly frequent the area.

> Fisherman's Landing (619) 221-8500
> Mission Bay Deep Sea Fishing (619) 224-3439
> San Diego Divers Supply Discount Outlet (619) 224-3439
> Seaforth Sportfishing (619) 224-3383

Oceanside   (see chart page 246)

NOAA Charts #18774, #18740

Latitude 33°12.1' N, Longitude 117°24.5' W (Offshore Buoy "OC")

Oceanside Harbor, thirty miles north of Mission Bay, is a small, quiet, friendly harbor with all boating services conveniently located around compact docks. On your way south this is a great place to stop off and insure that all your boat's systems are functioning properly.

Entrance to Oceanside Harbor

The original inhabitants of this area were the Luiseños Indians. They are re-lated to the Shoshone Indians of the plains and desert regions of Nevada and Utah. These gatherers and hunters migrated between the seashore and the San Marcos Mountains in the east. There were 10,000 Indians living around the Oceanside and San Luis Rey River Valley when the first Spanish explorers, the Portolá party, arrived in 1769.

Not long afterward, the Catholic church had established along the California coast a chain of missions designed to lie one day's journey apart (thirty miles). The seventeenth mission in this system, Mission San Luis Rey, known as the "King of the Missions," was named in honor of Louis IX, King of France. Founded in 1798 and dedicated in 1815, it was the largest, most populated, and most prosperous of all the missions.

In 1831 there were 3,000 Indians working church lands. After Mexican Independence these lands became large private tracts known as rancheros.

San Luis Rey Mission was known as "King of the Missions"

When San Diego became the terminus of the Transcontinental Railroad in 1885, the area began to boom. In 1888 Oceanside became a city, its downtown area clustered around the pier and beach, but with time the city expanded eastward.

Camp Pendleton Military Reservation was dedicated in 1942 and the Army Corps of Engineers built a jetty to protect Camp Pendleton Boat Basin, but the city claimed that this jetty caused beach erosion. The Federal Government responded by redesigning the harbor, which boosted the local economy. Oceanside Harbor was dedicated in 1963.

Today, the city is home to 160,000 residents, the largest employer being Camp Pendleton Marine Base. This 125,000-acre military reservation is home to one of the largest amphibious training centers in the world.

Quaint Seaport Village

The harbor, located at the northwest edge of the city, is actually two harbors protected by the breakwater and the southern jetty. The northern harbor is Del Mar Boat Basin, which is restricted to Camp Pendleton Marine Corps. The southern harbor contains Oceanside Harbor and the 950-slip marina operated by the City of Oceanside.

The harbor is in a park-like setting, with walking trails around the entire periphery. A seaport village with restaurants, shops, sport fishing boats, and rental concessions is located at the south end of the harbor. The launch ramp on the south peninsula is directly across from the surfing beach. A full service boatyard with a fourteen-ton travel lift is available for all types of maintenance and repair. The north end of the harbor is the site of the friendly Oceanside Yacht Club. All around the harbor are restaurants with ocean view dining. There are berths for forty-eight transient vessels, all under control of the Oceanside Harbor Department.

Oceanside Yacht Club

Land Approach

Exit Interstate Highway 5 at the "Oceanside Harbor" exit and proceed west down the hill to Harbor Drive. The harbor will open up in front of you.

Sea Approach

Approaching from the north, you will see the sandy beaches of the San Luis Rey River outlet, which extends to the Oceanside breakwater to the south. Waves commonly break over this seawall. Approaching from the south, the Oceanside pier is obvious 2.1 miles south of the harbor entrance. Proceed to lighted whistle buoy "OC" (latitude 33°12.1' N longitude 117°24.5' W) located about 1,000 yards off the south end of the breakwater. The large, lighted sign "OCEANSIDE" on the hill over-

Inner harbor and famous "Oceanside" sign

looking the harbor is directly in back of the harbor. Another landmark, a tall, singular apartment building, is on the east side of the harbor. The harbor opens to the southwest, so you cannot see the opening from the north or the west. Proceed northeast and enter between the two lighted jetties.

Buoys, lights, and day beacons mark the remainder of the channel. Exercise caution during heavy southerly swells, as waves break across the entrance under these conditions. Extra caution should be taken during night entries, because background lights of the city obscure the channel marking lights. Inside the breakwater, marked buoys to the north lead to Del Mar Boat Basin. An east turn leads to Oceanside boat basin. A danger buoy marks a submerged jetty on the north side of the channel. Once you are into the inner harbor, turn to the north and the guest dock will be directly on your starboard side. Tie up and report to the Harbor Master's office to secure a slip.

Local Weather Service	(858) 289-1212
SeaTow	(888) 473-2869
Tow Boat U.S.	(800) 493-7869
Vessel Assist	(800) 399-1921

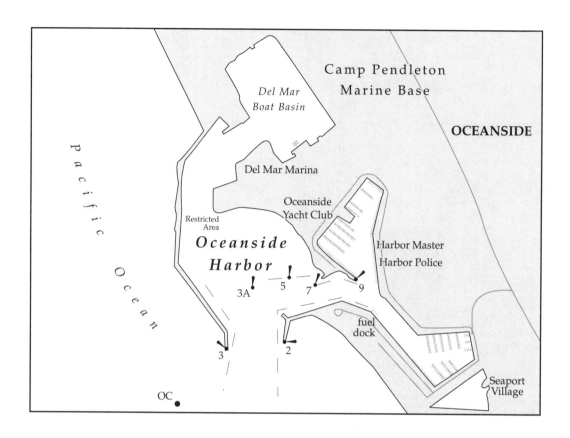

Anchorage and Berthing

No anchoring or mooring is permitted in **Oceanside Harbor**. The guest dock is directly across the street from the Oceanside harbormaster's office. If the harbormaster's office is closed, make arrangements with the harbor police in the adjacent office. Forty-eight city-controlled slips for transient yachts are located throughout the harbor. Space is provided on a first-come, first-serve basis; no reservations are accepted. These slips provide water, electricity, restrooms, showers, and laundry. The **Oceanside Yacht Club** has a guest dock for cruising yacht club members. Hotels, restaurants, boatyard, and chandlery are all within walking distance of any of the slips.

The **Del Mar Marina and Sailing Center,** located in the Del Mar Boat Basin, contains fifty-three slips accommodating boats from twenty-six to forty-five feet in length. This marina, on government property, is limited to active duty and retired military and their dependents only. The marina provides restrooms, showers, water, electricity, and boat rental facilities to qualified boaters. The Santa Margarita Sailing Club is also located within the facility.

Del Mar Marina and Sailing Center	(760) 725-2820
Oceanside Harbormaster	(760) 435-4000

Oceanside Harbor Police	(760) 435-4050
	(760) 535-0452 after hours
Oceanside Yacht Club	(760) 722-5751

Harbor Police and guest docks

Facilities

Bait and Tackle	Tackle Town (760) 721-2690
Boatyard	Oceanside Marine Center (760) 722-1833
Chandlery	Pablo's Crews (760) 721-1516
Convenience Store	
Fishing	
Fuel	
Hotel	Oceanside Marina Inn (760) 722-1561
Ice	
Launch Ramp	
Laundry	
Park	

Parking
Pool/Spa
Pumpout
Public Transportation
Rental Concessions
Restaurants   Monterey Bay Cannery (760) 722-3474
Shops
Slips
Showers
Surfing
Telephone

Del Mar Boat Basin and Del Mar Marina

Attractions and Transportation

The small, quiet harbor is adjacent to four miles of beautiful sandy beaches. On the bluff overlooking the ocean you will see "Top Gun House," the house used by Tom Cruise in the movie *Top Gun*. Across from the town center stretches the longest wooden pier (1600 feet) on the west coast. Oceanside is an excellent base from which to visit Mission San Luis Rey, Camp Pendleton Marine Base, California Surf Museum, San Diego Wild Animal Park, and Legoland California.

Public transportation, Oceanside Bus Route #314, runs on Harbor Drive at the east end of the harbor and goes to the Oceanside Transit Station. It connects with transportation to all areas of San Diego County and even Los Angeles, via Amtrak.

Attractions

California Surf Museum	(760) 721-6876
Camp Pendleton Marine Base	(760) 725-5569
Legoland	(760) 918-5346
Mission San Luis Rey	(760) 757-3651
Oceanside Visitors Center	(760) 721-1101
San Diego Wild Animal Park	(760) 747-8702

Transportation

Amtrak	(800) USA-RAIL
Coastal Cab	(760) 722-6786
Enterprise Rent-a-Car	(760) 966-9090
Oceanside Transit Information	(760) 722-6283

El Coral, B. C., Mexico   (see chart page 252)
NOAA Charts # 18766, #21021
Latitude 31°51.4' N, Longitude 116°40.0' W (Marina)

El Coral Hotel and Marina is located sixty-nine miles south of the U.S. border and one mile north of Ensenada. This small, luxurious, accommodating marina is the only hotel and marina between San Diego and the tip of Baja California. It is a great place to pass through Mexican Customs with the help of friendly, knowledgeable marina personnel.

Entrance to El Coral Marina

Many luxury hotels grace the coast between the international border and Ensenada, B.C., Mexico, but none is more modern and helpful than the El Coral Hotel and Marina Resort. This successful venture combined the efforts of two prominent Baja California families, the Lutteroth Valle family and the Curiel Amaya family. Both are involved in real estate, construction, and hotel management in Baja California. Construction of the breakwater, marina, and six-story hotel began in 1993; the facilities opened for business in 1995.

The harbor is located at the northwest edge of Ensenada; the new 370-slip marina has space available for boats thirty to sixty feet in length. It is a safe, secure location from which to explore all Ensenada has to offer. Procuring a slip gives you access to all resort facilities, including three swimming pools, spa, sauna, tennis courts, and gym. They offer recreational dive boats, fishing boats, and rental concessions and can provide transportation to horseback riding, golf, and scenic tours. The hotel has 147 deluxe suites with fine dining, lobby bar, and a nightclub on the property, making this an excellent place for friends and family to visit.

Land Approach

Five-star El Coral Hotel and Marina

Approaching from the United States, drive south on Interstate Highway 5 and cross the international border, following the signs to "Ensenada." The road takes you west along the border, but ultimately turns south and follows the beach to Ensenada. The toll road is the fastest (approximately ninety minutes) and most scenic route, with spectacular ocean views. After you pass three tollbooths, you will see the six-story hotel and marina on the right, one mile north of downtown.

Sea Approach

Continue south from San Diego sea buoy "SD." Passage inside the Coronado Islands is more direct; however, often more wind is found outside these islands. Pass by Punta Descanso, Punta Salsipuedes, and Punta San Miguel and enter Bahía de Todos Santos (All Saints Bay). Todos Santos Islands are nine and one-half miles west of El Coral Hotel and Marina Harbor. South of Punta del Morro is the small, rock breakwater protecting the El Coral Marina. The breakwater entrance faces south and is not readily apparent when approaching from the north or west. The marina is located at latitude 31°51.4' N, longitude 116°40.0' W fifty-seven nautical miles south of San Diego. Exercise extra care when entering the harbor at night, since there is no approach buoy outside the breakwater, and navigation lights on the ends of the breakwater are masked by the lights on shore.

Local Weather Service (858) 289-1212 (from USA)

SeaTow (888) 473-2869 (from USA)

Tow Boat U.S. (800) 493-7869 (from USA)

Vessel Assist (800) 399-1921 (from USA)

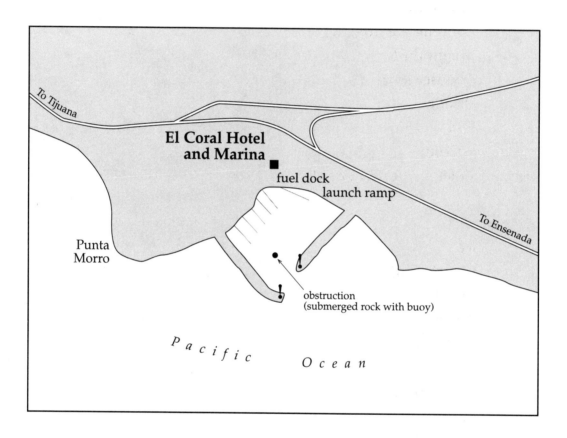

Anchorage and Berthing

No anchoring or mooring is allowed in El Coral Marina. The nearest anchorage is in Ensenada Harbor three miles south. A buoy marks a large rock directly inside the breakwater entrance.

This new marina has full hookups, including cable TV, phone, water, and thirty- and fifty-amp. electricity. Parking, twenty-four-hour security, showers, lockers, laundry, launch ramp, pumpout, fuel, and use of all the hotel facilities make this an excellent place to stay. Since it is a very popular harbor for California boaters, always call ahead to insure that space is available.

El Coral Hotel and Marina Resort (800) 862-9020 (from USA)
                                  (877) 233-5839 (from USA)
                                  01-800-026-3100 (from Mexico)

Facilities

Bait and tackle
Boat dock
Convenience store
Dinghy dock
Exercise room
Fishing
Fuel
Haulout
Hotel   El Coral Hotel and Marina (800) 862-9020 (from USA)
                                           (877) 233-5839 (from USA)
                                           800-026-3100 (Mexico)

Ice
Launch ramp
Laundry
Parking
Pool/Spa
Pumpout
Rental concession
Restaurant   Antares 175-0000
Security-24 hours
Shops
Showers
Slips
Snack Bar
Telephone
Tennis courts

Attractions and Transportation

El Coral Hotel and Marina Resort is within two miles of the tourist area of
Ensenada. A short taxi ride will take you to the center of town, where shopping,

eating, open-air fish markets, and historic museums await all visitors. The hotel can arrange for fishing, scuba diving, wine tasting, golfing, horseback riding, and archeological and mission tours.

A city bus runs in front of the hotel to take you downtown; however, taxis are plentiful, inexpensive, and the best way to see the sights. The hotel staff can help you negotiate a price with the taxi driver before you set out.

Attractions

Ensenada Visitor Bureau	(800) 310-9687 (from USA)
	178-3675
Hussong's Cantina	178-3210
Museo de Historia	177-0594
Museo Historico Regional	178-2531
US Consulate	(6) 681-7400

Transportation

Bus station	178-6680
Yellow Cab	178-3475

Fuel is available at El Coral

Ensenada, B.C., Mexico   (see chart page 256)
NOAA Charts #18766, #21021
Latitude 31°50.3' N, Longitude 116°37.7' W (Harbor Entrance)

Ensenada, or "Inlet," is a major tourist center of Baja California, Mexico, seventy miles south of the U.S. border. The marinas front the boardwalk near the busy center of town and the city's attractions. Being the first port of entry for cruisers traveling south, it is an excellent place to process all Mexican entry forms and the last place to buy fuel until Bahía de Tortugas, 275 miles to the south.

Entrance to Ensenada Harbor

The area was first visited by Portuguese explorer Juan Rodriguez Cabrillo on September 17, 1542. He named it Bahía de San Mateo. It was rediscovered sixty years later, November 2, 1602, and renamed Ensenada de Todos Santos (All Saints Inlet) by Sebastian Vizcaino. The original inhabitants of the land were Cochimi Indians, who were known for their cave painting in the local areas. In 1824 the Mexican government tried to colonize the area but failed because of the lack of water. Private companies from the United States and Britain attempted in 1886 to develop real estate in the area, but protests from the Mexican government discouraged success. Today Ensenada, home to over 300,000 residents, has a first rate seaport. It is Baja California's largest harbor (one mile long and a half mile wide) and is Mexico's second most visited port of call for major cruise lines. Ensenada contains a large commercial fishing fleet and is home to a sardine canning industry.

Protected by a rock breakwater, the harbor area, which fronts the city of Ensenada, contains five marinas: Cruiseport Village Marina, Baja Naval Boatyard and Marina, Sergio's Sport Fishing Center and Marina, Juanito's Boats and Marina, and Bandido's Boats and Marina. Adjacent to the marinas are shops, fish markets, and miles of white sandy beaches. Public transportation and taxis are available along the boardwalk. Sights to visit in the area include wineries, museums, and missions with numerous restaurants along the harbor providing waterfront dining. A warm, friendly Mexican atmosphere abounds everywhere to welcome the visiting boater.

Land Approach

Approaching from the United States, drive south on Interstate Highway 5 and cross the international border, following the signs for "Ensenada." The road takes you west along the border, but ultimately turns south and follows the beach to Ensenada. The toll road is the fastest (approximately ninety minutes) and most scenic drive, with spectacular ocean views. After passing three tollbooths, continue six miles into town. The marinas are located on the harbor boardwalk.

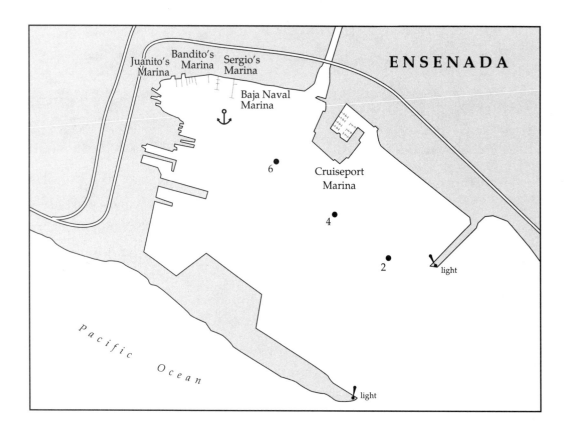

Sea Approach

Continue south from San Diego sea buoy "SD." Passage inside the Coronado Islands is more direct; however, more wind is often found outside these islands. Pass by Punta Descanso, Punta Salsipuedes, and Punta San Miguel and enter Bahía de Todos Santos (All Saints Bay). Todos Santos Islands are nine and one-half miles west of Ensenada. North of the harbor is a barren rock hill of an old rock quarry and extending south is the rock breakwater. The harbor entrance (latitude 31°50.3' N, longitude 116°37.7' W) opens to the south, and thus is not apparent from the north or the west. Enter the main harbor and continue north. The new Cruiseport Marina is located within the Cruiseport Terminal: the entrance is three-quarters of a mile north of the outer harbor entrance. The other four marinas are found in the outer harbor north of the Cruiseport Terminal among the sport fishing piers.

Local Weather Service (858) 289-1212 (from USA)

SeaTow (888) 473-2869 (from USA)

Tow Boat U.S. (800) 493-7869 (from USA)

Vessel Assist (800) 399-1921 (from USA)

Anchorage and Berthing

Anchoring is allowed off the beach, north of the Cruiseship Terminal, and in front of the municipal beach and boat-launching ramp. Good holding ground exists in fifteen to twenty-five feet of water in mud and sand. There are numerous mooring buoys in the area, but they are all privately owned and you will be charged a fee if you tie up. Berthing facilities are found at the small marinas within the harbor.

Cruiseport Marina

The first marina you encounter after entering the harbor is the new, 116-slip Cruiseport Marina. Nico Saad, owner of the nearby Hotel San Nicolas, completed the marina in 2001. Shore power, water, phone, cable TV, and twenty-four-hour security with fenced and patrolled property are provided. The basin is dredged to thirty feet, with a depth of twelve feet in the slip areas.

Baja Naval Marina, north of the Cruise Ship Terminal, has fifty slips. Its docks offer electricity, water, phone, and security. This marina is associated with the Baja Naval Boatyard, where a seventy-five-ton travel lift is available for haulouts and all types of maintenance and repair.

Sergio's Sport Fishing Center and Marina is just north along the boardwalk with thirty slips and all the amenities, such as water, electricity, showers, and restrooms. Two other small marinas–– **Juanito's Boats and Marina**, and **Bandido's Boats and Marina**––are further north along the boardwalk among the fishing boats. Always call ahead to determine if space is available for your boat.

Baja Naval Marina

Baja Naval Boatyard and
Marina   174-0020
Bandido's Boats and Marina
            174-0054
Cruiseport Village Marina
            178-8801
Juanito's Boats and Marina
            174-0953
Sergio's Sportfishing Center
and Marina   178-2185

**Sergio's, Juanito's, and Bandido's
Marinas
along the boardwalk**

Facilities

Bait and Tackle
Boat Dock
Boatyard
Chandlery
Convenience store
Cybercafé
Fuel

Naval Boatyard 174-0020

Grocery store
Hotel   El Cid 178-2401
Ice
Launch ramp
Laundry
Park
Parking
Rental concession
Restaurant   Casa Mar 174-0417
Restrooms
Shops
Showers
Slips
Telephone

Hussong's Cantina

Attractions and Transportation

The city of Ensenada has much to see and do; each marina is within walking distance to downtown, where most of the tourist activities are located. Shopping, Mexican cuisine, wine tasting, museums, the blow hole, sport fishing, beach activities, and golf can all be experienced here. Visit Hussong's Cantina, the oldest bar in California, established in 1892.

City buses run up and down the street in front of the harbor, and taxis are plentiful and inexpensive. It is best to negotiate a price before you set off in a cab.

Attractions

Ensenada Visitor Bureau	(800) 310-9687 (from USA)
	178-3675
Hussong's Cantina	178-3210
Museo de Historia	177-0594
Museo Historico Regional	178-2531
U.S. Consulate	(6) 681-7400

Transportation

Bus station	178-6680
Yellow Cab	178-3475

Famous Catalina Steamship derelict in Ensenada Harbor

Launch Ramps

"Have great hopes and dare to go all out for them. Have great dreams and dare to live them. Have tremendous expectations and believe in them."

Norman Vincent Peale

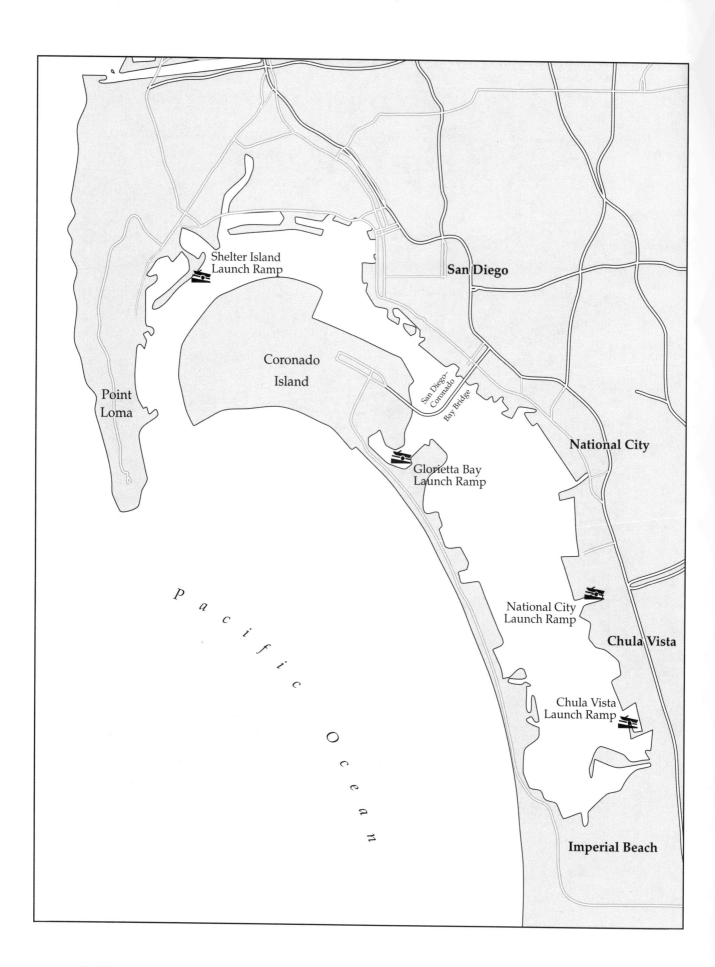

Shelter Island
Launch Ramp

San Diego

Coronado
Island

Point
Loma

San Diego–
Coronado
Bay Bridge

Glorietta Bay
Launch Ramp

National City

P a c i f i c   O c e a n

National City
Launch Ramp

Chula Vista

Chula Vista
Launch Ramp

Imperial Beach

14   SAN DIEGO BAY LAUNCH RAMPS

San Diego Bay Launch Ramps
NOAA Charts #18773, 18765

Shelter Island (Latitude 32°42.9' N, Longitude 117°13.4' W)
Glorietta Bay (Latitude 32°40.6' N, Longitude 117°10.1' W)
National City (Latitude 32°38.9' N, Longitude 117°06.6' W)
Chula Vista (Latitude 32°37.3' N, Longitude 117°06.2' W)

Shelter Island Launch Ramp

Latitude 32° 42.9' N, Longitude 117° 13.4' W (Outside launch ramp)

Shelter Island launch ramp near Point Loma is the closest ramp in San Diego Bay to open ocean. The free, eight lane, fourteen-percent grade, concrete ramp is open twenty-four hours a day. A small breakwater protects the ramp and dinghy dock from boat wakes and surge. Green grass, trees, and jogging and biking trails surround the area, making it a fine place for picnicking with an excellent view of the city and bay.

Fishing is allowed anywhere in the bay except in designated swimming, water skiing, and restricted military areas. In the bay, catch jack smelt, topsmelt, bass, halibut, croaker, opaleye, bonito, perch, shark, and ray. Anchoring is not allowed in the bay except in designated areas. In the ocean, catch croaker, rockfish, bass, mackerel, whitefish, barracuda, lingcod, sheephead, yellowtail, and albacore.

Local Weather Service (858) 289-1212

Shelter Island Launch Ramp

San Diego Harbor Police (619) 223-1133
SeaTow (888) 473-2869
Tow Boat U.S. (800) 493-7869
Vessel Assist (800) 399-1921

Land Approach

Two miles north of downtown San Diego, exit Interstate 5 at Rosecrans Street. Drive west on Rosecrans Street past the U.S. Naval Training Center; three miles from the freeway turn south onto Shelter Island Drive. The launch ramp and parking area are across from Humphrey's Restaurant on Shelter Island.

Facilities

Bait and tackle	Shelter Island Bait and Tackle (619) 222-7635
Chandlery	Boat US (619) 298-3020
	Downwind Marine (619) 224-2733
	West Marine (619) 225-8844
Dinghy dock	
Fresh water washdown	
Grocery store	
Hotels	Bay Club (800) 672-0800
	Island Palms (619) 222-0561
Launch ramp	
Restaurants	Fiddler's Green (619) 222-2216
	Humphrey's (619) 224-3411
	Sam Choy's Bali Hai (619) 222-1181
Restrooms	
Telephone	

Glorietta Bay Launch Ramp
Latitude 32°40.6' N, Longitude 117°10.1' W (Outside Launch Ramp)

Glorietta Bay launch ramp, one mile south of the City of Coronado, provides immediate access to central San Diego Bay. The free, three lane, fifteen percent grade, concrete launch ramp is open twenty-four hours a day. It is located in the southwest corner of Glorietta Bay, just north of Glorietta Bay Park. Adjacent to the ramp are a protected swimming beach and a green grassy park with play equipment. Across the road is surfing at Silver Strand Beach. This is a great area to take the family for an afternoon outing on the water.

Fishing is allowed anywhere in the bay except in designated swimming, water skiing, and restricted military areas. In the bay, catch jack smelt, topsmelt, bass, halibut, croaker, opaleye, bonito, perch, shark, and ray. Anchoring is not allowed in the bay except in specific designated areas. In the ocean, catch croaker, rockfish, bass, mackerel, whitefish, barracuda, lingcod, sheephead, yellowtail, and albacore.

Local Weather Service (858) 289-1212
San Diego Harbor Police (619) 223-1133
SeaTow (888) 473-2869
Tow Boat U.S. (800) 493-7869
Vessel Assist (800) 399-1921

Glorietta Bay Launch Ramp

Land Approach

Two miles south of downtown San Diego, exit Interstate 5 at Coronado, or State Highway 75, and proceed west across the Coronado Bay Bridge. Five blocks past the toll plaza turn south on Orange Avenue. Travel on Orange Avenue one mile past downtown Coronado. The launch ramp and parking area will be on the left just past the Coronado Municipal Swimming Pool.

Facilities

Boat dock
Fresh water washdown
Launch ramp
Hotels   Hotel del Coronado (619) 435-6611
                                Glorietta Bay Inn (619) 435-3101
Park
Parking
Restaurant   Coronado Boathouse (619) 435-4237
Restroom
Swimming
Surfing
Telephone

National City Launch Ramp
Latitude 32°38.9' N, Longitude 112°06.6' W (Off Launch Ramp)

National City Launch Ramp is freeway-close and provides easy access to south central and south San Diego Bay. The free, ten lane, fifteen percent grade, concrete, lighted launch ramp is open between 6 A.M. and 10 P.M. Located in Pepper Park next to the Sweetwater Channel with acres of green grass, trees, and an adjacent fishing pier, it is an excellent place to spend a boating weekend with the family. Enjoy watching the wildlife in the Sweetwater Marsh National Wildlife Refuge just south across the Sweetwater Channel.

National City Launch Ramp

Fishing is allowed anywhere in the bay except in designated swimming, water skiing, and restricted military areas. In the bay. catch jack smelt, topsmelt, bass, halibut, croaker, opaleye, bonito, perch, shark and ray. Anchoring is not allowed in the bay except in specific designated areas. In the ocean, catch croaker, rockfish, bass, mackerel, whitefish, barracuda, lingcod, sheephead, yellowtail, and albacore.

Local Weather Service (858) 289-1212
San Diego Harbor Police (619) 223-1133

SeaTow (888) 473-2869
Tow Boat U.S. (800) 493-7869
Vessel Assist (800) 399-1921

Land Approach

Six miles south of downtown San Diego, exit Interstate 5 on Bay Marina Drive. Drive west and turn south on Tidelands Avenue. Continue through the industrialized area until you reach Pepper Park. The boat ramp and parking area are on the south edge of Pepper Park.

Facilities

Boat dock
Fishing
Fresh water washdown
Launch ramp
Park
Parking
Restrooms
Telephone

Chula Vista Launch Ramp

Latitude 32°37.3' N, Longitude 117°06.2' W (Outside Launch Ramp)

Chula Vista Launch Ramp is freeway-close and provides ready access to south San Diego Bay. The free, ten lane, fifteen percent grade, concrete ramp is open from 6 A.M. to 10 P.M. Acres of trees, green grass, and walking trails of Bay Front Park adjacent to the ramp make it an excellent place for a family day outing.

Chula Vista Launch Ramp

Fishing is allowed anywhere in the bay except in designated swimming, water skiing and restricted military areas. In the bay, catch jack smelt, topsmelt, bass, halibut, croaker, opaleye, bonito, perch, shark, and ray. Anchoring is not allowed in the bay except in specific designated areas. In the ocean, catch croaker, rockfish, bass, mackerel, whitefish, barracuda, lingcod, sheephead, yellowtail, and albacore.

Local Weather Service (858) 289-1212
San Diego Harbor Police (619) 223-1133
SeaTow (888) 473-2869
Tow Boat U.S. (800) 493-7869
Vessel Assist (800) 399-1921

Land Approach

Six miles south of downtown San Diego, exit Interstate 5 at Marina Parkway. Drive west and turn left on Marina View: the launch ramp and parking are at the end of the road in Bay Front Park.

Facilities

Bait and tackle	Bay View Nautical (619) 442-9028
Boat dock	
Chandlery	Bay View Nautical (619) 442-9028
	West Marine (619) 422-1904
Fishing	
Fresh water washdown	
Launch ramp	
Park	
Parking	
Restaurants	Galley Restaurant (619) 422-5714
	Bob's By the Bay (619) 476-0400
Restrooms	
Telephone	

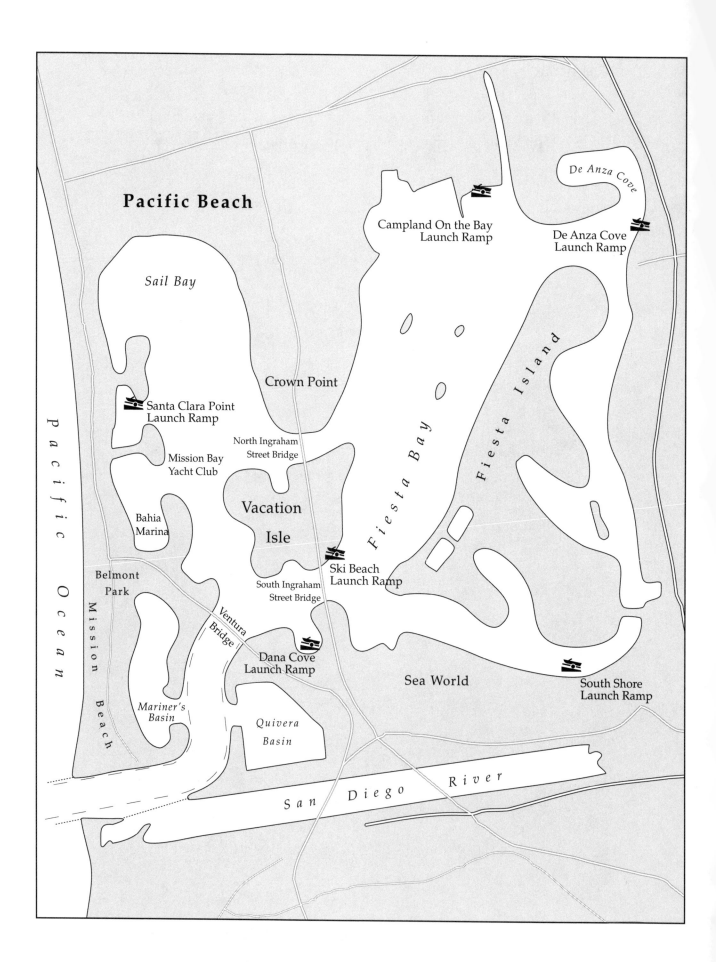

Pacific Beach

Sail Bay

Campland On the Bay
Launch Ramp

De Anza Cove

De Anza Cove
Launch Ramp

Crown Point

Santa Clara Point
Launch Ramp

Mission Bay
Yacht Club

North Ingraham
Street Bridge

Fiesta Bay

Fiesta Island

Bahia
Marina

Vacation
Isle

P a c i f i c   O c e a n

Belmont
Park

South Ingraham
Street Bridge

Ski Beach
Launch Ramp

Ventura
Bridge

M i s s i o n   B e a c h

Dana Cove
Launch Ramp

Sea World

South Shore
Launch Ramp

*Mariner's
Basin*

*Quivera
Basin*

S a n   D i e g o   R i v e r

15 MISSION BAY LAUNCH RAMPS

Mission Bay Launch Ramps
NOAA Chart #18765

De Anza Cove (Latitude 32°47.8' N, Longitude 117°12.6' W)
South Shore (Latitude 32°45.9' N, Longitude 117°13.0' W)
Dana Cove (Latitude 32°46.1' N, Longitude 117°14.2' W)
Ski Beach (Latitude 32°46.4' N, Longitude 117°13.9' W)
Santa Clara Point (Latitude 32°46.9' N, Longitude 117°15.0' W)
Campland On The Bay (Latitude 32°47.6' N, Longitude 117°13.3' W)
South Shore Launch Ramp (Latitude 32°45.9' N, Longitude 117°13.0' W)

De Anza Cove Launch Ramp
Latitude 32°47.8' N, Longitude 117°12.6' W (Off Launch Ramp)

De Anza Cove ramp is located in the northeast corner of Mission Bay Park adjacent to Interstate 5. The free, five lane, ten-percent grade, concrete ramp is open twenty-four hours a day. Grassy lawns, sandy beaches, swimming areas, and walking trails surround the popular ramp. Adjacent to popular Fiesta Bay water ski areas, it is a perfect spot to spend a day at the beach with the family.

Anchoring and fishing are allowed anywhere in Mission Bay except in designated swimming and skiing areas. In the bay, catch croaker, halibut, bonito, surfperch, sand bass, topsmelt, and jack smelt. In the ocean, catch mackerel, rockfish, kelp bass, bonito, whitefish, barracuda, lingcod, yellowtail, and white croaker.

Local Weather Service (858) 289-1212

Mission Bay Park (619) 221-8900

San Diego Lifeguards (619) 221-8899

SeaTow (888) 473-2869

Tow Boat U.S. (800) 493-7869

Vessel Assist (800) 399-1921

De Anza Cove Launch Ramp

Land Approach

Two miles north of downtown San Diego, exit Interstate 5 at Claremont Drive. Drive west and then turn north on North Mission Bay Drive. The launch ramp and parking area will be approximately 200 feet on the left.

Facilities

Boat dock
Fishing
Fresh-water washdown
Hotel   Hilton San Diego Resort (619) 276-4010
Launch ramp
Park
Parking
Restrooms
Swimming
Telephone

South Shore Launch Ramp
Latitude 32°45.9' N, Longitude 117°13.0' W (Off Launch Ramp)

South Shore is a new launch ramp located at the southeast corner of Mission Bay Park just east of Sea World. The free, lighted, twelve-lane, ten-percent grade, concrete ramp is open twenty-four hours a day. Green grass, swimming beaches, picnic tables, and walking trails surround the new, clean facility. The spacious parking lot provides excellent parking for large motor homes. Practice your first launch on the uncrowded, wide ramps.

South Shore Launch Ramp

Anchoring and fishing are allowed anywhere in Mission Bay except in designated swimming and skiing areas. In the bay, catch croaker, halibut, bonito, surfperch, sand bass, top smelt, and jack smelt. In the ocean, catch mackerel, rockfish, kelp bass, bonito, whitefish, barracuda, lingcod, yellowtail, and white croaker.

Local Weather Service (858) 289-1212

Mission Bay Park (619) 221-8900

San Diego Lifeguards (619) 221-8899

	(619) 221-8800 (after hours/weekends)
Tow Boat U.S.	(800) 493-7869
Vessel Assist	(800) 399-1921

Land Approach

Two miles north of downtown San Diego, exit Interstate 5 at Sea World Drive. Follow the signs to Sea World and turn right on South Shore Drive just before Sea World parking lot.

Facilities

Boat Dock
Fishing
Fresh water washdown
Launch ramp
Park
Parking
Restrooms
Swimming
Telephone

Dana Cove Launch Ramp
Latitude 32°46.1' N, Longitude 117°14.2' W (Off Launch Ramp)

Dana Cove Launch Ramp, located on the southwest side of Mission Bay Park, is the closest ramp to the ocean. The free, eight lane, ten-percent grade, concrete, lighted ramp is open twenty-four hours a day. Close ocean proximity and a nearby hotel, restaurant, and bait and tackle shop provide convenience for boaters. The beautiful park setting with bike paths and jogging trails adjacent to Sea World make this an excellent family holiday spot. The Dana Inn and Marina have water sport rentals, pump out, and fuel.

Dana Cove Launch Ramp

Anchoring and fishing are allowed anywhere in Mission Bay except in desig-
ated swimming and skiing areas. In the bay, catch croaker, halibut, bonito, surf-
h, sand bass, topsmelt, and jack smelt. In the ocean, catch mackerel, rockfish,
ass, bonito, whitefish, barracuda, lingcod, yellowtail, and white croaker.

Local Weather Service	(858) 289-1212
Mission Bay Park	(619) 221-8900

San Diego Lifeguards	(619) 221-8899
	(619) 221-8800 (after hours/weekends)
SeaTow	(888) 473-2869
Tow Boat U.S.	(800) 493-7869
Vessel Assist	(800) 399-1921

Land Approach

Two miles north of downtown San Diego, exit Interstate 5 at Sea World Drive. Proceed west past Sea World and follow the signs to West Mission Bay Drive. From West Mission Bay Drive turn right on Dana Landing Road; the launch ramp is east of the Dana Hotel and Marina.

Facilities

Bait and tackle	
Boat dock	
Fresh water washdown	
Fuel	
Hotel	Dana Inn and Marina (619) 222-6440
Launch ramp	
Park	
Parking	
Rental Concessions	
Restaurants	Dana Inn Restaurant (619) 222-6440
Restrooms	
Swimming	
Telephone	

Ski Beach Launch Ramp
Latitude 32°46.4 N, Longitude 117°13.9' W) (Outside Launch Ramp)

Ski Beach launch ramp is in the center of Mission Bay Park, adjacent to Fiesta Bay water ski area. The free, five lane, thirteen-percent grade, concrete, lighted ramp is open twenty-four hours a day. Grassy lawns, white sand beaches, and miles of walking and jogging trails make this an excellent place to picnic and water ski for the day.

Ski Beach Launch Ramp

Anchoring and fishing are allowed anywhere in Mission Bay except in designated swimming and water skiing areas. In the bay, catch croaker, halibut, bonito, surfperch, sand bass, topsmelt, and jack smelt. In the ocean, catch mackerel, rockfish, kelp bass, bonito, whitefish, barracuda, lingcod, yellowtail, and white croaker.

Local Weather Service	(858) 289-1212
Mission Bay Park	(619) 221-8900
San Diego Lifeguards	(619) 221-8899
	(619) 221-8800 (after hours/weekends)

SeaTow	(888) 473-2869
Tow Boat U.S.	(800) 493-7869
Vessel Assist	(800) 399-1921

Land Approach

Two miles north of downtown San Diego, exit Interstate 5 on Sea World Drive and proceed west past Sea World. Follow the signs to Ingram Street and drive north. Pass over the first bridge and turn right on Vacation Road. The launch ramp and parking area are on the south end of Vacation Isle.

Facilities

Boat dock
Fresh water washdown
Launch ramp
Park
Parking
Restrooms
Telephone

Santa Clara Point Launch Ramp
Latitude 32°46.9' N, Longitude 117°15.0' W (Outside Launch Area)

Santa Clara Point launch ramp is located on the northwest side of Mission Bay Park, adjacent to Sail Bay. The free, one lane, eleven-percent grade, concrete ramp is open twenty-four hours a day. Sandy beaches and walking and jogging trails abound in the area; surfing at Mission Beach is just across the street. Mission Bay Aquatic Center, near the ramp, has all types of watercraft for rent. This is a great place to sail, surf, and enjoy all types of water sports with your friends and family.

Santa Clara Point Launch Ramp

Anchoring and fishing are allowed anywhere in Mission Bay except in designated swimming and water skiing areas. In the bay, catch croaker, halibut, bonito, surfperch, sand bass, topsmelt, and jack smelt. In the ocean, catch mackerel, rockfish, kelp bass, bonito, whitefish, barracuda, lingcod, yellowtail, and white croaker.

Local Weather Service	(858) 289-1212
Mission Bay Park	(619) 221-8900
San Diego Lifeguards	(619) 221-8899

	(619) 221-8800 (after hours/weekends)
SeaTow	(888) 473-2869
Tow Boat U.S.	(800) 493-7869
Vessel Assist	(800) 399-1921

Land Approach

Two miles north of downtown San Diego, exit Interstate 5 at Sea World Drive and continue west past Sea World. Follow the signs to West Mission Bay Drive. Continue on West Mission Bay Drive to Mission Boulevard and turn north. Drive three quarters of a mile and turn right on Santa Clara Place. The launch ramp and parking area will be on the right.

Facilities

Boat dock	
Fresh water washdown	
Hotel	Catamaran Hotel (858) 488-1081
Launch Ramp	
Park	
Parking	
Rental Concessions	Catamaran Hotel (858) 488-1081
	Mission Bay Aquatic Center (858) 488-1036
Restaurant	Catamaran Hotel (858) 488-1081
Restrooms	
Surfing	
Telephone	

Campland on the Bay Launch Ramp
Latitude 32°47.6' N, Longitude 117°13.3' W (Off Launch Ramp)

Campland on the Bay launch ramp is located in the north side of Mission Bay Park adjacent to Fiesta Bay water skiing area. The four lane, thirteen-percent grade, concrete ramp is operated by Campland on the Bay. A fee is charged to launch; however, this fee provides access to all Campland facilities, such as camping, laundry facilities, fuel dock, bait and tackle, groceries, and hardware. The Northern Wildlife Preserve is just west of the ramp. Campland on the Bay is an excellent place to spend a vacation camping and using all the facilities in Mission Bay Park.

Campland on the Bay Launch Ramp

Anchoring and fishing are allowed anywhere in Mission Bay except in designated swimming and water skiing areas. In the bay, catch croaker, halibut, bonito, surfperch, sand bass, topsmelt, and jack smelt. In the ocean, catch mackerel, rockfish, kelp bass, bonito, whitefish, barracuda, lingcod, yellowtail, and white croaker.

Local Weather Service	(858) 289-1212
Mission Bay Park	(619) 221-8900
San Diego Lifeguards	(619) 221-8899
	(619) 221-8800 (after hours/weekends)
SeaTow	(888) 473-2869
Tow Boat U.S.	(800) 493-7869
Vessel Assist	(800) 399-1921

Land Access

Three miles north of downtown San Diego, exit Interstate 5 at Grand Avenue or Garnett Avenue and travel west. After one mile, turn south on Olney Street, continue three or four blocks, and turn east on Pacific Beach Drive. This will lead you to the entrance of Campland on the Bay.

Facilities

Bait and tackle	Campland on the Bay (858) 581-4224
Boat dock	
Convenience store	Campland on the Bay (858) 581-4215
Fresh water washdown	
Ice	
Launch ramp	
Park	
Parking	
Rental concessions	
Restaurant	Campland on the Bay (858) 490-3389
Restrooms	
R.V. Park	Campland on the Bay (858) 581-4260
Telephone	

INDEX

A

abalone 80, 116, 236, 238, 241
aids to navigation
  beacons 44, 245
  buoys
    #01 82, 148, 154
    #02 148, 154
    #05 61
    #08 148
    #15 61, 70
    #17 76
    #19 76, 82, 91, 99
    #21 105, 112, 118
    #23 138
    #32 160
    #39 176
    #40 166, 170, 185, 191
    #41 191
    danger buoy 245
    OC 244
    San Diego entrance 61
    SD 251, 257
  lights 160, 234, 245
  markers
    #01 166, 185
    #02 166
    #12 191
    #16 191
  navigation rules
    inland rules 44
    international rules 44
  publications
    Local Notice to Mariners 44
    nautical charts 43
    U. S. Coast Pilot 44
    U.S. Coast Guard Light Lists 44
    U.S. Aids to Navigation System 44

All Saints Bay 251, 257
All Saints Inlet 255
American Plaza Transfer Station 101, 107, 132
America's Cup Harbor 77, 80–84
anchorages
  Ensenada Harbor 252
  Gold Coast Anchorage 60, 63
  Half Moon Anchorage 60, 63

A anchorages cont.

  La Playa Cove 67
  overnight 223
  protected 67, 103, 210, 212, 235, 240
  quiet 67, 146, 164, 183, 210
  Silver Strand State Beach 164-168
  Sweetwater/South Bay 169-173

anchoring 45
  permits 53

anchors
  Bruce 45
  CQR 45
  Danforth 45

Anthony's Fish Grotto 107, 117
Anthony's Star of the Sea Room 107, 113
ARCO Olympic Training Center 193
Army Corps of Engineers 243
Atlantic Richfield Company 184

B

B-Street Pier 110
Babcock 146, 153
Babcock and Story 20, 183
Babcock and Story Wharf 109
Bahía de San Mateo 255
Bahía de Todos Santos 251, 257
Bahía de Tortugas 255
Bahía Hotel 218, 219
bait and tackle
    64, 72, 78, 85, 192, 205, 208, 218, 227,
    247, 253, 258, 265, 271, 278, 279, 284, 285
Baja Naval Boatyard and Marina 255, 258
Balboa Park 21, 65, 110
Ballast Point 61, 70, 74, 76, 88
Bandido's Boats and Marina 256, 258
barrier islands 27
bars
  Hussong's Cantina 259
  Shakespeare Pub and Grille 120
  The Waterfront 117

Bay Bridge Roadstead 141–145

B cont.

Bay Club Hotel 62, 78
Bay Club Marina 60, 62
Bay View Nautical 192, 271
Bayside Park 190
Beaufort Scale 30
Belmont Park 65, 202, 209, 213
Belt Line Railroad 137
Belt Train 164
Benchley, Belle 111
Berkeley 110
Bessemer Street 70
Birch Aquarium 202
boatyards
    Baja Naval Boatyard 258
    Driscoll Boat Works 78
    Driscoll Boatyard 64
    Driscoll Mission Bay 208
    Kettenburg Marine 64, 78
    Knight and Carver Boatyard 170
    Koehler Kraft Yard 64, 78
    Nielsen Beaumont Marine 64, 78
    Nielsen Beaumont Yard 64
    Shelter Island Boatyard 64, 78
    South Bay Boatyard 190

Boat/US Marine Center 208
Boathouse Restaurant 101
boats
    Berkeley 110
    commercial 125
    Della 136
    ferryboats
        Benecia 137
        Coronado 137
        Crown City 137
        Ramona 137
    Medina 110

Border Field State Park 162, 168, 184, 186
Brennan, Joe 110
bridge
    clearance
        thirty-eight feet 222, 225, 226
        thirty-one feet 221, 225
        thirty-six feet 221, 222, 225, 226
    Coronado Bay
        137, 138, 141, 142, 147, 160
    Ingraham Street 221
    North Ingraham Street 225
    South Ingraham Street 225
    Ventura 201, 205, 225

Brigantine Restaurant 150, 156

B cont.

Broadway Pier 20, 23, 109, 126, 137

C

Cabrillo Isle Marina 100
Cabrillo, Juan Rodriguez
    14, 152, 183, 200, 232, 238, 255
Cabrillo National Monument 65, 75, 202
California current 36
California Southern Railroad 174, 190
California State Park Commission 164
California State Park System 200
California Yacht Marina 190, 192
California/Panama Exposition 21, 110
Californian 96
Camp Pendleton Marine Base 243
Camp Pendleton Military Reservation 243
Campland Marina 199, 225-228
Campland On The Bay 225
Campland on the Bay Launch Ramp 284–285
Canalino Indians 237
Captain Vila 15
Carillo, Pedro 153, 183
Catamaran Resort Hotel 219
cave painting 255
Centennial Park 138
chandleries
    Bay View Nautical 192, 271
    Boat/US Marine Center 208
    Downwind Marine 64, 78
    Horizon Marine 100
    Pablo's Crews 247
    San Diego Marine Exchange 64, 78
    West Marine 64, 78, 208, 271

Chart House Restaurant 131
charts
    America's Cup Harbor 82
    Central Bay 134
    Chula Vista 188
    Coronado Ferry Landing 138
    Coronado Islands 234
    Dana Cove 217
    El Coral, B.C. 252
    Embarcadero 112
    Ensenada, B.C. 256
    Fiddler's Cove 161
    G Street Mole 124
    La Playa Cove 71
    Laurel Street Roadstead 118
    Mariner's Basin 211
    Marriott Marina 130
    Mission Bay 198

C charts cont.

Mission Bay Launch Ramps 272
Naval Sailing Center, Point Loma, 91
North Bay 56
Oceanside 246
San Diego Bay 12
San Diego Bay Launch Ramps 262
Shelter Island Roadstead 76
Shelter Island Yacht Basin 58
South Bay 180
Sweetwater/South Bay 170
West Mission Bay 217

China Camp 107
Chula Vista 189–195
Chula Vista Launch Ramp 270–271
Chula Vista Marina 190, 192
Chula Vista Nature Center 193
Chula Vista R.V. Resort 192
Chula Vista Yacht Club 190, 192
Clarion Hotel Bay View 131
coastal plains 27
Cochimi Indians 255
concessions
boat rentals 92, 158, 161, 207, 227, 251
Downtown Boat Rental 132
San Diego Yacht Charters 100
Seaforth Boat Rentals 209
Seaforth Coronado 150
watercraft rental
Mission Bay Aquatic Center 282

Conner, Dennis 81
controlling flood channel 28
Convair Lagoon 105
Convention Center 24
Coor's Amphitheater 193
Coronado 146, 152–157
Coronado Bay Bridge 137, 142, 148, 154, 160
Coronado Beach Company 20, 136, 146, 164
Coronado Beach Railroad 136
Coronado Boathouse 146, 148, 150, 156
Coronado Brick Company 136
Coronado Cays 183–187
Coronado Cays Channel 166
Coronado Cays Yacht Club 184, 185
Coronado Ferry 23
Coronado Ferry Landing 23, 136–140, 164
Coronado Golf Course 147
Coronado Hospital
Coronado Islands 232–236
Coronado Municipal Swimming Pool 267
Coronado Playhouse 151, 157
Coronado Railroad 153

C cont.

Coronado Railroad Company 164
Coronado Water Company 136
Coronado Yacht Club 148, 154
Cortez Fuel Dock 101
Courtesy Marine Examinations 52
Crown Cove 166
Cruise, Tom 248
Cruiseport Marina 257
Cruiseport Terminal 257
Cruiseport Village Marina 255
Cruising Anchorage 71, 77, 99, 103-109
Curiel Amaya family 250
current
California 36
range 36
rate of flow 36
cause 35
crosscurrent deflection 36
Davidson 36
range 36
definition 35
eddies 36
San Diego Bay 36
direction 36
velocity 36
sheer 36
slack water 36
wind-driven 36
velocity 36

Curtis, Tony 157
Cuyamaca Mountains 199
Cuyamaca Rancho 165
cybercafé 258
cyclones 33

D

Dana Cove 199, 216, 216–220
Dana Cove Launch Ramp 278–279
Dana Inn and Marina 219
Dana Point 68
Davidson current 36
De Anza Cove Launch Ramp 274-275
Del Mar Boat Basin 244
Del Mar Marina and Sailing Center 246
deltas 27
Derby Dyke 17, 27
derelict 260
Diegueños Indians 14
Discovery 15
docks

D docks cont.

dinghy
78, 85, 103, 104, 105, 106, 113, 119, 120, 125, 131, 143, 148, 149, 150, 156, 170, 172, 173, 174, 177, 253, 264, 265
fuel 207
Cortez Fuel Dock 101
Harbor Island Fuel Dock 101
High Seas Fuel Dock 85
Islandia Fuel Dock 208
guest 155, 192
Anthony's Fish Grotto Restaurant 113
public 207
transient 61, 125, 155
commercial 125

Downtown Boat Rental 132
Downwind Marine 64, 78
Driscoll Boat Works 78
Driscoll Boat Yard 64
Driscoll Mission Bay 208
Driscoll Mission Bay Marina 207
Driscoll's Wharf 84
Dutch Flats 21, 89

E

El Camino Real 189
El Coral 250–254
El Coral Hotel and Marina 250
Eleventh Naval District 90
Embarcadero 109–115
Embarcadero Marina Park 131
Embassy Suites San Diego 125
embayed coasts 27
Ensenada 255–260
Ensenada de Todos Santos 255
Ensenada Harbor 252
estuaries 27

F

False Bay 17, 200
Father Jayme 15
ferries
Coronado Ferry 23
San Diego-Coronado Ferry 145

ferry 141
Ferry Landing 136, 153
Fiddler's Cove 158–163
Fiddler's Cove Marina 158
Fiddler's Cove RV Park 158
Fiddler's Cove Yacht Club 159

F cont.

Fiddler's Green 64, 78
Fiddler's Green Restaurant 65
Fiesta Bay 225, 226, 228
fishing industry 116
Chinese 80
Italian 81
Portuguese 81
sardine canning 255
tuna 20, 117, 122
United States Tuna Association 122
whaling 17

fishing pier 131, 137, 177, 191, 257, 268
Fleet Anti-Submarine Warfare Training Center 90
Flying Leatherneck Aviation Museum 65
Foreign Miner's Tax 18
Fort Cobblestones 88
Fort Guijarros 15, 88
fuel
51, 65, 85, 97, 99, 205, 207, 218, 219, 247, 252, 253, 254, 255, 258, 278, 279
fur seals 116

G

G Street Mole 122–127
Gaslamp District 128
Gaslamp Quarter 123, 126
Gaspar de Portolá 68
Ghio family 116
Glorietta Bay 146-151
Glorietta Bay Inn 147
Glorietta Bay Launch Ramp 266–267
Glorietta Bay Marina 148, 154
Glorietta Bay Park 148
Glorietta Boulevard 142
Gold Coast Anchorage 63
Golden Triangle 24
Goodrich 190
Governor Edmund (Pat) Brown 142
Grand Caribe Island 185
Great White Fleet 20
Gruendike 153
Grumwald 146

H

Half Moon Anchorage 63
Harbor House Restaurant 132
Harbor Island 23, 31, 71, 95–99
Harbor Island Fuel Dock 101
Harbor Island Park 100

H cont.

Harbor Island West Marina 99
Harbor Police 33
harbors
   protected 190, 255
   quiet 189, 242, 248

hazards to navigation
   background lights 245
   chop 116, 141, 172
   debris 172
   derelicts 169, 172
   kelp 61, 234, 235, 238, 240
   lee shores 235
   lights 191, 245, 252
   obstruction 37, 170, 172
   sandbar 59
   shallow water
     35, 37, 43, 171, 190, 201, 211, 217
   sheer 36
   shipping lanes 239
   shoal
     36, 37, 59, 82, 131, 143, 148, 154,
      176, 191, 201, 206, 211, 217, 222, 226
   shoal water 37
   strong currents 234
   submerged objects
     jetty 37, 61, 245
   surge 77, 208, 233, 235, 240
   waves 245
   wind 141, 172, 190, 240, 251

Hedgecock, Roger 131
Henry, Richard Dana 16
High Seas Fuel Dock 85
Hilton San Diego Airport Hotel 101
Holiday Inn at the Embarcadero 120
Holiday Inn on the Bay 106, 113, 125
Holiday Inn San Diego Bayside 85, 93
Horizon Marine 100
Horton, Alonzo 18, 122, 190
Horton Plaza 123, 126
Horton Wharf 109
Horton-Grand Hotel 123
Hotel del Coronado
   20, 137, 146, 148, 152, 154, 157, 164, 183
Hotel San Nicolas 257
hotels
   Anthony's Star of the Sea Room 107
   Bahía Hotel 218
   Bay Club Hotel 62, 78
   Catamaran Resort Hotel 219
   Clarion Hotel Bay View 131
   Dana Inn and Marina 219

H hotels cont.

   Embassy Suites San Diego 125
   Glorietta Bay Inn 156
   Hilton San Diego Airport 101
   Holiday Inn at the Embarcadero 120
   Holiday Inn on the Bay 106, 113, 125
   Holiday Inn San Diego Bayside 85, 93
   Horton-Grand Hotel 123
   Hotel del Coronado 156
   Hotel San Nicolas 257
   Humphrey's Half Moon Inn and Suites 63, 78
   Hyatt Hotel 207
   Hyatt Islandia Resort 201, 208, 211, 213
   Hyatt Regency San Diego 131
   Island Palms Hotel 62, 78
   La Avenida Inn 156
   Lowe's Coronado Bay Resort Hotel 184
   Lowe's Coronado Resort 185
   Oceanside Marina Inn 247
   Pacific Inn Hotel 106, 113, 120
   Residence Inn by Marriott 106, 113, 120
   San Diego Marriott Hotel 131
   Shelter Point Hotel 78, 85
   Shelter Point Hotel and Marina 62
   Sheraton Harbor Island 101
   Travel Lodge Point Loma 93
   U.S. Grant Hotel 125
   Vagabond Inn Point Loma 85, 93
   Westgate 125

Howland, Charles 238
Humphrey's Half Moon 78
Humphrey's Half Moon Inn 78
Humphrey's Half Moon Inn and Suites 63
Humphrey's Restaurant 64, 78, 265
Hussong's Cantina 259
Hyatt Hotel 207
Hyatt Islandia Resort 201, 208, 211, 213
Hyatt Islandia Restaurant 209, 213
Hyatt Regency San Diego 131

I

Imperial Beach 137, 164
indigenous people
   Canalino Indians 237
   Cochimi Indians 255
   Diegueños Indians 14
   Jamacha Indians 189
   Kumeyaay Indians 13
   La Jollan Indians 13
   Luiseños Indians 14, 242

Ingraham Street bridges 221

I cont.

inspection 52, 169
inspection dock 52
Island Palms Hotel 62, 78
Islandia Fuel Dock 208
Islandia Marina 207

J

Jamacha Indians 189
Jamul Mountains 191
Japanese Garden and Friendship Bell 60
Juanito's Boats and Marina 256
Julian 18
Junípero Serra, Father 15, 68, 189
junks 18

K

Kansas City Barbeque 125
Kendall Frost Wildlife Preserve 228
Kettenburg Marine 64, 78
Kimball, Frank 18, 174, 190
Kimball Wharf 109
Knight and Carver Boatyard 170
knots 45
Knott's Soak City 193
Koehler Kraft Yard 64, 78
Kona Kai International Yacht Club 62
Kumeyaay Indians 13, 174, 200

L

La Avenida Inn 156
La Jolla 23, 201
La Jollan Indians 13, 200
La Playa 68, 80
La Playa Cove 67–73, 77, 83
La Victoria 238
Lamb's Players Theatre 150, 157
landmarks
    apartment building 245
    evaporation ponds 191
    Hotel del Coronado 152
    Hyatt Islandia Resort Tower 201
    Marriott Towers Hotel 128
    municipal fishing pier 201
    Oceanside sign 244
    power generating plant 191
    radar dome 239
    rock breakwater 257
    rock quarry 257
    salt mounds 191
    San Diego Convention Center 128
    San Miguel peak 191

L landmarks cont.

    Sea World tower 201
latitude 43
launch ramps
    Campland on the Bay Launch Ramp 284
    Chula Vista Launch Ramp 270
    National City Launch Ramp 268
    Shelter Island Launch Ramp 264
    South Shore Launch Ramp 276
    twenty-four hour
        Dana Cove Launch Ramp 278
        De Anza Cove 274
        Glorietta Bay 266
        Santa Clara Point Launch Ramp 282
        Shelter Island 264
        Ski Beach Launch Ramp 280
        South Shore Launch Ramp 276

launching 50
Laurel Street Roadstead 116-121, 130
Legoland California 249
Liberty Carousel 209
Lifeguard Services Division 207
lighthouse 17, 75
    Ballast Point 17
    Cabrillo National Monument 75
    Point Loma Light 75

lights 160, 191, 234, 245, 252
    north jetty light 201
    south jetty light 201

Lindbergh Field 21, 95, 103, 107, 117
lines 45
Little Italy 116
lobster 233, 236, 241
Local Notice to Mariners 44
Local Weather Service 61
Loews Crown Isle Marina 184, 185
longitude 43
low pressure centers 29
Lowe's Coronado Bay Resort Hotel 184
Lowe's Coronado Resort 185
Luiseños Indians 14, 242
Lutteroth Valle family 250

M

March Air Base 159
Marina Cortez 99
Marina Parkway Pier 192
Marina View Park 190
Marina Village Marina 207

marinas
Baja Naval Boatyard and Marina 255, 258
Bandido's Boats and Marina 256
Bay Club Marina 60, 62
Cabrillo Isle Marina 100
California Yacht Marina 190, 192
Campland Marina 225-228
Chula Vista Marina 190, 192
close to ocean
Dana Cove 216
West Mission Bay 216
Coronado Cays Yacht Club Marina 184, 185
Cruiseport Marina 257
Cruiseport Village Marina 255
Del Mar Marina and Sailing Center 246
Driscoll Mission Bay Marina 207
Driscoll's Wharf 84
El Coral Hotel and Marina 250
Fiddler's Cove Marina 158
Harbor Island West Marina 99
Islandia Marina 207
Juanito's Boats and Marina 256
Loews Crown Isle Marina 184, 185
Marina Cortez 99
Marina Village Marina 207
military
Fiddler's Cove 158
Marine Corps. Recruit Depot Boathouse 88
U.S. Naval Sailing Center 88
Montego Bay Marina 184, 185
protected 160, 206
quiet 88, 193
Seaforth Marina 207
Sergio's Sport Fishing Center and Marina 256
Shelter Cove Marina 84
Shelter Island Marina 60
Shelter Point Hotel and Marina 60, 62
Sheraton Harbor Island Marina 100
Sun Harbor Marina 84
Sunroad Resort Marina 100

Marine Corps. Recruit Depot 89
Marine Corps. Recruit Depot Boathouse 88
Marine Corps. Recruit Depot Museum 65
Mariner's Basin 199, 210–214
Marriott Coronado Island Resort 142
Marriott Marina 128–133
Marriott Towers Hotel 128
Marston, George 21
Maytime Band Review 173, 178
Medina 110
Mexican border 30
Mexican Customs 250

Mexican fishing license 232, 236
Mexican-American War 153
Middle Town 80
Miguel's Cocina 86, 150, 156
military reservation
Camp Pendleton 243
San Clemente Island 237
Millinix Drive 142
Miramar 26
Mission Basilica San Diego de Alcalá 65
Mission Bay 17, 22, 26, 199–203
Mission Bay Aquatic Center 282
Mission Bay channel 211, 222, 226
Mission Bay Golf Course 228
Mission Bay Park 65, 202, 205
Mission Bay Park Headquarters 207
Mission Bay Yacht Club 218
Mission San Diego de Alcalá 15, 69
Mission San Luis Rey 243
missions
Mission San Diego de Alcalá 15, 65, 69
Mission San Luis Rey 243
San Diego Mission 68

Mona Lisa 113, 117
Monroe, Marilyn 157
Monte Carlo 147
Montego Bay Marina 184, 185
Monterey Bay Cannery 247
Montgomery, John 20
monument 168
mooring buoys 211
mooring office 52
San Diego Unified Port District Mooring
Office 53, 61, 67

mooring permit 52
moorings
busy 77
Mediterranean 119
protected 77
quiet 141, 158

Mother of Missions 15
Mount Soledad 26

N

National City 80, 137, 164, 174–178
National City and Otay Railroad 190
National City Boat Basin 177
National City Launch Ramp 268–269

N cont.

National City Marine Terminal
    166, 170, 175, 176, 185, 191
National City Railroad Museum 173, 178
National Ocean Atmospheric Administration 43
National Steel and Ship Building
    160, 166, 176, 185, 191
National Weather Service 33
nautical charts 43
Naval Amphibious Base 89, 148, 157, 162
naval flight training school 20
Naval Repair Facility 89
Naval Sailing Center, Point Loma 88–90
navigation
    charts 43
    definition 43
    nautical charts
        description 43
    rules 44

Navy destroyer base 89
Navy Electronics Laboratory 89
Navy Frogmen 159
Navy Hospital 89
Navy pier 109
Navy SEALS 159
Navy Supply Corps 89
New Town 80, 122
Nielsen Beaumont Marine 64, 78
Nielsen Beaumont Yard 64
no-wake zone 206
North China Restaurant 93
North Island 74, 89, 152
North Island Naval Air Station
    20, 152, 157, 162
North Sails 64, 78
Northern Wildlife Preserve 284

O

Ocean Beach 201
Oceanside 242–249
Oceanside Marina Inn 247
Oceanside Yacht Club 244, 246
Old Town 17, 80, 95, 122
Old Town San Diego State Historical Park
    66, 97, 202
Old Town Transfer Station 65
Over-The-Line Tournament 202
overnight anchorage 223

P

Pablo's Crews 247

P cont.

Pacific Inn Hotel 106, 113, 120
paddleboat restaurant 105
parks
    amusement
        Belmont Park 65, 202, 209, 213
    Balboa Park 21, 65
    Bayside Park 190
    Border Field State Park 162, 168, 184, 186
    Centennial Park 138
    Embarcadero Marina Park 131
    Harbor Island Park 100
    Marina View Park 190
    Mission Bay Park 65, 202, 205
    Old Town San Diego State Historical Park
        66, 97, 202
    Pepper Park 170, 269
    Presidio Park 97
    RV 225, 227
    Shelter Island Park 60, 74
    theme
        Sea World 23, 205, 209, 213, 224
        Wild Animal Park 112
    Tidelands Park 141
    water
        Mission Bay 22
        Soak City 193

Pepper Park 170, 269
Perez Cove 199, 221–224
Pico, Pío 17, 153, 183
piers
    B-Street Pier 110
    Broadway Pier 20, 23, 109
    fishing 131, 137, 177, 191, 201, 257, 268
    Marina Parkway Pier 192
    Navy Pier 109

Pilgrim 16
Pizza Nova 93
Point Conception 30
Point Loma 26, 61, 67, 70, 75, 76, 80
Point Loma Light 61, 75
Point Loma Seafoods 86
Port Royal Swim and Tennis Club 184
Portolá, Gaspar 15
power generating plant 191
Presidio 15
Presidio Hill 88, 122
Presidio Park Historical Site 66
procuring a berth 51
provisions
    64, 72, 78, 86, 93, 99, 101, 125, 131,
    150, 156, 161, 186, 192, 208, 219, 223,

P provisions cont.

227, 247, 253, 259, 284, 285
public dock 207
pumpout
        161, 162, 193, 205, 207, 248, 252, 253
Punta del Morro 251
Punta Descanso 251, 257
Punta Salsipuedes 251, 257
Punta San Miguel 251, 257

Q

Qualcomm Stadium 66
Quivera Basin 199, 205-209, 211

R

radar dome 239
radio
    license 194
    permits 194
        Mexican 194
    VHF Channel 16 238
    weather announcements 33
    weather channels 33

railroad
    Belt Line Railroad 137
    California Southern Railroad 174
    Coronado Beach Railroad 136
    Coronado Railroad 153
    National City and Otay Railroad 190
    Southern Pacific Railroad 18
    Transcontinental Railroad 243

Rancho Carrillo 184
Rancho de la Nación 174, 190
Reagan, Ronald 142
recreation
    aquariums 202, 224
    ball park 24
    beaches 62, 67, 68, 71, 74, 75, 142,
        143, 157, 158, 166, 167, 190, 199, 210, 213,
        220, 256, 259, 266, 274, 276, 280, 282
        La Playa Cove 70
        Silver Strand Beach 266
        Silver Strand State Beach 6, 162
        Ski Beach 7
    bike paths
        95, 117, 142, 162, 168, 186, 207, 220,
        264, 278
    camping 165, 167, 225, 284

R recreation cont.

golf
    140, 147, 150, 156, 157, 200, 202, 228,
    251, 254, 259
horseback riding 251
jogging trails 210, 264, 278, 280, 282
Legoland California 249
museums
    California Surf Museum 249
    Flying Leatherneck Aviation Museum 94
    Marine Corps. Recruit Depot Museum 94
    Maritime Museum 94
    Museum of Contemporary Art 202
    National City Railroad Museum 178
    San Diego Maritime Museum 66, 94
playground 60, 142, 227, 266
rides 224
scuba diving 254
sightseeing
    monuments 60, 65, 75
surfing
    150, 156, 158, 162, 164, 165, 166, 167, 186,
    212, 213, 219, 220, 244, 248, 266, 267, 282,
    283
swimming
    Coronado Municipal Swimming Pool 267
tennis 93, 132, 150, 156, 186, 218, 251
tours
    archeological 254
    mission 254
walking trails
    97, 140, 162, 166, 168, 186, 207, 209, 210,
    212, 220, 223, 225, 244, 264, 270, 274, 276,
    278, 280, 282
water skiing
    164, 199, 223, 225, 227, 274, 280
wildlife viewing
    Kendall Frost Wildlife Preserve 228
    Northern Wildlife Preserve 284
    Sweetwater Marsh National Wildlife
    Refuge 170, 174, 268
    Tijuana River Estuary Nature Reserve
    162, 184, 186
windsurfing 190, 199
wine tasting 254, 259

Red Sails Inn 86
rescue 104
Residence Inn by Marriott 106, 113, 120
restaurants
    Anthony's Fish Grotto 107, 117
    Anthony's Star of the Sea Room 107, 113
    Bahía Hotel 218-219

R restaurants cont.

Boathouse 101
Brigantine 150, 156
Catamaran Resort Hotel 219
Chart House Restaurant 131
China Camp 107
Coronado Boathouse 148, 150, 156
Dana Inn and Marina 219
Fiddler's Green 65
Harbor House Restaurant 132
Humphrey's Restaurant 64, 78, 265
Hyatt Islandia Resort 213
Hyatt Islandia Restaraunt 209
Kansas City Barbeque 125
Miguel's Cocina 86, 150, 156
Mona Lisa 113, 117
Monterey Bay Cannery 248
North China Restaurant 93
Pizza Nova 93
Point Loma Seafoods 86
Red Sails Inn 86
Reuben's 101
Roger's on Fifth 131
Ruth Chris Steak House 113
Sam Choy's Bali Hai 64
Sam Choy's Bali Hai 78
Shakespeare Pub and Grille 120
The Field 132
The Old Spaghetti Factory 132
The Waterfront 117
Tom Ham's Lighthouse 101

Reuben's 100
Ritter, William 146
Rockwell Field 158
Roger's on Fifth 131
Rohr Industries 190
roller coaster 213
Roosevelt, Franklin D. 159, 165
Rose Canyon Fault 26
Rose Inlet 226
Roseville 80
Ruth Chris Steak House 113
RV park 164
Chula Vista R.V. Resort 192

S

Saad, Nico 257
safety
boat equipment 38, 40
checklist 39
fueling 39
towing service 42

S cont.

sail lofts
North Sails 64, 78
Ullman Sails 65, 78

Salk Institute for Biological Studies 202
salt mounds 191
Sam Choy's Bali Hai 64, 78
San Andreas Fault 26
San Antonio 15
San Carlos 15
San Clemente Island 237-241
San Diego 15
San Diego and Coronado Ferry Company 136
San Diego Convention Center 128
San Diego Land and Town Company 190
San Diego Marine Exchange 64, 78, 82
San Diego Maritime Museum 66, 110
San Diego Marriott Hotel 131
San Diego Mission 68, 70
San Diego Mooring Office 61
San Diego Naval Station 89
San Diego Port District 52, 169
San Diego River 15, 17, 199
San Diego Roadstead 75
San Diego Rowing Club 131
San Diego Sports Arena 66, 202
San Diego Trolley 132
San Diego Unified Port District Mooring Office 52, 67
San Diego Visitors Center 66
San Diego Water Taxi 65
San Diego Yacht Charters 101
San Diego Yacht Club 70
San Diego Zoo 21, 66, 111
San Diego-Coronado Bay Bridge 23, 141
San Diego-Coronado Ferry 126
San Luis Rey River 244
San Miguel 14
San Miguel Peak 191
San Salvador 14, 238
San Thomas 14
Santa Ana 31, 32
Santa Catalina Island 238
Santa Clara Point Launch Ramp 282, 282–283
Santa Fe Train Depot 114, 132
Santa Margarita Sailing Club 246
Scott Street 70
Scripps Institute of Oceanography 146
SCT permit 194
sea cliffs 27
Sea World 23, 66, 200, 205
Sea World Park 209, 213, 224
Seaforth Bait and Tackle 208

Seaforth Boat Rentals 209
Seaforth Coronado 150
Seaforth Marina 207
seamanship
   anchoring 45
     scope 46
   chain 46
   definition 45
   instruction 46
   knots 45
   lines 45
   rode 46

Seaport Village 23, 66, 126, 128, 129
Secularization Act of 1833 15, 69
Sergio's Sport Fishing Center and Marina 256
Shakespeare Pub and Grille 120
Shelter Cove Marina 84
Shelter Island 23, 31, 33, 67, 71, 132
Shelter Island Bait and Tackle 78
Shelter Island Boatyard 64, 78
Shelter Island Drive 76
Shelter Island Launch Ramp 76, 264-265
Shelter Island Marina 60
Shelter Island Park 74
Shelter Island Roadstead 74–79
Shelter Island Yacht Basin 59-66, 77, 83
Shelter Point Hotel 78, 85
Shelter Point Hotel and Marina 60, 62
Sheraton Harbor Island Hotel 101
Sheraton Harbor Island Marina 100
shopping centers
   Horton Plaza 123
   Seaport Village 23, 66

Shore Towers Condominiums 147
Silver Gate Yacht Club 62
Silver Strand Beach 75, 159, 266
Silver Strand Boulevard 160
Silver Strand Peninsula 160
Silver Strand State Beach Anchorahe 164–168
Ski Beach Launch Ramp 280–281
slip fees 189, 192
Soak City 193
Some Like It Hot 157
South Bay Boatyard 190
South Ingraham Street Bridge 222
South Shore Launch Ramp 276–277
Southern Pacific Railroad 18
Southwestern Yacht Club 70
Spanish Bight 152, 159
Spirit of St. Louis 123
Spreckel's 141

Spreckles, John D. 20, 146
stadium
   ball park 24
   Coor's Amphitheater 193
   Qualcomm Stadium 66
   San Diego Sports Arena 66, 202

Star of India 21, 109, 110, 112
Story 146, 153
Submarine Repair Base 89
submerged objects 37, 61, 245
Sun Harbor Marina 84
Sunroad Resort Marina 100
surge 208
Sweetwater Channel 170, 191
Sweetwater Marsh National Wildlife Refuge
   170, 174-175, 268
Sweetwater Marsh Refuge 170, 175
Sweetwater River Channel 171, 175
Sweetwater/South Bay Anchorage 161, 169-
   173, 192

T

Tall Ship 96
Tent City 146, 165
terraces 27
the Del 148, 154
The Field 132
The Giant Dipper 209
The Old Spaghetti Factory 132
The Russian Spring 152
The Waterfront 117
theaters
   Coronado Playhouse 151
   Lamb's Players 150

Thunder Boat Races 202
Tidelands Park 142
tides
   causes 34
   definition 34
   ebb 35
   flood 35
   forecasts 35
   inequity 35
   maximum 35
   periodicity 34
   range
     diurnal 35
     mean 35

Tijuana 154, 193

T cont.

Tijuana River Estuary Nature Reserve
    168, 184, 186
Todos Santos Islands 251, 257
toll road 251, 256
Tom Ham's Lighthouse 101
Top Gun 125
Top Gun House 248
towing services 42
trailer
    attachments
        tiedowns 47
        winches 47
    ball 48
    boat support 47
    heavy duty 47
    hitch 48
    hubs 50
    lightweight 47
    maintenance 50
    safety chains 48
    safety checklist 49
    selection 47
    tires 47
    tongue weight 48
    wheel bearings 47
    winch
        antireverse lever 48

Transcontinental Railroad 175, 243
Travel Lodge Point Loma 93
Tres Reys 14
Tuna Fisherman's Monument 60
tuna fishing industry 20
tuna fleet 81, 122
tunnel 141, 166

U

U.S. Aids to Navigation System 44
U.S. Civilian Conservation Corps 164
U.S. Coast Guard 103
U.S. Coast Guard Auxiliary 46, 52
U.S. Coast Guard Light Lists 44
U.S. Coast Guard Station 104
U.S. Coast Pilot 44
U.S. Consulate 260
U.S. Grant Hotel 125
U.S. Naval Amphibious Base 159
U.S. Naval Base 160, 166, 185
U.S. Naval Sailing Center 88
U.S. Naval Station 22, 176, 191
U.S. Naval Submarine Base 61, 70, 76

U cont.

U.S. Naval Training Center 21, 82, 90
U.S. Navy 20, 22, 88
U.S. Power Squadron 46
Ullman Sails 65, 78
Underwater Demolition Team 159
United States Tuna Association 122
University of California at San Diego 23
USS *Cyane* 17

V

Vagabond Inn Point Loma 85, 93
Vancouver, George 15
Ventura Bridge 201, 205, 217, 222, 225
VHF radio Channel 16 238
Victoria 14
Vizcaino, Sebastian 14, 233, 238, 255

W

weather
    anemometer 30
    average temperatures 31
    barometer 29
    fog 31
    fronts 29
    Pacific high 30
    rainy season 31
    storm tracks 30
    wind
        afternoon sea breezes 31
        apparent 30
        cyclones 33
        land breezes 30
        moderate 31
        offshore 32
        onshore 30
        Santa Ana 31, 32
        sea breezes 30
        strong 31
        true 30
        velocity 30
        violent 32
    wind direction 31
    winter storms 31

weather reports 33
weather warning flags 33
Wegeforth, Harry 21, 110
weir 201
West Marine 64, 78, 208, 271
West Mission Bay 216–220

W cont.

Western Salt Company 191
Westgate 125
Whaler's Bight 152, 159
whales 116
whaling business 17
wharfs
    Babcock and Story Wharf 109
    Horton Wharf 109
    Kimball Wharf 109

Wild Animal Park 111
winch 48
wrecks
    Monte Carlo 147

Y

yacht charters
    San Diego Yacht Charters 101

yacht clubs
    Chula Vista Yacht Club 190, 192
    Coronado Cays Yacht Club 184, 185
    Fiddler's Cove Yacht Club 159
    Kona Kai International Yacht Club 60
    Mission Bay Yacht Club 218
    Oceanside Yacht Club 244
    San Diego Yacht Club 60
    Silver Gate Yacht Club 60
    Southwestern Yacht Club 60

yacht harbor 23
yard services
    dry storage 62, 223
    hoist 207, 223, 227
    travel lift 244, 258

Z

Zoological Society of San Diego 110, 111
zoos
    San Diego Zoo 66

Zuñiga Jetty 61, 74, 158

DOWN

2804 CANNON